Developing Higher Order Thinking in the Content Areas K–12

Frances S. O'Tuel and Ruth K. Bullard

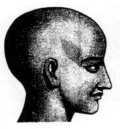

© 1993
**CRITICAL THINKING
PRESS & SOFTWARE**

(formerly Midwest Publications)
P.O. Box 448 • Pacific Grove • CA 93950-0448
800-458-4849 • FAX 408-372-3230
ISBN 0-89455-499-9

Contents

Preface

The purpose of this book is to help classroom teachers, staff-development personnel, and instructors of courses and training in developing higher order thinking for K–12, adult education, and business and industry. The content is to be used to design and/or redesign instruction, which increases participation by the learners in performing more complex processes. The development of critical and creative kinds of thinking is a major goal for education in the 21st Century.

The intent of the authors is to furnish the reader with all of the scaffolding and assistance s/he will need to be able to involve learners in developing their abilities to engage in higher order processes. There are blank forms (which may be copied), outlines, verbal maps, external organizers, instructional models, and model units and lessons to assist the reader. We hope it is user friendly.

Many readers will have engaged their learners in activities which require higher order thinking, but they may not have directly taught the skill or strategy. Research results show that the learner needs to know what skills and strategies s/he has, label them, and learn when to use them. The authors hope this book will assist you in providing more emphasis on (1) the direct teaching of skills and (2) integrating strategies into your content.

Part I (Chapters 1–8) of the book contains background information; theoretical and research bases; instructional design and techniques; aspects of higher order thinking such as metacognition and creativity; explanations about problem solving, decision making, and transfer; and descriptions of assessment and evaluation processes.

Part II (Chapters 9–13) contains the steps for designing or redesigning units of instruction in various content areas and examples of unit plans, and, in some areas, the actual lesson plans for the complete unit.

Finally, Part III (Chapters 14–18) addresses related topics such as how to help students do research; curriculum development; commercial programs; technology and higher order thinking; and a teacher's guide to use when conferencing with parents.

Acknowledgments

The authors are grateful for the assistance of the graduate students in their classes on developing higher order thinking over the past seven years. Their feedback has been invaluable in this manuscript's evolution. We particularly want to acknowledge the professional assistance of Drs. Margaret Gredler and Joan Gallini and graduate student Neal Helman in the preparation of the chapter on technology. Ms. Margaret Roberts allowed us to take the whole language unit for 8th graders she developed and adapt it to the format for units and lessons set forth in this book. She also furnished us with the outline for the Spanish unit. We appreciate her willingness to share her expertise. We also used many ideas from student's projects, which we combined or used as springboards for other instructional materials. Dr. Mary Louise Hunley devoted many hours to reading the manuscript for accuracy and adequacy; we appreciate her efforts. Robert Bullard also spent long hours reading the materials for their correctness and readability. To these individuals and others not named who contributed, we acknowledge our appreciation.

About the Authors

Dr. Frances S. O'Tuel is an Associate Professor of Educational Psychology at the University of South Carolina where she teaches classes in human growth and development, instructional design, and cognition. She has also given teacher-training courses on the gifted, instructional design, and curriculum development for special populations (gifted, at-risk, advanced placement, etc.)

Dr. O'Tuel has served as a presenter, staff developer, workshop director, and consultant at all levels, elementary through college, both nationally and internationally. She has conducted workshops and taught courses on developing higher order thinking in the content areas, human development and learning situations, and human growth and development in the United States, Japan, Myanmar (formerly Burma), Korea, Kenya, Ethiopia, and Mexico.

A frequent conference presenter, Dr. O'Tuel has authored and co-authored numerous books, articles, and papers in the education field.

Dr. Ruth K. (Rawl) Bullard received her doctorate in Early Childhood/Elementary Education from the University of South Carolina, Columbia. She teaches at the Irmo Middle School, Lexington District Five and also serves as an Adjunct Professor in the College of Education, University of South Carolina, where she teaches graduate courses in developing higher order thinking and human growth and development. She has been an elementary school principal and an elementary school-district consultant.

Involved in staff development, curriculum development, and program evaluation as a developer, consultant, and workshop presenter, Dr. Bullard has conducted workshops and taught courses on integrating thinking skills into the curriculum, curriculum development in math, science, reading, and social studies, using Bloom's taxonomy, and assessment. She has also presented workshops on parenting.

Dr. Bullard has presented papers at numerous conferences and has authored and co-authored books and articles in the education field.

PART I
Basics of Higher Order Thinking

Chapter One

Overview of Higher Order Thinking

Educators have begun to wonder if they know what higher order thinking and thinking skills are. The professional journals have been filled with articles about the development of thinking skills, higher order thinking, critical thinking, and problem solving. Those of us who thought we knew what they were and were trying to help students develop them have started to doubt our understanding. To relieve confusion, we begin with a few definitions.

- **Thinking skills** are specific processes by which we organize, interact with, and adapt to our environment.

- **Higher order thinking** (HOT) refers to the more complex processes such as analysis, synthesis, and evaluation.

- **Critical thinking** is a term used by some as a synonym for higher order thinking. Critical thinking implies the individual is inferring or concluding something based on some specified criteria such as critical reading or critical analysis. In practice, however, the term is sometimes used to mean to "think hard" or "deeply" about some topic or issue.

- **Strategies** are mental processes which facilitate our actions. They usually include various combinations of thinking skills.

- **Cognition** is another term we see frequently in connection with higher order thinking. Webster's Dictionary defines cognition as the "act or process of knowing, including both awareness and judgment." Thus, a good working definition of cognition is the act or process of thinking.

Rationale

Now that we have reviewed the terminology, we will turn to the question, "Why all the fuss?" There are some very good reasons for educators' concern about thinking skills.

The rationales below justify not only the thinking skills movement, but also activities which are important and necessary parts of good instruction, even though they may not appear to be tied directly to basic skills objectives—practices which require students to think through a problem, explore an issue, debate, induce, engage in guided discovery, create, synthesize, and evaluate with justification, to name a few.

The rationales are divided into four sections: (1) definition of literacy, (2) information explosion, (3) education reform movements and assessments, and (4) research. Each will be discussed briefly. More detailed articles are listed in the bibliography at the end of the book.

Literacy

Resnick and Resnick (1977) developed the definition of literacy as rational thinking. This is a step further than the expanded definition of literacy as "functional competencies" which was developed in the '70s. Historically, literacy was the ability to read at a minimum level. Literacy as functional competency meant one could read, write, listen, orally communicate, and compute. In the Resnicks' article, the argument is set forth that processes such as being able to analyze information, draw conclusions, generate hypotheses, and find solutions are also necessary for a literate individual in today's society.

Information Explosion

The explosion of information and the obsolescence of much past information is not in doubt. According to Seif (1981), in the past 60 years—1/800th of the 50,000 years of human development—the most profound changes in history have taken place. In order to deal with these and future changes, Seif urges that curricula include opportunities for students to do the following:

- Think convergently and divergently;

- Investigate challenges and problems of today and tomorrow;

- Think in complex and creative ways; and

- Synthesize, analyze, and evaluate.

All of these require the higher order thinking skills referred to earlier. The inference is clear: process is as important as product in education. Note that the words "as important as," not "more important than," were used. This is because students need an information base upon which to build. In the recent research studies on novices and experts and on good and poor problem solvers, the findings repeatedly show the need for a sound information base.

Bruner (1968) argued for process when he set forth his discovery (inductive) instructional model. Research on inductive models has not been particularly encouraging if one is looking for superior scores on evaluation measures currently in use. Unfortunately, most of these standardized achievement tests primarily measure information and comprehension and not the more complex processes. Until processes are measured, the jury should remain out as to the effectiveness of such programs.

Educational Reform

Reform in education has been one of the hottest domestic issues in the United States. The issue is prevalent in other countries as well: Japanese educators are concerned about the need for developing more creative thinking in their students; the USSR, before it broke up, invited educators from the United States to consult with their counterparts about how to improve student achievement. From *A Nation at Risk*, the Carnegie Report, the National Assessment of Educational Progress, the Governors' Report, and numerous other studies of our educational system, there is agreement that reforms are indicated. There is not consensus on just what those reforms should be or how they should be implemented. There is agreement probably on the statement that students need to learn more, learn more effectively, and utilize their learning better in academic and real-life situations.

The Education Commission of the States (1982) set forth what it considered to be the "Basics of Tomorrow." The following is a summary of those "basics":

- Evaluation and analysis skills

- Critical thinking

- Problem solving strategies (including mathematical problem-solving)

- Organization and reference skills

- Synthesis

- Application

- Creativity

- Decision making given incomplete information

- Communication skills through a variety of modes

A quick examination of the above list reveals that the processes needed are again the ones called higher order thinking.

One of the most active organizations in promoting the development of higher order thinking in the United States is the Association for Supervision and Curriculum Development (ASCD). It adopted this area of interest as one of its foci and has produced numerous materials including books, videotapes, audiotapes, manuals, and overheads. In addition, ASCD has sponsored many training opportunities through its National Curriculum Study Institute Program and regional and state conferences. Several entire issues of its professional journal, *Educational Leadership*, have been devoted to articles on thinking skills and issues concerning the teaching of such skills. Many other articles on these topics have appeared in this journal in issues not specifically focusing on the area of thinking.

Another national organization that has published a number of articles on critical and creative thinking is Phi Delta Kappa. The *Kappan*, the official publication of Phi Delta Kappa, has offered its readers a series of articles on higher order thinking. The Piaget Symposium, International Reading Association, National Science Teachers Association, National Council of Teachers of Mathematics, and the National Council of Teachers of English are additional professional organizations which have held sessions, conferences, and/or published material addressing thinking. The bibliography at the end of this book lists many of the published articles. For additional information one can write these organizations or, in the case of articles, can check the *Current Index of Journals in Education* (CIJE) in a professional library for teacher preparation or do an ERIC search for periodical articles and research reports. The library may require an appointment if one of their staff is needed to assist the investigator.

In some states, the legislatures have passed bills mandating that teachers offer students opportunities to develop higher order think-ing. The legislation in one state (South Carolina) stipulated that a committee would be named by the State Department of Education to define higher order thinking. The Committee used the following guiding statements to assist them in developing the definition and dimensions (minutes of committee 1989):

1. All students can learn to be better thinkers.

2. Higher order thinking can be taught at all grades, with consideration for developmental differences.

3. Higher order thinking applies to all subject areas. There is a link between the skills/processes and content.

4. Motivation, or the will to learn, is critically important to the improvement of higher order thinking.

5. Knowledge and prior experience are necessary for higher order thinking. Basic and higher order skills cannot be clearly separated, and they operate in an integrated manner.

6. Problem solving is one component of higher order thinking.

7. Higher order thinking can be directly taught and facilitated in the classroom.

8. The effective teacher models higher order thinking. Thinking cannot be taught solely by worksheets or by devoting short periods of time to its instruction.

9. Higher order thinking should be assessed and evaluated in a variety of ways beyond traditional assessment measures such as multiple choice.

10. The nurturing of higher order thinking in the classroom should be rewarded by the education system and by society.

Some of these ideas came from work in other states, such as Maryland, and were merged to forge these guides. The following definition and dimensions resulted:

- Higher order thinking is the ability and willingness to manage the mental processes necessary to reach decisions, make judgments, solve problems, and construct and communicate meaning.

• Higher order thinking involves many processes, yet it is more than the sum of its parts. Higher order thinking includes, but is not limited to, the following: questioning, interpreting, analyzing, synthesizing, organizing and integrating information, generalizing and inferring, estimating and predicting outcomes, creating, and evaluating.

• These processes must be selected, combined, and used at the appropriate time. Students must believe they can think well and must learn to monitor and regulate their own thinking, and they must also understand how skills and processes relate to different kinds of content and situations.

In summary, higher order thinking includes these dimensions:

1. Skills, strategies, and processes.

2. Selection, organization, and use of the skills, strategies, and processes.

3. Application within and across subject areas and real-world tasks.

4. An inquisitive and positive "can-do" attitude.

5. Managing and regulating one's own thinking processes.

Research

In an analysis of student item performance (Ryan & Rowls 1986), the responses of students on a state's basic skills assessment program in reading in grades 1, 2, 3, 6, and 8 were studied. The items for objectives not mastered by students who failed to meet the state standard for their grade level were those designed to measure drawing inferences, making comparisons, finding the main idea, predicting outcomes, summarizing, and concluding. All of these tasks require a student to use one or more higher order thinking skills or strategies. Strangely enough, most compensatory programs are designed to work on more basic skills such as decoding and word meaning—ones on which the students who scored below the state standard were successful.

Conclusion

Whether one considers the expanded definition of literacy, the dilemma of information explosion, the educational reform movements, or research, the results are the same. We need to be doing a better job of preparing students to *function* and it would appear that the logical place to address our efforts is in the developing of higher order thinking and the strategies which facilitate these processes. Perkins (1985) stated that there were three components to intelligence: power, tactics, and knowledge. He suggested that there is little we can do to alter power—which is our genetic endowment, including our neurophysiological equipment. He also contended that we are effective in our encoding of a knowledge base, a base which must be updated constantly. Perkins made it clear that the component which showed the most useful and successful promise for improving intelligent performance was the area of tactics or strategies. These tactics are what many call thinking skills. How to plan instruction in order to facilitate students' abilities to use these skills is what this book is all about.

Issues in Teaching Thinking

As different approaches to teaching higher order thinking have been tried, several recurring issues have arisen. One of the most important for schools and districts is the decision of whether to present thinking skills as a separate course or whether to integrate the skills into one or more content areas.

Issue I: Separate or Integrated?

An issue never becomes an issue unless there are good arguments on either side. In the case of how to offer the instruction in higher order thinking, there are some strong arguments for presenting thinking skills as a separate course.

First, as a separate course, it permits the students to focus on the skill without being sidetracked by the content of the subject matter. Second, assessment of progress may be made more easily. Third, some of the skills are so basic that they need to be mastered before they can be used with any content. Fourth, there is more freedom in selecting activities and subject matter with which to illustrate and interact.

Several commercially available programs have been developed with this format. The material is highly interesting and novel for the most part. Students enjoy the activities and participate willingly. De Bono's CoRT program, Feuerstein's Instrumental Enrichment, and the Harvard Project Intelligence program in Venezuela called Odyssey are examples of this approach. To their credit, some empirical data have been published on their effectiveness.

Transfer

The major question as yet not answered about these separate programs is, "Do the skills transfer to content areas and real life situations?" Will the student recognize the appropriateness of a skill when confronted with a specific situation not like the material with which he or she was working in the thinking skill activities? The transfer of such skills, learned in nonacademic and sometimes nonreal-life activities, probably has a slim chance of happening. In fact, transfer from one academic area to another seldom happens unless the teacher consciously presents examples and illustrations of appropriate skill-usage in other subjects, and situations are specifically mentioned or are generated by the students.

Pogrow (1990) has reported achievement gains for his HOTS program for Chapter I students although he did not teach for transfer; however, his research is the exception to the findings in the majority of the literature.

Some disadvantages of a separate course, in addition to the issue of transfer, relate to scheduling, personnel, and costs.

Scheduling

Most school schedules are so packed with state-mandated minutes for basic skills and certain subjects (sometimes called Defined Minimum Programs) that it is very difficult to find a time to add anything.

Personnel

A teacher must be obtained and probably trained to teach the course. To plan staff development in the teaching of higher order thinking for all teachers may be a more desirable approach for a school to take if the objectives are long-range and comprehensive. However, it too poses problems. Some of the disadvantages of separate programs may be diminished as schools experiment with deregulation and restructuring.

Cost

A curriculum, syllabus, materials, requirements, etc. must be developed locally or must be purchased commercially. Either requires an outlay of funds. Some of the programs available commercially require extensive training of the teacher, and the programs themselves are costly. It may be difficult to convince a school board that such expense is the best use of the district's limited funds and resources. Some districts which have purchased these programs have used funds for gifted education and used the programs with this group of students. This solves problems of scheduling a separate course, a source of funding, and the need for an additional teacher; unfortunately, it offers the program to a group of students who need it least. Gifted students should be engaged in higher order thinking, but so should all the other students. In fact, some of the strategies taught in thinking skills programs are already being used by gifted students, who generated them spontaneously and then use them for more efficient learning, remembering, and processing. Below-average students seldom spontaneously generate strategies, except perhaps very basic rehearsal and a little self-referencing to improve their memory. They need specific instruction the most.

Conclusion

For all of the reasons mentioned above, we take the position that the most practical and the soundest theoretically-based approach is to teach thinking skills in the context of subjects and disciplines the students are studying. Transfer among subjects must still be addressed by the teachers who are teaching, or having students use, higher order thinking in their subject. Transfer does not occur by osmosis. It must be consciously taught. However, once the students have learned one context, the particular subject in which the process may be applied, it appears then to be easier to assist them in seeing other situations in which they might use the thinking skill or strategy.

There is little research which has been done with integrated-subject-area programs to support conclusively that they are more effective than separate programs. The difficulty arises from the lack of valid measures and the problem of intervening variables which may be affecting the outcomes. Much more research is needed.

We are biased in the direction of teaching higher thinking within the content areas of the school subjects, preferably in an interdisciplinary approach. More about how to do this will be found in subsequent chapters.

Issue II: Teach for, of, or about Thinking Skills

The second issue which has received much attention is the decision of whether to teach *for* thinking (Part II), to teach *of* thinking (Chapter 7), or to teach *about* thinking (Chapter 4). Each of these is a worthwhile activity and all are recommended. The process in the classroom will differ, however, depending on which of these outcomes you have selected.

Costa (1985) explained that teaching *for* thinking refers to the integration of thinking skill(s) in a lesson of content material; students engage in a higher order thinking process, but we may not give it a name or measure whether or not they can carry out the skill.

When we ask students to compare and contrast two literary selections on specified dimensions, such as plot, characterizations, mood, organization, or use of literary devices, we are assuming that they can analyze. We offer no instruction in analysis, a higher order thinking process. The task contributes to the students' understanding of the content, and that is the purpose of giving the task.

On the other hand, if you are not sure students can participate in analyses and you decide to teach the process within the content area (teaching *of* thinking), the approach is somewhat different. To teach any process skill—thinking skills or other types—the students must actively participate in the process and have opportunities for practice and feedback. If our objective is to teach analysis deductively, we would probably begin by naming and defining the process, giving examples and illustrations (declarative knowledge), modeling the behavior or process by doing it in class for them, having them participate as a group with us in another example, allow them to try the process in small groups and/or pairs, give them feedback on how they are doing, and have them reflect upon what they have done. Additional practice to maintain and enhance the skill is also necessary.

Several cautions should be noted about this activity. First, because we want them to concentrate on acquiring the skill, we should consider choosing content to which they have already been exposed. If the material is new or novel, the students may be so caught up in learning the content that they do not focus on the process. Second, we must create as nonthreatening a situation as we can for them. We are asking them to take risks because they do not know how to do it, and we are asking them to expose their less than perfected performance. Nonthreatening also means we *never* grade such activities. How would we like it if someone told us to stand up in front of 300 people and speak extemporaneously and told us that they would criticize and grade us on our performance?

Risk taking must be nurtured in an accepting climate where it is all right to try and make "mistakes." This is probably more obvious when we look at motor skills such as writing or swimming; processes must be practiced and feedback must be received for mastery to occur. The use of groups for the activities allows individuals to share the risk and to support one another.

The third approach, to teach *about* thinking, refers to a particular kind of thinking which is called metacognition or executive control. This is truly higher order thinking because it involves the processes of planning, monitoring, and evaluating our thinking. We engage in metacognitive activities when we do any of the following:

- Plan a set of activities,
- Sequence them in a particular order,
- Predict the outcome or consequences,
- Implement the activities,
- Monitor how well they are going,
- Make adjustments when necessary, and
- Match the outcomes with the criteria of performance we had established in our planning.

As one can see, these are really combinations of many other less complex skills which are integrated into a problem-solving procedure. Because metacognition, or thinking about thinking, is critical in decision making and problem solving, it will be addressed again in a later chapter. Metacognitive activities will be tempered by the developmental level of the learners. Younger children may have difficulty expressing their thoughts, but they should be given numerous opportunities to examine their own thinking.

All of the above approaches to the teaching of thinking are recommended. It should be apparent, however, that the goal or purpose of our endeavor will drive the lessons. This decision needs to be made in advance (a little metacognition on our part) in order to accomplish the outcomes we expect.

Issue III: Objections to Teaching Higher Order Thinking

One of the most interesting issues to come out of the movement to teach higher order thinking to students is the objection by some parents to the teaching of higher order thinking. Some of these parents, from conservative religious groups, expressed concerns that certain programs, particularly Tactics for Thinking, were fostering New Age Religion. They cited examples from a manual, which they then related to techniques recommended in various books written by proponents of New Age Religion. These parents see a program in higher order thinking as introducing techniques which will condition their children to be susceptible to New Age Religion. Their objections are primarily to any activity which might involve relaxation or imagery by students. Progressive relaxation is a technique used in New Age Religion to set the stage for meditation which, if successful, could lead to "altered states of consciousness."

When teachers ask students to clear their minds of other ideas and concentrate on the lesson or when teachers ask students to take deep breaths and settle down, no altered states of consciousness are desired or obtained. It is hoped that the students have focused their attention on the lesson or activity and are paying attention.

The objection to using imagery is a serious one; it suggests that we should not ask students to pretend they are with Hannibal as he crosses the mountains or to experience vicariously what is happening around the world, in history, and literature. What a loss! Why would we teach the past if we were not to learn from it? Where would creative writing come from? Our imaginations are frequently what makes abstract ideas more realistic so that we can understand them. Trying to feel what it would be like to walk on the moon is not New Age Religion. The use of imagery in classrooms has been a hallmark of good teaching for hundreds of years.

If New Agers have borrowed teaching techniques that work and use them as part of their procedures, that does not make the techniques New Age. Guilt by association should have gone out with McCarthyism. The problem has been exacerbated by the fear of these parents that their children will be influenced in their moral development by someone other than themselves. These parents appear to be threatened by other points-of-view.

The solution is not clear. A small group of parents, whoever they are, should not dictate the curriculum to professional educators. This would probably not be in the best interest of the rest of the students and is not likely to be as sound educationally as a curriculum developed by teachers and administrators who have spent years learning what works, what is appropriate, and how to implement it. Yet districts do not want to be unhearing to parents who are conscientiously afraid of what their child is learning in school. It may be that these parents will need to consider home schooling or banding together to form a private religious school where they can have more control over the curriculum.

Some objections to the teaching of higher order thinking have come from teachers who express their discomfort in being asked to teach skills and strategies they have not been taught. Some teachers believe classes where these activities are going on will be less teacher directed and controlled; they prefer to maintain their role as the director of their students' learning. Some subculture groups where authoritarian parental child-rearing is practiced, want there to be more "control" in the class. There are also groups of teachers, parents, and administrators who do not want any change and tend to reject what is "new." Even though these groups exist, there are others, including business executives, educators, government leaders, and civic groups, who are unwavering in their requests for this shift in emphasis in the curriculum of public schools.

Chapter Two

Theoretical Bases of the Thinking Skills Movement

As teachers, we have many techniques which we use and which we know are effective in certain instructional situations. We do not need a theory to use these techniques, but what happens when we are in a new situation or dealing with a new topic or process and we do not have a plan? This is where a theory is helpful. If we understand a learning theory, then we can relate the new situation to the basic tenets of the theory and come up with a "best scenario" guess of what should work. Knowing how individuals learn helps us to plan effective instruction.

Two theories will be presented in this chapter: Constructivism (Piaget and Bruner) and Information Processing. Since both of these approaches to learning try to explain what goes on in our minds, and since thinking is a mental process, these theories should help us in teaching thinking. Although these theories differ from each other, they are compatible; each explains our cognitive processes by taking different perspectives, like looking at the same event from different windows of the mind.

Constructivism

Piaget is a familiar name. According to several of our highly respected educators, Piaget has had more impact on our educational systems than any other single person. He called himself a genetic epistemologist, someone who studies the origin of knowledge and knowing. As a result of this focus, Piaget did not address applying his theory to education. Thousands of individuals who studied with him or about him have addressed the implications of his theory to instruction and curriculum. Many of these followers have carried out research in school settings. Although the general outline of the theory has been validated, some specific areas of extension have been modified to accommodate the findings of later research studies. Piaget continued to modify the specifics himself until his death in 1980. He would, doubtlessly, have approved of such continued study. Inhelder, Case, Pascual-Leone, Gelman, and Fischer are some of the investigators who have continued to refine and expand Piaget's theory.

Piaget's theory is classified as an interactionist theory in that he believed our cognitive development is a result of the interaction of the individual with the environment. Some other theorists, for example, Skinner, explain behavior primarily from the environment's effects on the individual; others, such as information processing theorists, focus more on the mind and its processes. The information processing theories will be discussed in more detail in the next section.

Piaget has also been called a cognitive developmental psychologist (by others, not himself). This classification has been used because Piaget was concerned with how we develop cognitively as we progress through a series of stages. He explained that children respond differently to the same stimulus at different stages of development because they process the information in progressively more complex ways. This is possible because of changes in the structures of the mind. The stages are invariant—you cannot skip one or change the order.

His theory states that each of us constructs reality in our minds. What one person perceives is not the same as another person's interpretation of the stimulus. For example, if the stimulus at a particular point in time is a large dog, one person may approach the dog because he has a similar dog at home, but another person may head for the nearest tree because last week he was bitten by a dog that looked very similar to this one. The stimulus is the same. What is different is how it fits into one's schema, or previous experiences and actions, and the resulting interpretation. Thus, each of us is taking in stimuli and processing them, but because we each construct our reality, no two perceptions are the same.

Constructivism influences teaching through encouraging exploration, inquiry, direct experience with materials and information, and structuring the curriculum around primary concepts (Brooks 1990).

Piaget wrote of four components in learning. Each must be present in order for learning to take place. The diagram below shows the interrelationship of these four components:

- maturation
- physical experience
- social transmission
- equilibration

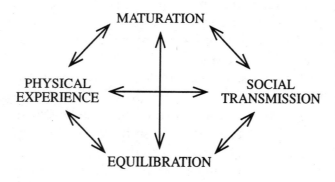

Maturation

Maturation refers to the developmental level of an individual—physically, cognitively, emotionally, and socially. There are lower limits as to when we can perform certain tasks or exhibit certain behaviors. For example, you would not try to teach a child to skip if he cannot yet walk; you would not try to train a child to form letters with a pencil if he cannot yet hold such an object. In each case, the behavior is not potentially in the repertoire of the child; therefore, you would not try to teach it.

This can be true of cognitive abilities also. Teaching reading would not be very successful if a child has not yet acquired the ability to discriminate differences in objects and pictures.

Environment obviously affects a child's readiness to perform certain tasks. Prior learning and familiarity with an event or subject are examples of environmental influences. Equally important is the consideration of whether the child is maturationally ready to perform the task. According to Piaget, children who have not reached the stage of concrete operations would lack the ability to conceptualize the process of subtraction; they would not be able to recognize that the subtraction process is the reverse of addition. They can be taught number facts by the memorization of the combinations. Abundant repetition and practice is required. This may be adequate for them to perform simple subtraction problems, but not be sufficient for them to be successful in multidigit problems with regrouping.

Maturation serves to set the lower limit of when a child can function in a certain way. When the child reaches a point when a function or conceptualization is potentially within his repertoire, he will not necessarily do it. Instruction and/or learning must still occur.

Physical Experience

The component of physical experience refers to what each of us learns through our senses. We each bring with us an individual set of impressions and actions associated with the object, event, and/or person at hand. We have internal categories or classifications that we test the stimulus against. If the object is round and rolls, it may match our category of balls. If we have had no previous physical experience with balls, and therefore no "ball category," then we will have another classification for this object. Maybe we have a category in which we group things we roll or throw. Objects are often categorized by what we do with them.

This does not mean that we have an actual

mental label called "objects we roll or throw"; rather, we generalize stimuli into categories based on our perceptions of them. Perception is the process of interpreting what we take in through our senses.

Piaget states that thought is rooted in *action*. Actions and objects, and persons or events associated with the actions, form memories. Piaget calls these "connected" actions and objects schema. Thus, our first schemes are memories associated with various actions we can perform or are performed upon us. Through seeing, touching, hearing, smelling, and tasting, we learn about those things which are external to ourselves and the properties that they have. During infants' second year of life, they learn object permanence. This means they understand that objects have properties of their own. These properties exist separate from the infant and his or her actions.

Any experience is processed by fitting it into what we already know (assimilation) and modifying the scheme to accommodate any new information. Physical experience is the total of what we have taken in through our senses and processed.

Social Transmission

Social transmission is the process of learning from those around us. We imitate models both present and absent at a given point in time. We develop an arbitrary symbol system which we use for communication (language) by hearing others speak and by interacting with symbols we have learned. Acquiring language is perhaps the most amazing of all examples of social transmission. It, too, has developmental limits. For example, we are aware that children understand more words than they can speak during their acquisition of language. At the time, they do not have sufficient voluntary control over the vocal mechanisms to reproduce all the meaningful units which they understand. This lag between performance and comprehension is well accepted. The lag points to the interaction of the components above—more learning is still taking place.

Equilibration

The last of the four components is equilibration. This concept is the most difficult to explain because it lacks observable behaviors to exemplify it. Basically, the term refers to executive processes in the mind which balance what we are taking in from physical experiences and social transmissions, oversee the assimilation and accommodation processes, reflect upon our own actions and abstractions, compare ideas, and, in general, keep us functioning mentally.

Disequilibration is usually described as a mismatch between what we are experiencing and what we have in our schemes. Without disequilibration learning may not be occurring. If everything fits into place, then you have no reason to try to make things work or fit together. Only when there is distinction and/or variety do we have to accommodate the new experience and our scheme changes. In learning, we need to arrange the environment so children experience a mismatch or disequilibration. This way the child will feel the need to solve the problem or comprehend the situation.

Learning Process

All four components interact in the learning process. We need to consider the maturational level of our learners so that we do not needlessly frustrate them with tasks they are likely to be unsuccessful in completing. Maturation is not something we can change; it is a given. We need to arrange the physical environment to offer learners sensory experiences such as the use of tangible materials for hands-on interactions. We need to serve as models or furnish models of processes, objects, etc. which will allow the child or adult to observe the characteristics or the accomplishment of a given task. Finally, we need to encourage students to reflect upon their own thinking and to evaluate their planning, progress, and results.

Piaget's concern was that the individual have the opportunity to observe, explore, experiment, interact, reflect, and construct schemes which include physical and social experiences, actions and their consequences. He contended that if we tell something to the learner, we rob that person of finding out for himself or herself. We also may be limiting the understanding to just what we imparted. Learners need to engage actively in the learning process. The participation is what is critical to the Piagetian, not the correct answer. Children's errors may reveal much more about their understanding and processing than the correct response. Their participation may assist them in constructing more complex schemes even when they do not get the "right" answer.

Developmental Stages

Piaget also developed descriptions of the stages of cognitive development which he found individuals pass through. Although most of you have seen these stages presented with ages of onset and end, Piaget was not concerned with age but stage of development. As teachers, we begin to work with children from about age four up. At this age they are in a preoperational stage of development.

Preoperational

In the preoperational stage, language development and the rudiments of reasoning are developing. During this period, children learn all they need to know in order to communicate in their native language. Language acquisition is one of the most remarkable accomplishments of childhood. This is not to say that language development stops after this stage, but that the child has extracted rules and syntax from social experiences and is able to communicate effectively with other individuals. Of course, the vocabulary varies greatly at this time; speech by native-language models influences the rapidity and complexity of a child's language acquisition.

Children are perception-bound during this stage of development—what they see is what it is. Because they are not capable of logical, sequential thought and reasoning, they can be

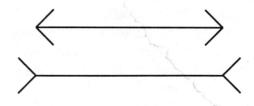

fooled by ambiguous stimuli. To them, something is longer than something else if it looks that way, even if we show them by measuring that the two are the same, as in the case of the arrows above.

Because they do not think logically, they are likely to associate cause and effect with proximity of time or place. For instance, it's bedtime because I've had my bath. It is difficult for them to hold more than one new idea in their memory at one time. Thus, if we give them instructions to go to the bathroom, wash their hands, and get in line, they are likely to do only one or none of the above until such time as these actions are chained together as one sequence. The neo-Piagetians, such as Robbie Case, have explained this phenomenon in terms of information processing theory, and it will be discussed further in the section on information processing.

Concrete Operational

There is more variability in age of onset for this period than for the last one. Most normal children move from sensorimotor to preoperational between 18 months and two years. In Western cultures, children as young as five and as old as nine may move into the concrete period. Children are not preoperational one day and wake up the next morning at concrete operational. There is usually a period of transition. Sometimes they operate on the concrete operational level and other times they revert to preoperational behaviors. The latter is more likely to occur when the child encounters something novel. Interaction with the physical and social world is crucial for the unfolding of concrete operational thought.

Conserving is one of the major acquisitions of concrete thought. This means that the individual knows that something is the same even if we move it around or it looks different.

Children conserve number first, then liquid and mass follow. For example, if we pour liquid from one container into another, the child is conserving if s/he tells us the amount is the same and gives as his or her justification that we did not add or take away anything, so it must be the same, or if we poured the liquid back into the original beaker, it would be the same as before. The mental process of transferring the liquid back to its original container Piaget called reversibility.

The lack of reversibility in young children has been used as one explanation of why many first graders have difficulty with subtraction, the reverse of addition. They have not yet arrived at the concrete operational stage.

Concrete operational children can hold more than one idea in their heads at one time. They can take a group of objects and classify them by different sets of criteria into different categories. It has been suggested that preoperational children can do this on a limited basis but may have trouble holding in conscious memory the criteria with which they started.

Concrete operational children can reason logically and sequentially about concrete objects, events, and people. They can understand how an object can belong to one group which is part of another group. Piaget called this *class inclusion*. For instance, the child may identify an object as an orange. He can also understand that oranges are fruits and that fruits are foods. Class inclusion of this type is called *hierarchical classification*.

Over time, activities of the mind develop the structures necessary for children to become better thinkers. Piaget's insistence on children experiencing and exploring paves the way for the development of their capabilities to think more logically and productively.

Formal Operational

The major difference between concrete and formal is the content of the mental operations. Formal operators are able to think logically about ideas; that is, they can have ideas about ideas. They are not bound to the physical world. They can think about all the possible combinations of several variables or exhaust all the possible elements in a situation. They are able to differentiate the variables that might affect a given problem and then plan how to control them in order to see what effect a particular one has on the outcome. When adolescents spend much time and conversation on topics such as world problems, religion, politics, philosophical issues, and social issues, they are exercising their new found capabilities.

The onset of formal operations is even harder to pinpoint than the previous stage. Although the literature lists ages 11 to 15, several research studies have found that only 50 per cent of adults were operating at formal thought on the measures they administered. This has been true of college freshman as well as samples from the general population. A partial explanation of these results may be the instruments used, and another factor may be how familiar the person tested is with the kinds of problems s/he is given.

Constructivists' Theories

Piaget is only one of the theorists in the category of constructivists. Jerome Bruner is another. He, too, is a stage theorist, and his stages are similar to those described by Piaget. Because he believes language plays a more crucial role in thought than Piaget did, his stages are more related to the development of language, but the descriptions of what children do and think at his stages have parallels with Piaget's stages. Where Piaget looked on language as a tool of thought, Bruner believes language is necessary for the construction of meaning.

What are the implications of constructivists' theories for critical thinking or higher order thinking? Their theories might be seen as suggesting that younger children should not be asked to engage in higher order thinking; however, that is not the case. They should be given opportunities to evaluate and give their reasons, but the standards or expectations of their performance level should be tempered by our knowledge of their developmental level. Very complex tasks can lead to frustration; however, Vygotsky (1966) explained that teachers can offer scaffolding to students which will enable them to be successful in tasks which they could not yet do independently. This range of teacher-assisted activities was called by him the *zone of proximal development*.

One Piaget-based program is the *Cognitively Oriented Curriculum* (Weikart, D. P., Rogers, L., Adcock, C. & McClelland 1971). It demonstrates appropriate metacognitive activities for preschoolers. They plan their day with an adult at the beginning of the session, and at the end of the day, they report on what they did (or did not) do and how it went. These activities of planning, monitoring, and evaluating are laying the foundation for children to think about their own thinking and activities in reflective ways.

Information Processing Theories

The focus of information processing theories is the way the central nervous system handles information. All of these theories consider stimuli which impinge upon the system, the processes we use to interact with the stimuli, and the output of the system. This output may be a motor response (such as throwing a ball), a verbal response, or a covert action (such as turning ideas over in ones mind). Thus, not all responses are observable.

At one time, electroencephalograms (EEGs) were all we had to measure brain action. This was analogous to measuring someone's height with a measuring stick that is only calibrated in feet. With the development of methods to observe evoked potentials (brain waves caused by external stimuli), neurophysiologists have been able to measure electrical impulses and localize certain processes by tracing them at the time of stimulation and response. Information processing theorists are also able to utilize computers to simulate some mental processes. The sophistication of the computers that are now available has made more complex processing possible. These and more refined measurement tools have led to a large body of literature which has allowed information processing researchers to compare their findings and to interpret their data better.

Information Processing Model

Each information processing theorist has a model interpreting the information processing sequence. These models may differ in terminology or in the explanation of long-term memory storage, but all include input, process, and output in the information processing sequence.

Below is a composite model of how information is processed; the model closely resembles Robert Gagné's 1974 model which is reproduced in Gagné and Driscoll (1988) and in Gagné, Briggs, and Wager (1992).

In addition to the components shown in the model, there are two other concerns in an information processing model: executive control, or metacognition, and expectations based on previous experiences. These will be discussed later in the chapter on metacognition.

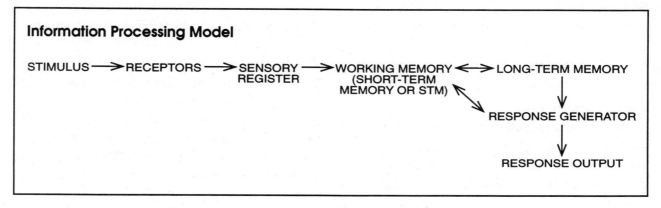

Information Processing Model

STIMULUS ⟶ RECEPTORS ⟶ SENSORY REGISTER ⟶ WORKING MEMORY (SHORT-TERM MEMORY OR STM) ⟷ LONG-TERM MEMORY ⟶ RESPONSE GENERATOR ⟶ RESPONSE OUTPUT

Stimuli

A stimulus can be anything that activates a receptor in the body. It may be chemical, thermal, pressure, visual, auditory, or anything which will set off a receptor. The stimuli may originate internally or externally. For example, an internal stimulus might be the digestive juices of the stomach sending a message to the brain, which is then interpreted as hunger; or a cramping in the intestines, resulting in a message of an upset there; or the secretion of adrenaline or noradrenaline setting off the autonomic nervous system, resulting in increased heart beat, respiration, etc. and a state of fear or flight.

External stimuli are usually observable through the senses. Some, like atmospheric pressure or gravity while in flight, may not be as obvious but are also external stimuli. The body receives multiple stimuli every moment. Even though these may activate receptors, this does not mean we will attend to all of them. We have a characteristic called selective attention which determines which stimuli will be dealt with consciously. Since this comes later in the sequence, it will not be discussed here.

Receptors

As mentioned above, we have many receptors and certain receptors are sensitive to certain kinds of stimuli. Our hand has receptors which respond to pressure, others which respond to temperature, others which respond to chemicals, etc. When receptors are stimulated, electrochemical waves travel to the brain on neural pathways that only carry impulses in one direction. We have many receptors, and all that are stimulated will send impulses. If the stimulation is intense and of long duration, the brain receives a strong and persistent wave of impulses.

Because there are some stimuli which need immediate response in order for an individual to survive, there are bundles of the neural pathways that the body covers in a sheath (myelin) much like the covering of insulation on an electrical cord. This myelin sheath insulates so that the impulses will lose less potency en route to the brain. Electrochemical impulses can travel up to twenty times faster through these enclosed pathways. Thus, all stimulation is not transmitted equally. A receptor is activated by a stimulus and sends an electrochemical charge to the central nervous system for as long as the stimulus continues to impinge upon it.

Sensory Register

The sensory register is a holding pad for sensory input. Its ability to hold is very limited in time. If some of the input is not moved into working memory within less than a second, it is dumped and lost. We all engage in selective perception in which we choose the sensory input we will work on in our working memory (Gagné, Briggs & Wager 1992). Only the impulses that are transferred to working memory or short-term memory are retained for further action. For instance, what we are viewing visually may be so interesting or dramatic that the visual input may mask auditory or other sensory input that is being received simultaneously.

Working Memory (Short-term Memory, STM)

Working memory (STM), as the name implies, is where the categorizing, transforming, encoding, decoding, etc. goes on. It works in tandem with long-term memory (LTM) to accomplish its tasks. When input from the sensory register is selected for attention, it is in working memory. Working memory sends out to long-term memory for any information, declarative knowledge, images, and/or procedures which may be cued for recall. All of these are activated in working memory. This is where we run into a problem which has particular implications for teaching/learning situations.

Working memory has a very limited capacity as to the number of chunks of information it can handle at one time. A computer, on the other hand, can call up any data stored in its memory bank at the same time. If we try to do that in working memory, we get information overload. Estimates of how many chunks we can handle at one time have varied. Early on, George Miller (1960) talked about the magic number seven (plus or minus two) which a Scottish philosopher had suggested was about our capacity as adults. Children have much smaller capacities. Some research (Simon 1974) has suggested that seven may be optimistic for adults and that a more realistic number of chunks might be five plus or minus two. Again, this capacity refers to adults; children's efficiency is less.

When we tell children in a classroom to hang up their coats, wash their hands, get in line, and be quiet, and most of those do not happen, we should not be discouraged; as soon as these are chained together in a sequence of "getting ready to go to lunch," which is one chunk, they will be able to do them all. At first, each instruction is taking up space in working memory, and they simply do not have room for all of them. Just being aware of why they do not follow our directions may at least reduce our frustration. We can help them by giving each instruction separately, then gradually helping them to put the sequence together. This bottleneck that we have, and computers do not have, is very useful to us.

The human brain is, indeed, a marvelous machine. What it can do that computers cannot do is to process parts and wholes. The computers either have data or they do not; it is all or none. The brain, on the other hand, can recall partial information which may be useful in solving a problem. For instance, we may not remember someone's name, but we can remember the beginning sound. This may help us look it up or further prompt us until we retrieve it.

When we hear that someone acted intuitively, it probably means that at that moment they did not consciously recall what they knew; yet they had enough of a sense of the situation to respond correctly. Many times we cannot explain our actions; if all behavior is purposeful, then we must assume that we were responding to a partial retrieval of related information or procedures. This type of recall is important in creative problem solving.

Long-term Memory (LTM)

Processes and the results of them from working memory (STM) are stored, or encoded, in long-term memory (LTM). Given proper cues, the brain can retrieve these at later points in time. There is research support for the proposal that short-term memory is chemical in form and that long-term memory is a result of structural growth of the neural cells. That is, the endings of the cells that were activated during the encoding grow closer together at the synapses (although they never touch). The next time any of these cells is activated, there is a spread of activation to the other cells as well. This makes it possible for us to recall the information. There are many ways we can assist students in improving their retrieval abilities. Most of them are related to the meaningfulness of the data being encoded and the data's organization. These will be discussed under strategies in subsequent chapters.

At one time it was thought that we lose information in long-term memory that we do not use. Currently, a more plausible explanation is that we may not be able to retrieve something because we lack the cues to activate it, but it is still there.

There is much debate about how we store memories. Are they all stored in some verbal way? Or are they stored in a dual system which has verbal and spatial systems? Or do we transform all images, procedures, and declarative knowledge into some other code or system? Some researchers propose a network of nodes (declarative knowledge) and sets of arguments (procedures) (Anderson 1980). Others talk about schemas which are made up of all the declarative information as well as images and procedures related to that particular scheme or idea. Declarative knowledge is the things we know and have concluded; procedural knowledge is the things we can do, the processes we can execute (Gagné, E. 1985). One exposure to declarative information may be sufficient for us to remember it forever. We do not need to witness more than one hurricane in order to have vivid recollections about a hurricane. One exposure to a process, however, is not usually sufficient for us to be able to execute it, particularly if it is complex.

The most important ingredients for the acquiring of procedural knowledge are practice and feedback. In fact, one of the short cuts we develop with procedures is to overlearn them to the point of automaticity. Thus, when something is in short-term memory which recalls an overlearned response, we may simply plug in the response without having to belabor it in the response generator.

Response Generator

Working memory and long-term memory collaborate to generate a response. The response may be overt or covert or both. The response generator sends the necessary instructions and activates the muscles, body systems, and neural processes needed to carry out the response. It appears that these activations may be localized in specific areas of the brain: some involve speech, some motor movements, etc.

Response Output

The response is carried out in various parts of the body by effectors such as muscles. At this point, we are no longer attending to the initiating stimulus or the content of long-term memory which we retrieved; we have turned our attention to another stimulus which we have selected from the sensory register, and the sequence begins again.

Implications for Teaching

Many of the proponents of teaching higher order thinking skills emphasize the importance of the teaching process. Piaget and Bruner repeatedly supported the active participation of the learner in the learning process. Bruner comments that process not product should be the emphasis in instruction.

Some curriculum developers of programs for the gifted which have focused on active engagement of the learner have implied that the majority of academically engaged time should be spent on doing something with the knowledge we have instead of acquiring information. They have suggested that Bloom's taxonomy be used, but that it should be inverted so that instead of spending the major portion of the instructional time on information and comprehension, it should be spent on the higher levels of analysis, synthesis, and evaluation.

This rationale is not faulty because gifted students generally acquire information and comprehend it at a much faster rate than other students. The problem arises, however, in translating the rationale into teaching strategy. Some teachers have interpreted this in their curricula to mean that knowledge acquisition is not critical, but that the higher level processes are. Nothing could be further from the truth. Knowledge and process are both important and, if anything, the acquisition of knowledge must precede acting upon that knowledge in new and different ways.

The growing body of research on problem solving has repeatedly pointed out that one of the differences between novices and experts is the amount of knowledge and the organization of that knowledge in their memory systems (Gagné, E. 1985). In other words, one cannot carry out a process in a vacuum; there must be information upon which the process is applied.

Instructional techniques or strategies for helping students recall their previous knowledge and/or relate it to new material, i.e., through analogy, external aids to assist the student in organizing the information, spatial displays and outlines, self-referencing prompts, mnemonic devices, etc., will be discussed in later chapters, particularly in Models of Instruction in Chapter 3.

Chapter Three

Frameworks and Models for Higher Order Thinking

The constructivist and information processing theories suggest that knowledge needs to be organized, that certain ways of presenting processes and information facilitate learning, that practice and feedback are necessary for processes to be learned, that a base of information is needed on which processes may be carried out, and that much of what we say about how the brain works is inferred from a variety of measures and deductions. These all have implications for instruction, particularly for instruction in higher order thinking processes. This chapter addresses the considerations in selecting an instructional model and some of the better articulated approaches to using these models.

Bloom's Taxonomy

There are many ways of organizing the field of knowledge and the processes of thinking. Although we will list several taxonomies, or classification systems, which the reader may want to explore, we will begin with the *Taxonomy of Educational Objectives: Cognitive Domain* (Bloom et al. 1956) also known as "Bloom's Taxonomy."

Many teachers have heard of or worked with Bloom's Taxonomy in other settings. For example, this taxonomy is used in planning instruction in mastery learning programs. Mastery learning has been combined successfully with thinking skills in Maryland and New York (Arredondo & Block 1990).

Bloom's Taxonomy is hierarchical in that the lower levels are considered inherent in the higher levels; that is, the students can perform the activities of the levels under the one with which they are working. For example, if we ask students to apply a formula to solve a mathematics problem (application), we assume they could define the terms (information) and tell us in their own words what the formula means and recognize instances where they might use it (comprehension).

The verbs we use when asking questions or giving instructions will determine at which level of thinking students will function. Sample lists of verbs at each level are included in this chapter (p. 41). These lists are not all inclusive.

Using verbs at the various levels can assist us in preparing questions which will take students to higher levels of thinking. This is not to imply that we should avoid asking the who, when, what, how, and where questions; they are basic. The problem is that many times those are all we ask and all we test. Questions such as Why do you think so? and What would happen if...? will engage students in processing the material in more meaningful ways. Some teachers post the levels and several verbs from each category in their classroom to serve as prompts when they are asking oral questions.

The six levels of Bloom's taxonomy starting with the lowest level and moving up are knowledge or information, comprehension, application, analysis, synthesis, and evaluation.

Knowledge or Information

This category refers to what one can remember from previous learning or experience. It involves simple recall and recognition; the learner may have acquired the information by rote learning. This is the lowest level of understanding; for example, naming and defining three parts of a cell.

Verbs which describe what we ask students to do at this level include

- list
- define
- describe
- label
- identify
- recall
- state

Comprehension

This category indicates some understanding of the knowledge the learner has acquired. If one can paraphrase or translate knowledge, put it in his or her own words, s/he comprehends it. It may involve recognizing or giving examples of a category. When one translates from words to numbers, comprehension is being demonstrated. Changing a word problem in mathematics to a number sentence is one example of translation, reading a graph or chart is another.

Verbs which refer to this level include

- paraphrase
- translate
- extend
- give examples

Application

This is the ability to use previously learned material in new situations. The material may be facts, rules, methods, concepts, or generalizations. The person understands the material and recognizes the appropriateness of using it in a new and concrete situation. This is considered the beginning level of higher order thinking.

Verbs which indicate the activities at this level include

- compute
- operate
- solve
- use
- apply

Analysis

As the name of the category implies, analysis is the process of breaking into parts, making comparisons, finding similarities and differences between parts of a whole or separate sets, and seeing organizational patterns and structures. Many of the most interesting activities in which we ask students to participate fall in this category. Even kindergartners can observe objects, events, or persons and discern differences and similarities. In fact, this ability to discriminate differences is a forerunner of being ready to read. Ability to recognize organizational patterns and break large amounts of material into smaller segments would seem a necessary precursor to being able to put elements or components together in meaningful new ways (synthesis).

Verbs which illustrate the activities at this level include

- differentiate
- discriminate
- infer
- outline
- relate
- compare
- contrast

Synthesis

Some educators think of synthesis as the other side of the analysis coin since in synthesis we put things together in new and different ways, and in analysis we take them apart. Some analysis is necessary, however, in order to synthesize. Synthesis is a critical skill in academic settings and in the world beyond. It includes the ability to organize, to arrange elements in meaningful relationships, and to make inferences about those relationships. Another important activity of synthesis is composing. When students write compositions, regardless of the type, they are creating something new based on what they know. Constructing an organizational pattern for a body of material or developing plans and sequences of events are other synthesis activities. Verbs for this category include

- compose
- create
- generate
- organize
- plan
- construct
- design

Evaluation

The top level in terms of complexity, difficulty, and abstractness is evaluation. The processes here involve making judgments based on some type of criteria. The major difference between analyzing and evaluating is the necessity to have an *a priori* standard against which one makes the evaluation. Because evaluation implies valuing in the decision making, some characteristics of the affective domain may be included. Judgments based on personal likes and dislikes cannot be ruled out, as those are still standards, albeit personal ones. If justification of a decision can be explained, then evaluation is present. This is the level where many of the "WHY" questions we ask fit. Why do you believe that? What is the reason you have for that choice? How do you know that is so?

Verbs which are used to ask for processes at this level include

- defend
- rate
- judge
- decide
- debate
- appraise
- justify
- evaluate

Other Taxonomies

Quest

Another taxonomy which focuses on processes is one developed by Carolyn Hughes for the Quest program. The lowest level is data-gathering skills, which include observing, recalling, comparing, and contrasting. The second level is organizing ideas and lists, conceptualizing, and classifying. The next level is inferencing; this group of processes includes inferring attributes, inferring meaning, inferring cause-effect relationships, and concluding. The top level (most complex) is called application; the processes here are inquiring, anticipating, making choices, and solving problems. One of the values of this hierarchy is that it classifies by what the students will be doing.

The very basic level of observing is sometimes overlooked. If one does not make accurate and precise observations, the data are garbage and no amount of sophisticated processes will change the outcome—more garbage. This taxonomy probably more closely follows the kinds of activities we scope and sequence in our curricula.

Rankin and Hughes

More recently, Rankin and Hughes (1987) have developed another classification system for thinking skills (Rankin-Hughes List of Selected Thinking Skills) which organizes the thinking skills needed to reach certain objectives. These objectives include concept formation, comprehending, principle formation, composing, problem solving, decision making, and research. They list seven steps in the generic process as focus, gather information, organize information, analyze information, generate ideas, synthesize, and evaluate.

O'Tuel and Bullard

We have developed a taxonomy to describe the processes we see as important (p. 22). The emphasis in this taxonomy is on processing, so verb participles have been used to describe the hierarchy. The chart moves from least complex (collecting data) to most complex (using multiprocesses).

IMPACT

Many of the commercially available programs have hierarchies of processes which are taught from the bottom up in their curricula. One example is IMPACT, which also starts with observing and moves up to more complex procedures.

Thinking Frames

Another approach to thinking skills is that of Perkins. To organize the way we look at thinking skills, Perkins (1985, 1990) introduced the concept of *thinking frames*. He defines thinking frames as representations you make to guide your thinking. The frame helps you focus on the task at hand by organizing your thinking, assisting you in focusing on the product you are producing, giving you a process (or tactic) to use to carry out a task, characterizing your treatment by a certain style, or in some way catalyzing your thinking processes. The frame may be an image, a verbal representation, or even a motoric procedure. If it functions to give meaning and focus, then it can be classified as a thinking frame. Perkins suggests that prior to tackling a situation or task, we should stop and consider how we might place it in perspective to product or process. Such a frame should include how to proceed

A TAXONOMY OF THINKING SKILLS AND STRATEGIES (O'Tuel and Bullard)		
Category	**Processes**	**Applications**
Collecting Data	Observing	senses—appearances, materials, origins; feelings—emotions, value, personal significance; recording—preciseness, recall, reliability
Relating/Clarifying Data	Describing	physical properties; functions; relationships; analogies
	Classifying	critical attributes; compare/contrast; class inclusion; hierarchaical
	Pattern Recognizing	processes; events; objects; persons
Conceptualizing	Evaluating Data/Relations	data source, authority, reliability; data/relations; cause/effect; fact/opinion; reliability/likelihood; valuing; relevance
Using Processes on Data/Concepts/ Relations	Summarizing	concluding, annotating
	Inferencing	generalizing, if...then; estimating; predicting consequences/likelihood
	Organizing/Planning	developing frameworks, scaffolds; relating pieces to whole
	Analyzing	breaking whole into parts; relating parts to each other; compare/contrast
	Hypothesizing	generating solutions, ideas; what if
Using Multiprocesses on Data/Concepts/ Relations	Problem Solving	using processes above to clarify problem, generate solutions, test hypotheses, evaluate
	Decision Making	using processes above to weigh choices, predict consequences, evaluate, decide
	Valuing	evaluating how comfortable one's actions and/or choices are with one's value system
	Synthesizing	abstracting/combining bodies of knowledge and/or series of procedures into coherent wholes
	Creating/Inventing	generating new products and/or procedures which go beyond what is already known and understood

NOTE: *Categories in this taxonomy are listed from least complex (collecting data) to most complex (using multiprocesses on data/concepts/relations).*

and when to proceed as well as the goal and direction we are to take.

* * *

Whatever taxonomy, plan, or procedure we use to make order out of our thinking can be an organizational tool. We may not need to use a taxonomy for ourselves, but using one may provide a support system, allowing less-sophisticated students to make sense out of the material. Such systems help novices, both teachers and students, to organize their thinking.

Models of Instruction

We all need some structure in our lives. Each of us knows someone who seemingly floats (or stumbles) from one series of events to another as a cork bobs on the water. These individuals may appear to have little structure to their lives; however, looks may be deceiving. We do not actually know that their behaviors are not planned and purposeful. Other individuals around us demonstrate a strong need for external structure, an explicit plan and sequence which they may follow in a way that appears to be somewhat rigid. We refer to these explicit plans, sometimes, as security blankets; the person may not be rigid in the execution of the plan, but s/he feels less anxious because there is a "plan."

One place that our society seems to be adamant about us having plans of action is in the act of teaching. Thus, the teaching act is described as involving three segments: planning, implementing, and evaluating (Eggen & Kauchak 1988). As we look at models of instruction, we realize that there are a number of models, some which vary greatly from others, and that no model is the best one for all types of educational outcomes (Joyce & Weil 1972).

Before we select any model of instruction, we must decide what the learning outcomes are to be for the lessons and the unit of instruction. *Purpose drives instruction.* We decide first what the students will be able to do at the end of the unit that they cannot do now. Then it is helpful to determine what level of complexity and proficiency they are expected to reach. When we have these clearly in mind, we are ready to select a delivery system which we think is most likely to lead to the successful achievement of the outcomes we set. The instructional model we choose should facilitate student learning, learning in the context of our outcomes or objectives (Joyce & Weil 1972).

Deductive Models

To say a model of instruction is deductive or inductive is useful in the context of higher order thinking because the names imply both a general structure and sequence. Models which we call deductive begin with a stated concept or general statement and then break it down into its parts. We go from the general to the specific. "Direct instruction," a term frequently used in educational literature, is a deductive model.

Deductive models of instruction have several advantages. The straightforward presentation of general then specific tells you where to store the specific information you are receiving. If external aids to organizing the material, for example, an outline (verbal) or a structural display (spatial/visual), are to be used, they may be furnished to students at the beginning of the instruction. Using external organizers, we have a structure for organizing all of the related pieces in one meaningful "chunk" of information for our long-term memory. This is one of the strategies recommended for improving the storing of information (declarative or procedural) in long-term memory. Because we have put the "chunk" in as a meaningful whole with its pieces, retrieval of all or part is enhanced.

Little time is wasted in a deductive approach to instruction. Its efficiency in the temporal realm is no small plus. We are asked to teach more and more in the same or less amount of time. When we use a deductive model, we can observe rather easily what percent of the instructional time our students are spending on task (time-on-task).

If we increase our students' academically engaged time, the research results report that we should also see an increase in achievement. With our monitoring of the students' time-on-task, we can pickup on lapses in concentration, keep them attending, and move in a logical, sequential manner. When information is clear, focused, and logically structured and time is short, deductive teaching may be our most efficient approach. It also lends itself to the teaching of facts, principles, and concepts.

The deductive model has been used effectively in the direct teaching of thinking skills. When this is done, the objective is to teach the skill. The teacher introduces the thinking skill, defines it, gives examples of the process, and asks the students to suggest examples. This is usually followed by the teacher modeling the behavior for the class. Such a demonstration is then followed by having the students work through the process as a class with the guidance of the teacher.

Since a thinking skill is a procedure, it must be practiced in order to be learned. The information processing theories emphasize the need for practice and feedback when learning any procedure. After the students have had the experience of working through the process, the teacher should give them further opportunities to practice. Trying new processes is a risk-taking task for most students. Therefore, the first opportunity for practice can best be accomplished in small groups or pairs. Feedback, through discussion, is essential. In subsequent classes, the students can be given opportunities to try the skill on their own. During the practice and feedback segment, the students need to have the experience of reflecting on what they have done and how they did it. Another activity that aids in the acquisition of a skill is to have the students generate other situations in which they might use it.

In order for a skill to transfer from a specific context, the usefulness of it in other activities must be consciously addressed. This applies to any skill, not just thinking skills. As noted earlier, transfer does *not* occur by osmosis!

Procedures and forms to use in the planning of the general deductive and Ausubel models can be found on pages 30 and 32. In addition, Beyer (1987) is a good source of information on the direct teaching of thinking skills.

Inductive Models

Inductive models of instruction have not been articulated and promoted as much as deductive models. An inductive model moves from the particulars to the general. If our objective is teaching for thinking, inductive approaches are particularly suitable. Suppose we want our students to understand a particularly important concept, and we feel they will accomplish this best by getting involved in the material or content which surrounds this concept. Because the concept is complex, we would like for them to "chunk" all of this together in some meaningful organization. They must participate in activities that will promote this long-term storage outcome.

The phrase "interact with the material" is often heard. When we allow students to think about the relationships between the various subsets of the concept through the processes of comparing and contrasting, we are using an inductive approach (see model unit in Social Studies, Chapter 10, for example). The techniques of brainstorming and semantic mapping are other examples. When we allow the students to do something with the content, interest is usually heightened, attention is increased, and encoding into long-term memory is enhanced.

If inductive models are so effective, why do we not use them more often? The major reason is *time*. It takes more class time to engage in activities where we are guiding, but not directing, the process. Students' thinking is not necessarily rapid and focused. Many teachers will tell us they do not have enough time to use inductive models; they have too much material to cover. All teachers are feeling the pressures to teach more and do it faster. Many teachers are not familiar with inductive approaches and feel uncomfortable with the less teacher-controlled situation that occurs when students are actively involved in constructing their understanding.

The justification for investing the time it takes to use an inductive model is that it improves understanding and increases retrieval at a later time. In addition, students are engaging in higher order thinking, which they need now and will need, perhaps even more, in the future. If much of what we teach now may be obsolete in ten years, what will current students do with the new information that replaces or modifies current content? Teachers of literature and history may argue that their content will not change. In some respects this is true; we will still be studying the treasures of literature and the chronicles of our past. This outlook does not suggest what the individual will do with new publications and occurring events in our world. How will the individual analyze, critique, evaluate these if the thinking skills needed are not learned and practiced in his or her school experiences?

Inductive teaching appears less structured when it is implemented. This appearance is deceptive because the teacher must do extensive planning to organize the activities and direction of the lesson (Joyce & Weil 1972). It does permit students to introduce ideas and inferences. Teachers who feel the need for explicit structure or who lack confidence in their teaching abilities, particularly in the area of classroom discipline, may find inductive teaching threatening and/or unsettling. This does not have to be the case. Preplanning is the key. Once a teacher has tried an inductive approach which s/he has carefully orchestrated in advance, the momentum of student participation and the enthusiasm of students will usually convince the teacher of its viability. The class will be noisier, and there may be more student movement, but these are the by-products of effective learning.

The steps in the inductive process are generally described as follows:

- The teacher selects the concept to be taught by an inductive model.

- The teacher then "thinks backward" from the concept to all of the relevant facts, principles, examples, etc. which contribute to his or her understanding of the concept.

- Several are selected to present to the students, or the teacher may ask students to generate all the information they can about a topic.

- Once these particulars are before them, the students must make inferences, draw conclusions, and/or generalize from them.

- Depending on the complexity of the concept, these inferences may only arrive at subsets of the general concept.

- These are then processed in similar ways to arrive at the general concept.

One criticism of inductive models is that they do not work well on students who do not have a broad information base or who do not have a fair amount of prior knowledge of the subject. This does not have to be a stumbling block if during the process of collecting or being exposed to the facts, principles, examples, etc., some way of displaying all this information is employed. For instance, in the Taba Model (1966) a data retrieval chart is constructed so that all students have access to the information on which they are working. This permits students with less prior knowledge to participate in the thinking processes. These less well-informed students might not be able to make inferences on the knowledge they have in their memory, and they might not have a format for making generalizations/inferences. By supplying an information base and the format, the teacher makes it possible for each student to become involved.

More specific procedures on particular inductive models, as well as forms to use in planning and developing the general inductive and Taba models (Eggen & Kauchak 1988; Joyce & Weil 1972), can be found on pages 35 and 38.

Inductive or Deductive

Although it may appear that we are promoting inductive models over deductive models, we are not. They are used much less often and are particularly appropriate for stimulating student involvement in learning.

The necessity of selecting an instructional model which most nearly supports the kind of learning in which the students are engaged should not be in doubt. How to select the appropriate model may not be apparent. Again, the outcome of the instruction should help determine the model. It is important to remember that variety is also an important factor in maintaining interest and attention.

Variables Which Affect Instruction

When the instructor embarks on developing a program of study, unit, lesson, demonstration, or whatever, four variables must be taken into account:

- the characteristics of the students
- the characteristics of the teacher
- the nature of the content and the desired outcomes
- the environment in which the instruction will take place, i.e., the physical setting

Other factors which may have an impact on learning include parents, community, administrative policies of the school or state department of education, national educational issues or mandates, and the economy, to name a few. We will deal with the four major considerations only, since they are always of concern.

Student Characteristics

The most important student characteristic is the student's developmental level. In the section on Piaget in Chapter 2, it was stressed that stage, not age, is the critical concern. We will touch on some of the considerations and limitations that someone's stage of development may impose on the learning situation.

Preschool programs modeled after cognitively oriented curricula such as High Scope (a Piaget based program) have many excellent activities and procedures which encourage children to become self-initiated learners, explorers, planners, etc. K–12 scope and sequence plans and curriculum frameworks take developmental levels into account. Trainers in industrial settings have become increasingly aware of the potential to improve the effectiveness of their training by employing basic principles about how people learn.

One important student characteristic is whether s/he can deal with abstract situations. Teaching a highly abstract concept to a concrete operational child may not succeed. A general learning principle is that if you can teach something using concrete examples and objects and hands-on experience, do it! Any new learning is learned quicker and more easily if concrete referents (objects, persons, events) can be used, no matter what the age or stage of the learner is. Another caution that comes from Piagetian theory and information processing theories is how many "pieces" can this learner be expected to hold in short-term or working memory at one time. A 6-year-old may only be able to deal with one or two; an adult may be able to deal with five or six.

Students' learning style preferences may be another characteristic to be considered (Carbo 1990; Dunn, Beaudry & Klavas 1989; McCarthy 1990). Modality preferences—visual, auditory, or kinesthetic—could help us in deciding the way we demonstrate or present content. Also, some students seem to take in new situations in a "global" or wholistic fashion and others in an analytical or discrete way. The global learner may be quicker at seeing relationships between elements, and the analytical processor may focus on the major element and its characteristics. For example, if we ask students to draw three things, the global learner may draw a tree, a bench, and a flower; the analytical learner may draw three trees or three balls, etc.

Motivation is always a concern of teachers. If a teacher can use examples to which students can relate themselves or in which they are interested, attention will be increased. The more we have the students actively participating in the learning activity, the more motivated they will be. The two major sources of motivation are internal and external (Weiner 1974). The internally motivated student enjoys doing an activity for its own sake or for the satisfaction of mastering it or for the joy of solving the puzzle. The externally motivated student is looking for some good reason or payoff outside himself or herself to engage in the task. The internally motivated student is more persistent and more likely to engage in similar activities during free play or nonclass time. Some of the research has found that tangible external reinforcers may actually reduce internal motivation and the likelihood of the student engaging in the activity outside of the class task. Since higher order thinking is what we want all students to use in many different settings, we want to use high-interest, hands-on, self-rewarding (mastery) tasks whenever possible.

Another affective component in instruction is students' self-concepts. How confident are they about their abilities? How successful are they in school? Do they perceive the activity as highly risky? Are they likely to be embarrassed by their performances? These attitudes that students hold about themselves are important (Marsh & Parker 1984). All of us strive to maintain and/or enhance our self-concept. The affective domain is an important consideration. Up to 25% of the variance in achievement can be attributed to affective characteristics (Bloom 1976). Some recommended suggestions are (1) allow students to work in groups, (2) do not grade them on thinking skills (although you may later assess the content they have learned in the subject area), (3) give them constructive feedback and encouragement, and (4) choose developmentally appropriate tasks on which they have a reasonable chance of being successful.

Some sex differences have been found among students and adults (Hyde 1984; Macoby & Jacklin 1974, 1980). Most of them are not consistently shown across studies. There is the most support for the following findings: (1) boys are more aggressive than girls, and this is consistent from infancy on, (2) in adolescence and after, boys tend to perform better on tasks involving visual/spatial abilities than girls, and (3) from adolescence on, girls tend to perform better on verbal tasks than boys. When planning thinking skills tasks, you may want to keep these characteristics in mind.

Socioeconomic status (SES) of students usually impacts on their performance in school. In fact, several studies have found that if socioeconomic differences are partialled out of the performance of groups of students in school, no other variable left was significant, not race, sex, teacher, school, etc. (Mussen, Conger & Kagan 1979). Unfortunately, SES is a Pandora's box; so many things contribute to it that we cannot usually address it directly. For instance, family stability may be as important as family income; the number of children and the living space they have may be significant; certainly, nutrition and health care are components in SES; and the list goes on. Nevertheless, we need to know as much as we can about our students and their backgrounds in order to plan instruction better. The variety and distinctiveness of cognitive experiences that preschoolers have affect the level of their cognitive abilities when they enter school (and the family setting continues to be a stumbling block for many of them). Low SES children have many experiences, but these experiences may lack the variety and distinctiveness of their middle class counterparts.

Teacher Characteristics

Teacher characteristics are seldom considered when curricula and instructional designs are developed, but they are important also. As noted earlier, a teacher's preference for a highly structured learning environment will affect that teacher's choice of instructional approaches. The teacher's learning style preference may be observed in his or her teaching. A friend of ours (Hunley 1989) was presenting models of instruction to a class of graduate students. She used an inverted tree (visual display) to outline the content. Because she noted some uncomfortableness in some of the students, she asked several of them to explain their confusion. They said that they had trouble following the display. She then went to the chalkboard and translated the visual display into a verbal outline with Roman numerals and capital and lower case letters. The students were delighted and said they had no trouble understanding the verbal outline. The two organizations had identical information in them, but the verbal was preferred to the spatial by these students. In the same class were other teachers who found that the visual gave them an image they could call up so that they had all the information simultaneously. They preferred the visual.

Teachers have varying levels of competency in their subject areas. This is particularly true in elementary schools where teachers are asked to be all things to their students. Our feelings of adequacy and expertise will affect whether we are willing to let students generate data. If we are afraid they may introduce something we do not know, and need for self-esteem will not permit us to say we do not know, then we are not likely to choose an instructional approach that introduces that possibility.

Training and experience in questioning is another teacher characteristic which is considered in choosing an instructional design. When Bloom's taxonomy was introduced earlier in this chapter, the use of verbs which ask students to engage in higher order thinking was suggested as a way to expand the teacher's questioning skills. The use of action verbs instead of the verb "to be" may be helpful. In addition to the usual five "w's" and the "h" (who, what, when, where, why, and how), questions which start with the following may generate some thoughtful replies:

- What do you think would happen if....

- Why do you think that is more likely the case....

- What reasons can you give for....

- How would this be different if....

- If you had to make the decision, what would you do and why....

- Can you think of a way that....

Questions may be categorized by the level of thinking they involve or by several other ways such as the content area, their sequence in the instructional plan, or whatever method makes sense to the teacher. The need to ask students to do something with the content rather than just regurgitate it is the focus of questions which require higher order thinking.

Content

The discipline to be studied might be one content consideration. When units are interdisciplinary, the particular parts of the various disciplines may need to be taken into account. Some parts of a subject may lend themselves to student participation while others may seem better presented in lecture form. The educational outcomes of the unit should be the guiding light as to what instructional model is used and what kinds of activities are planned for the learners. Again, these outcomes will vary when the lesson involves new material over when the students are reviewing and relating previously learned information, concepts, and procedures. These differences will be more apparent when the outcomes for lessons and units are shown in the model units and lessons in Part II of this book.

Learning Environment

The learning environment includes the physical arrangements, the psychological aspects, and such variables as time constraints and student grouping. The physical setup may place some constraints. These may be overcome in some cases by taking the students to another setting or moving the furniture in the room. The teacher has the opportunity to arrange the learning environment with posters, charts, outlines, displays, specimens, maps, preinstructional organizers, attention getters, audio-visual aides such as films, video cassettes, audio cassettes, and filmstrips, and computer programs. Whatever is to be used in the lesson should be chosen and obtained during the planning.

Class organization must also be decided. Will the children work individually, in small groups, or as a total class? Will the task be pencil-and-paper seat work, hands-on construction, observation and oral discussion, demonstration, sociodrama, debate, etc.? What is the role of the teacher in the segments of the lesson? Is s/he a facilitator, monitor, or director?

The school schedule imposes some constraints on the time available. Pullout programs, special areas (music, art, physical education), staggered lunch periods, recess, library access are some of the considerations in elementary schools where there are self-contained or semi-departmental arrangements for instruction. In middle schools and secondary schools, the limitations of a certain number of minutes is more structured and uniform across classes.

Community and parents may make demands or offer assistance, and the building administrator may place limitations in addition to those mandated by district and state policies. Most of these can be integrated into instructional plans with minimal effort. One constraint which may not be as easily considered is a financial one. Fortunately, higher order thinking activities and instruction do not require materials and equipment in excess of what is needed for adequate instruction. We may be limited in the use of computers, for instance, but computers are not a necessity, although they can enhance interest and access to activities.

Outlines for Models

The next section presents several teaching models. Inductive and deductive models are presented separately; we hope it might help to highlight the differences between the two.

Generic outlines developed by the authors for planning a unit and a lesson are found in Chapter 9 on pages 104 and 110. Outlines adapted for use with particular instructional approaches are included in the discussions in this chapter.

Deductive Models

Three deductive models will be described: the general deductive model, Ausubel, and PET. There are others, but these will serve to show the deductive approach. Remember that deductive instruction is where we start with the principle or main idea and develop the supporting information and/or break it into parts.

General Deductive Model

The general deductive model (see below) is a direct instruction model in which the major idea is expressed first, and the material to be presented about it is noted. Then the material is presented in a very direct way from the general to the specific.

If the topic is a concept, a five-step model might be used:

(1) give the concept name
(2) define it
(3) enumerate the characteristics
(4) give exemplars of the concept
(5) relate it to any superordinate, subordinate, or coordinate concepts

Again, this is a very direct method of presenting material and may only require students to recognize or repeat the information. You could ask students to give other examples

---

General Deductive Model

NAME ——→ DEFINE ——→ ENUMERATE CHARACTERISTICS ——→ GIVE EXEMPLARS ——→ RELATE

GENERAL DEDUCTIVE MODEL

TOPIC: TIME NEEDED:

GRADE LEVEL:

CONTENT OBJECTIVE:

PROCESS OBJECTIVE:

STUDENT
GROUPING _____ Individual _____ Pairs _____ Group _____ Total Class

MODEL STEPS

1. Introduce: state content and process objectives to students.

2. Define/illustrate/give examples of ideas and concepts.

3. Model any processes.

4. Walk students through process.

5. Expand, relate content.

6. Students practice process and summarize content.

7. Evaluation: students reflect on process/content, perform process on new content, apply or recall content.

or to suggest how they might use the concept in another situation. Any questions you ask can be implemented orally or in writing. You could solicit applications of the concept from the students. The lesson on longitude discussed below in the section on Ausubel could be taught by this model.

A general deductive planning guide developed by the authors is presented on page 30. The steps to use in teaching a general deductive model are listed.

Ausubel

Ausubel believes that students will remember verbal information more easily if it is tied to information already stored in their memories (Ausubel 1963). The technique he recommends is an "advance organizer." It may relate what is being introduced to a similar concept or to an overarching or superordinate concept which includes both the similar concept and the new concept. The advance organizer may be an analogy, giving the students something they already understand as a model for the new information. If we have taught a lesson on latitude and now we are going to introduce the concept of longitude, we can remind them (or have them tell us) what they know about latitude. We can explain the differences and similarities. We could also use a superordinate concept about how we spatially section our globe in order to locate places and their relationships to each other. The analogy of sections of an orange might be used to help them understand longitude.

Ausubel might use a spatial array to illustrate the relationships between parts of a major idea or concept (Eggen, Kauchak & Harder 1979). In this case, it might look like the Global Sectioning graphic below.

After presenting the "advance organizer," start with the main idea, then define, develop, etc. Then present each of the subsections. In this case, latitude has already been introduced. If the teacher used this spatial array before introducing latitude, then the array could serve as the organizer. The total lesson does not have to be deductive if you want to introduce some variety. One of the subsections can be taught inductively. With young students, teachers may not want to give them the whole array at the beginning but add each element as they go along. The younger the children, the easier it is for them to be distracted. If all the array is visible, some may be attending to some other part rather than the one under discussion. For older and more sophisticated students, presenting the full array gives them the big picture and helps them understand the purpose, relationship, or importance of each part.

Since we all have different modality preferences, the spatial array may be disconcerting to verbal/auditory learners. We might want to have a conventional outline with Roman numerals, capital letters, Arabic numbers, lower case, etc. available for those who prefer it. Latitude would be Roman numeral I and longitude would be Roman numeral II. For

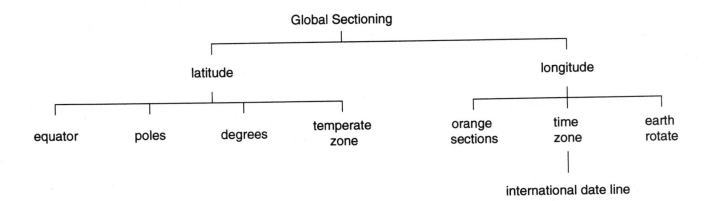

AUSUBEL

TOPIC: TIME NEEDED:

GRADE LEVEL:

CONTENT OBJECTIVE:

PROCESS OBJECTIVE:

STUDENT
GROUPING _____ Individual _____ Pairs _____ Group _____ Total Class

MODEL STEPS

1. Advance organizer (teacher develops spatial array, analogy, or organizational relationship that relates new to old array):

2. Present subsets and examples and fill in array

3. Analysis of array, analogy, or relationships

4. Evaluation

Follow-up activities suggested:

further explanation of the classical verbal outline, read the section later in this chapter under Strategies and Techniques.

Eggen, Kauchak, and Harder (1979) used the spatial display all through their book on teaching strategies and devoted a complete chapter to Ausubel. Since this is a deductive or direct teaching model, it can be used to deliver information without asking students to transform or do anything with the content. Thus, in using this model you must plan to include questions or activities which will engage the students. The active involvement of the students is not apparent in the outline; you must plan for it.

The authors present their planning outline for Ausubel on page 32. As suggested above, the steps are similar to the general model, but the differences of this particular model are indicated.

PET

The Program for Effective Teaching (PET) is one of several systems based on Madeline Hunter's learning system. Other programs based on her system are Instructional Theory Into Practice (ITIP) and the UCLA plan. Although Hunter did not intend that instruction based on her delivery system include only direct or deductive teaching, most of the systems have been presented in that way.

The PET model is a six-step model (see diagram below):

(1) presenting an anticipatory set

(2) stating the objective
(3) teaching to the objective
(4) monitoring and adjusting
(5) maintaining the focus of the learner
(6) closure

During the beginning, the teacher may introduce or have students recall relevant information. The teacher states the objective and then proceeds with the instructional techniques that s/he has selected. The end of the lesson involves review and summary, usually by students, of what they have learned. If this outline omitted the statement of the objective or stated the objective as learning to think like a "scientist," it could be designed as an inductive lesson.

Many evaluators of PET lessons or demonstrations will mark down anyone who does not state the objective within the first two minutes of the lesson. Unless you can establish in a pre-lesson conference that the evaluator is comfortable with you leaving out the objective, it is best not to plan an inductive PET lesson for evaluation purposes.

The various techniques from which the teacher selects the activities for instruction may include any number of higher order thinking skills. For instance, during teacher questioning, s/he could ask students to compare, to evaluate, to speculate, to estimate, etc. Student generated questions frequently are more probing than some of our inquiries. The main consideration, again, is that we plan to ask

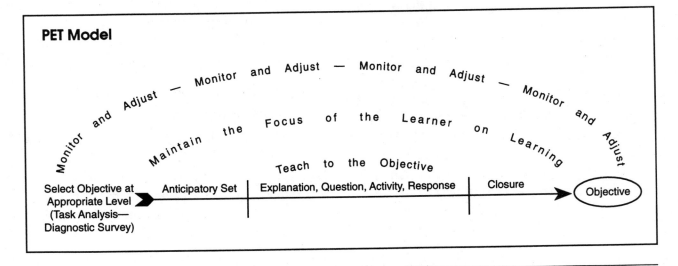

PET Model

Monitor and Adjust — Monitor and Adjust — Monitor and Adjust — Monitor and Adjust

Maintain the Focus of the Learner on Learning

Teach to the Objective

| Select Objective at Appropriate Level (Task Analysis— Diagnostic Survey) | Anticipatory Set | Explanation, Question, Activity, Response | Closure | Objective |

students to engage in higher level thinking by our questions and the activities they are asked to do.

Inductive Models

Inductive models require the student to construct, infer, generalize, evaluate, and/or analyze the content. These thinking processes encourage students to develop their own ideas and strategies. These models are particularly effective when processes need to be internalized and when relationships between events, places, people, etc. need to be understood. Because the students construct the concepts and relations, most of the cognitive activities in these lessons are at the higher levels of Bloom's taxonomy.

Two inductive models will be described; they are the general inductive model and Taba. The discovery models used by Bruner and others in the sciences, mathematics, and social studies are examples of the general inductive model. Should you want to read an example of this, see Bruner (1968) for a chapter on "Man, A Course of Study." In the science curriculum, the students become "scientists" and carry out experiments and research. From these they draw their conclusions and build their conceptual understanding. The hands-on experiencing assures the students' active participation in the learning process.

Criticism of discovery and inductive techniques in general is that they work best with students who have a good knowledge base, such as many gifted groups (Olson 1976). Process is emphasized, and critics point out that you have to have some knowledge base in order to have anything to process. There is some truth to this. Some of the research on problem solving found that experts have a larger knowledge base, and it is better organized, than that of novices (Gagné 1985). Models need to address the need for background or declarative knowledge and to include the acquisition of the knowledge as part of the model; this is particularly well done in the Taba model. The choice of the inductive ap-proach, which does take more time, should be made based on the desired outcomes of the unit.

General Inductive Model

Many teachers have experimented with inquiry and discovery learning. They report mixed feelings about the experience. Anytime we try something new, we may not feel as comfortable as we do when we use what we are accustomed to. For students to engage in activities which culminate in their constructing the concepts or relationships or making the desired inferences, the teacher must do much planning and guidance prior to the lesson's implementation.

The model begins with the teacher planning the outcomes and selecting student activities which will lead to the desired outcome. The teaching differs from the deductive models in that the outcome is not stated at the beginning. The introduction may include some interest-arousing questions or dilemmas which start students on their quest. A simulation of a situation with which the students are not familiar may allow them to develop ideas about how to go about some process and give them an analogy to draw upon. A planning guide for the steps in a general inductive unit is presented on page 35.

The inquiry method, a variation on the inductive model, is described as having these steps:

- identify a problem
- generate an hypothesis (or develop a research objective)
- collect data
- interpret data in relation to hypothesis
- develop tentative conclusion
- verify or replicate
- generalize results

The students may set up a data bank for their group. In the process, they may find it necessary to organize their information. When the students have to do something to the information, they are more likely to remem-

GENERAL INDUCTIVE MODEL

TOPIC: TIME NEEDED:

GRADE LEVEL:

CONTENT OBJECTIVE:

PROCESS OBJECTIVE:

STUDENT GROUPING	Individual	Pairs	Group	Total Class
_____	_____	_____	_____	

MODEL STEPS

1. Teacher writes content and process objectives and plans student activities to achieve them.

2. Teacher introduces topic to students without stating objective or merely stating a process objective.

3. Students participate in guided discovery activities.

4. Evaluation: As a result of activities students demonstrate understanding of concept and/or process.

5. Follow-up plans

ber it. At the end of the set of activities, the students should be able to discover the outcomes intended for them. Inductive models take more time than deductive models because the students are developing ideas, not being told them. These inductive models should probably be reserved for important bodies of information where you want students to develop their own ideas about the material. A verbal sequence of the lesson might look like the diagram at the bottom of the page.

Taba

In the Taba model, the students learn the declarative knowledge as they engage in thinking processes such as analysis, inferring, and generalizing. This model is best used when a large body of content needs to be examined and the emphasis of the objectives is for the students to see the relationships among the components and engage in the higher order thinking processes of analysis and inferring. If one follows the whole model, the time required is much more than would be needed to present the material in a deductive model such as Ausubel. Therefore, the process objectives would need to be critical to justify the implementing of the entire model. However, there is a compromise available in that the teacher can enter the model at several points depending on which processes are to be developed. The steps will be described first, then variations will be suggested.

The topic is introduced to students, and they are asked to generate as many ideas and words or collect as much information as they can about the topic. Each suggestion is placed on the board or overhead. Hints and cues are permissible. If this is the first time the students have addressed brainstorming by name and process, and you are going to structure their doing it by directions and feedback, then one of your process objectives may be that the students will be able to brainstorm effectively. You do not want to introduce too many new processes in one lesson.

The list may also be generated by collecting objects (rocks, leaves) or observing events. Once the list is generated, the students are asked to group the items that are alike in some way. When the groups are displayed, the students generate a name for each group. These group labels become bases of the titles for columns or rows in the Retrieval chart. This process or classification or categorization may also be a process objective in your lesson. This Retrieval chart is the heart of the model. The Chart is used to display factual information about the components the students will compare and contrast, and about which they will then make inferences and generalizations.

When the titles for the rows and columns have been selected, the students gather the data to fill in the Chart. An individual, a pair, or a group may be assigned one of the cells or a column or a row. This will be determined by the developmental level of the students, the availability of information, the time to be allowed, the number of groups who will work on the tasks.

If the development of research skills is one of the unit objectives, then the students have the opportunity to hone those skills by seeking data from materials in the classroom, the

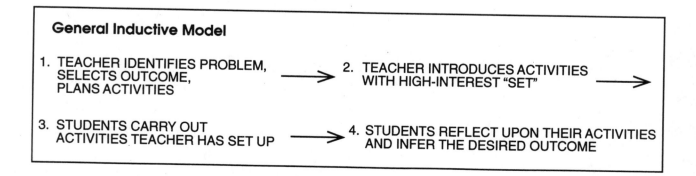

General Inductive Model

1. TEACHER IDENTIFIES PROBLEM, SELECTS OUTCOME, PLANS ACTIVITIES → 2. TEACHER INTRODUCES ACTIVITIES WITH HIGH-INTEREST "SET" →

3. STUDENTS CARRY OUT ACTIVITIES TEACHER HAS SET UP → 4. STUDENTS REFLECT UPON THEIR ACTIVITIES AND INFER THE DESIRED OUTCOME

library, individuals in the community, or by writing for additional documents or references. It is their job to find the "observable" information to place in their cell(s) or row. Opinions and generalizations are not put in the cells.

Once there are data for all the cells, each student receives a copy of the Chart. Actually, the Chart could be put on the board, but the analysis of the Chart content will take several days, and the Chart might get erased. The Chart can be put on an overhead and used during the analysis process. This is recommended. The reason it is advisable for each student to receive a copy is that they will then have it for review of the factual information which may be evaluated later on a summative test. The matrix can be as simple as 2×2 and use pictures instead of words for nonreaders, or be an adaptation of the periodic table in chemistry or the phylogenetic scale in Biology, or be some set of complex relationships in social studies. The size of the cells can be expanded depending on how much information will be put in the various cells. An example of a blank 4×4 matrix is shown at the top of the next column.

After the information is entered in the chart, the students are ready to begin analyzing and inferring. Since all students have the same information (the Chart), all students are able to participate in the process. This is a major advantage in using such a chart. Students who may not have enough information to participate in a class discussion ordinarily have all the information at their fingertips.

The teacher selects one cell for analysis. S/he asks the students to study the information in the cell. They may do this as a class or in cooperative groups. They are then asked what they can infer from the information in that cell. Each time they make an inference, they are asked to tell on what they based their inference. This justification step is a pivotal stage in the strategy.

Once students have gotten the idea of looking at a set of facts and making predictions or generalizations about the set, they can examine a column of cells. What happens at this level is that the students discern likenesses and differences between the components on that particular characteristic. They should be told that this process is called analysis.

After comparisons and inferences are made about the rest of the columns, the students are asked to generalize about the major topic based on the data in all of the Chart. The teacher may be fearful that the students will not be able to do this. As a result, s/he may spend time writing down generalizations s/he hopes the students will make. This is a good practice to follow. The surprise has been that, typically, the students generate more than those written down! Each generalization must be justified by, or based on, information in the Chart.

Textbooks and teacher resource materials

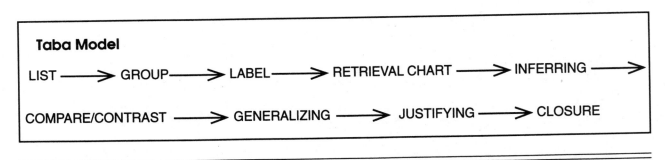

Taba Model

LIST $\longrightarrow$ GROUP $\longrightarrow$ LABEL $\longrightarrow$ RETRIEVAL CHART $\longrightarrow$ INFERRING $\longrightarrow$

COMPARE/CONTRAST $\longrightarrow$ GENERALIZING $\longrightarrow$ JUSTIFYING $\longrightarrow$ CLOSURE

TABA INDUCTIVE MODEL

TOPIC: TIME NEEDED:

GRADE LEVEL:

CONTENT OBJECTIVE(S):

PROCESS OBJECTIVE:

STUDENT
GROUPING _____ Individual _____ Pairs _____ Group _____ Total Class

MODEL STEPS

1, 2, & 3. Brainstorming, observing/classifying/labeling

4. Data Collection (show chart):
   Select column and row headings:
   Assign students or groups to find factual information to go in the cells or rows they are assigned:
   Assist students in locating resources (room, library, school, community):
   Students assemble their information:
   Students enter their information on Chart:

5. Analysis and inferencing (with justification):
   Within cells:
   Among cells:
   Across all cells:

6. Evaluation: Predictions?

7. Closure: Summarize. Follow-up activities?

are filled with charts, graphs, and maps. Any of these can become a Retrieval chart, á la Taba. Although the matrix may be the easiest organizer for students to develop, the construction of graphs, maps, etc. is a viable alternative.

As was mentioned at the beginning of this section, it is possible to enter this model at several places. If the teacher begins at the first step above, the students retrieve their prior knowledge about the topic. This will help in giving them a place to store the information in a meaningful manner. The grouping and labeling which were described next give excellent practice in classification or categorization. The filling-in of the cells on the Retrieval chart (by finding the information) develops the students' research skills. If the objectives of the lesson focus on analyzing and inferencing, the teacher could produce the Chart as a *fait accompli* by handing out a copy of the Chart and start with the analysis of the cells. All steps require students to be actively involved in the learning. Most students find this approach appealing and interesting although they may complain of having to do too much work. A planning guide for the steps in the Taba model is presented on page 38. Based on your objectives, you must decide at what step you will access the model, 1, 2, 3, 4, or 5.

Strategies and Techniques

In addition to the major instructional models outlined above, there are strategies and techniques which can be used in some aspect of teaching regardless of which model or approach is selected. These will be developed below and referenced in the chapters on content-area applications. Chapter 9 has detailed suggestions on unit planning. This is a context in which many of these strategies and techniques might be used.

Questioning with Bloom's Taxonomy

Whenever a question is asked, it is at one of the six levels of Bloom's Taxonomy. The key is for the teacher to be aware of what level s/he is using and have an understanding of the intent and power of these questions.

Many times the teacher may ask a question and feel it is requiring the student to do some "real" thinking when the question may be only requiring the student to recall information that has just been taught and do nothing else with the information. When the student is asked a question, s/he may answer that question, but the teacher thinks the question requires a more in-depth answer. "You get what you ask for!" The general intent of the question is what counts, but the awareness of the verbs we use in our instruction will help us understand the questions we are asking in so far as the levels of thinking. For a review of the Taxonomy, please go back to the beginning of this chapter.

For a chart of which verbs correspond with which thinking levels, see page 41.

K–2nd Examples

The following examples about bears show several questions or activities to be used to represent each level of the Taxonomy with children in kindergarten, first, and second grade.

Knowledge
- Name different kinds of bears.
- What do bears eat?

Comprehension
- Describe a bear to someone who has never seen one.
- Explain how a bear catches fish.

Application
- Classify teddy bears by size, shape, or color.
- Act out your favorite bear story.

Analysis
- Tell how a bear's home is different from an elephant's home.
- How are these three kinds of bears alike? How are they different?

Synthesis

- Draw a picture about a bear's alarm clock which forgets to go off at the end of winter.
- Make a poem about a bear.

Evaluation

- Would a bear make a good pet? Why do you think that?
- Decide if you would like to have a bear as a house guest.
- If so, describe what might be needed to make him comfortable and tell me why.

3rd–6th Examples

This set of questions/activities might be used with students in elementary grades on the topic of colonial history.

Knowledge

- List the 13 colonies.
- Record the date each colony was established.

Comprehension

- Locate and label each colony on the map.
- Explain why each colony was settled.

Application

- Construct a matrix which shows the following about Virginia, Massachusetts, Rhode Island, and Pennsylvania: the reason each was formed; the government each had; the leaders; occupations of colonists; geography and climate.
- Demonstrate butter-making or weaving as done by the colonists.

Analysis

- Using the previously constructed matrix, compare the effect of climate and geography on occupational options.
- Contrast the work force of the southern colonies with that of the New England colonies during the 1760s.

Synthesis

- Plan and hold a colonial fair based on New England, middle, and southern colony life in the 1750s. Include booths, games, food, displays, and period clothing.
- Predict how the continent would be different today if it had not been colonized by Europeans.

Evaluation

- Appraise the effect of the creation of the House of Burgesses on the future decision to declare the colonies free and independent of British rule.
- Justify the cultivation of tobacco by John Rolfe or argue against its cultivation.

Secondary Examples

- Questions/activities that could be used with secondary students on the topic of the Renaissance might look like these.

Knowledge

- What were the approximate dates of the Renaissance?
- In what area of the world did the Renaissance take place?

Comprehension

- Summarize the main events that led to the emergence of the Renaissance using a graphic organizer.
- Explain the importance of perspective in the artistic movement of the Renaissance.

Application

- Select a saint and dramatize the story which his or her symbol represents.
- Sketch your partner's body and have him or her sketch you. Relate this activity to the Renaissance.

Analysis

- Using the knowledge of the Fibonacci Theory and cooperative learning strategy, select and analyze natural objects (pine cones, sunflowers, roses, etc.) to determine the Fibonacci sequence in each.
- Compare and contrast the Renaissance with the Middle Ages.

Taxonomy
LEARNING/PROCESS VERBS

KNOWLEDGE	COMPREHENSION	APPLICATION	ANALYSIS	SYNTHESIZE	EVALUATION
explain	explain	organize	take apart	add to	interpret
show	translate	group	part of…	predict	judge
list	group	collect	fill in	assume	justify
observe	conclude	apply	take away	translate	criticize
demonstrate	summarize	summarize	put away	extend	solve
uncover	describe	order	combine	hypothesize	decide
recognize	restate	classify	differentiate	design	infer
discover	discuss	model	divide	reconstruct	verify
experiment	describe	construct	isolate	rename	conclude
define	express	relate	order	reorganize	appraise
memorize	identify	code	separate	regroup	evaluate
repear	locate	translate	distinguish	restate	rate
record	report	interpret	dissect	systematize	compare
recall	review	use	subtract	symbolize	value
name	call	demonstrate	associate	vary	revise
relate		dramatize	relate	formulate	select
		practice	pattern	substitute	choose
		illustrate	analyze	modify	assess
		operate	apraise	minimize	estimate
		schedule	calculate	maximize	
		shop	experiment	alter	
		sketch	test	connect	
			compare	compose	
			contrast	plan	
			criticize	propose	
			diagram	arrange	
			inspect	assemble	
			debate	collect	
			inventory	construct	
			question	create	
			solve	set up	
				organize	
				manage	
				prepare	

* * *

Synthesis

- Use an event in your own life and invent a symbol to represent the event and create a "stained glass" window (black paper and colored tissue) to portray your symbol.
- A famous person from the Renaissance makes a "Quantum Leap" into the present. Hypothesize his or her reaction to any of the technology of today. Record their impressions.

Evaluation

- What does the term Renaissance Man/ Woman mean? Justify your interpretation. Select present-day persons who exemplify the term.
- How would the world be different if the printing press had not been invented? Explain your answer.

You may have noticed much similarity in the three sets of questions. Remember, when you ask open-ended questions (those that have more than one right answer), they may fit across grade levels.

As you have found in your teaching, answers to questions at the knowledge and comprehension levels require specific answers and those at the application level require students to do something with the specific information.

Answers get more interesting as they come from the upper levels. The analysis level, the beginning of the critical thinking levels, asks the student to pick the subject or information apart and look at it critically. The student will begin to understand that s/he and other students can all have a correct answer, yet each answer is different. This occurrence continues through the next two levels as well. The student will be asked to think creatively at the synthesis level and make judgments at the evaluation level.

As the teacher plans a unit of instruction, s/he will want to make sure the student has been provided the opportunities to operate at all these levels. This does not mean that you must plan to do all the levels everyday in every lesson. Some lessons, particularly introductory ones, may not ask students to do something with the material. At that point, they may not have any information on which to do something. But as their information base expands, it is critical that they do something more than repeat the information or just put it in their own words. It is possible for students in all grades to address all levels of the Taxonomy, but they must be given the opportunity. The older and more capable the student, the more complex the responses, but *all* ages, regardless of their abilities, need to be given opportunities to develop these skills.

Table of Specifications

In planning a unit, the teacher may want to make a grid or use an old lesson plan book with six blocks across. Each block can be labeled with the Taxonomy level while areas of study are listed down the side. As plans of activities are made, they can be filled in at the appropriate level. This gives the teacher a chance to see, at a glance, if s/he has provided as much instruction and/or activity at each level as s/he had thought. It takes out the guesswork. In mastery learning, this is called a Table of Specifications. It would look something like the grid below.

There may be times that more time and emphasis will need to be put on some levels and not on others, depending on the objectives and the work that is going on in other subject areas.

Questions do not need to be asked at all levels in all lessons, but all levels should be addressed within all units. The amount of time spent on each level will depend upon the objectives, prior knowledge of the students, and the levels to be emphasized in other subject areas. For instance, if the students do not have a broad information base, it will be necessary to spend a longer time providing that for them.

If many creative activities are going to be used in Social Studies, the time constraint may require you to do less of this in other subjects at this time. Every opportunity should be made to compact and combine activities across subject areas. A report written in social studies could be accepted as an English paper.

LESSON GRID

(place an X under each level to be covered on topic)

Topic	Information	Comprehension	Application	Analysis	Synthesis	Evaluation

42

Science process skills could be identified and reinforced within the social studies area when appropriate. Interdisciplinary and/or integrated units are highly desirable, particularly when you are teaching various process skills and strategies which you want to transfer across subjects.

A more detailed description of unit planning is in Chapter 9.

Verbal Charts

Teachers may find it useful to put up a verb chart in the classroom to assist them in becoming conscious of asking questions at the upper levels of the Taxonomy instead of knowledge level questions. The teacher may want to post six small charts, one on each level with a few key verbs under each. Tell the students why they are there. They may want to use the cues in their own questioning.

File Folder Activities

Another activity might be to take that old collection of pictures you have been saving for a picture file and have students do something with them. They can work in small groups or independently to select a picture, paste it on the front of a colored file folder, and then use the verb charts or copies of the verb list to help them construct a question, dealing with the picture, at each level of the Taxonomy. They should be asked to sign the inside of the folder before it is laminated. These folders are a great source of topics for creative writing. Students can also select folders which would fit within social studies and science units that are to be studied. Folders offer opportunities for research as well as creative writing.

In rooms where space is at a premium, file folders that can be kept on a table or ledge, selected by the student(s), used at the desk, and then returned to the table offer additional variety to tasks the students are asked to do.

"The Real Thing"—Using Concrete Objects

When available, real objects (specimens, artifacts, etc.) should be used to enhance learning in science and social studies. These can be handed out to small groups of students for them to construct questions using the verb charts. These questions can then be answered by their classmates.

Because Bloom's Taxonomy is one of the most easily identifiable instructional aids, many teachers feel comfortable using it. It is a

Cognitive Map

great tool for teachers and students to use in monitoring their own thinking.

Cognitive Mapping

This model has been called by a number of titles such as semantic mapping, webbing, and concept mapping. All of them refer to the same type of process although some are more detailed or elaborate. The technique uses brainstorming, classifying, and graphic organizing.

One of the important aspects of brainstorming is the second set of activities which comes after the initial free-wheeling generation of related ideas to the topic. In the second set of activities, the students organize and, in the process, discard some of the ideas. For this evaluation, the students must remember to save ideas based on the objectives and outcomes. For instance, if a list of possible solutions to a problem has been generated, the students select the ones which they predict are the most likely to lead to success. They must evaluate evidence as to the likelihood of each happening based on the information they have at the moment. While the list of ideas was being generated, the teacher could develop a cognitive map—a graphic organizer which looks like a conglomerate of Tinkertoys or a spider web or a model of the planets in orbit around the sun. A generic example of a cognitive map is shown on page 43.

Place the main topic in a circle in the center of the board and group the ideas into subgroups out from it like spokes on a wheel. Some ideas will have a number of related thoughts, where others may have no other associated thought; the cognitive map may take on an asymmetric shape. The other alternative is to list all the ideas on the board and, as in the Taba model, have the students organize the subtopics. These webs or maps are then used as organizational devices for written compositions, oral presentations, planning of a project, or other process outcomes. This process also helps student to relate the current activity with their prior knowledge, a sound educational practice. In addition, it serves as an organizational tool to help students sequence and revise.

Verbal Outline

The verbal outline is one of the most commonly used organizational devices. It breaks the topic down into parts and then subdivides those into smaller pieces. The topic is placed at the head of the page. A thesis statement may be stated before beginning the breakdown of ideas. Next Roman Numeral I is listed on the left and filled in with the first major part of the topic to be dealt with. Under I, there may be two or more subcategories labelled A, B, C, etc. If there are subdivisions under these, they are numbered with arabic numerals, 1, 2, 3, etc. Lower case letters can further subdivide the parts below the arabic numbers. An example of the format is shown on page 45.

Examples/Nonexamples

This technique is useful in helping students internalize a concept. It can be used with very young children as well as older ones. The concept is "discovered" through the studying of examples and nonexamples of the concept. Research in concept development supports the idea that one does not understand a concept until s/he understands what is *not* an example of the concept as well as what is.

The first step is to present a set of examples and nonexamples. Usually, the teacher begins with one example and one nonexample, telling which is which. By using pictures or objects, the teacher can use this technique with nonreaders. After the presentation, the students hypothesize as to what the concept might be. They may be asked why they think that is the concept. Then additional examples and nonexamples are presented, frequently two at a time.

One way to make it easier for the students to hypothesize is to put two column headings on the board. Label one "yes" and one "no." As each item is presented, the teacher places it under the correct column. Then the students hypothesize again using the new information. This recycling occurs until the students arrive at the concept. The application step occurs

Higher Order Thinking

I. Rationales for teaching students higher order thinking

  A. Information explosion

  B. Reform movement

   1. ASCD

    a) Wingspread Meeting

    b) National Training Institutes

    c) Publications/Materials

     (1) <u>Educational Leadership</u>

     (2) Yearbooks

     (3) Curriculum materials

   2. NCTE

   3. NCTM

   4. Governors Committee

   5. Professional books

    a) Goodlad

    b) *A Nation at Risk*

    c) The Carnegie Report

  C. Research studies

  D. Literacy definition

next. The students name as many other examples of the concept as they can.

The example on p. 46 illustrates pairs that are presented simultaneously under "yes" (an example of the concept) and "no" (a nonexample of the concept).

* * *

A summary of some of the more common external organizers that we use in presenting instruction and assisting students to learn how to organize their materials can be found on page 47.

In this chapter, taxonomies were presented as a useful tool in lesson planning. Models of instruction were described with some of the characteristic considerations in instructional planning. Under the deductive models, a general deductive model, Ausubel, and PET were briefly explained. Inductive models included a general inductive model and Taba. These will be revisited in chapters where more specific instructional situations are developed. In addition, a variety of devices to assist teachers in their planning and instructing were included as techniques. Examples of many of the above will be found in the chapters devoted to specific subject areas.

Example/Nonexample

External Organizers

Verbal Outline

I.

    A.

    B.

II.

    A.

    B.

      1.

Spatial Array

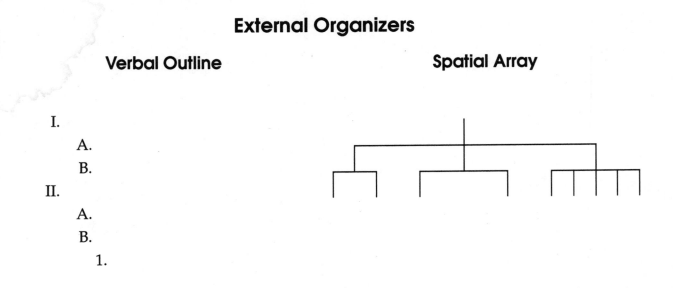

Diagram, Graph, Images, Pictures

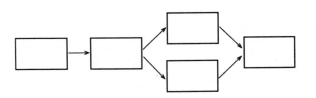

Semantic or Cognitive Mapping

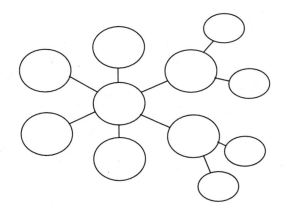

Matrix

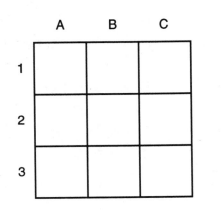

Three-dimensional Model

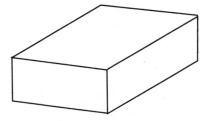

Chapter Four

Metacognition

The term metacognition means different things to different people. The act of metacognition is thinking about thinking. In particular, it refers to thinking about one's own thinking. When one reflects, that is metacognition. In the cognition literature, metacognition is the broad term used to refer to processes where you manage your own thinking.

Flavell (1978) divided metacognitive knowledge into three parts: person, task, and strategy. Although metacognitive activity is probably a product of two or more of these, we will focus on the metacognitive experiences which fall under strategy. Flavell believes that much of our metacognitive activity can be automatic and unconscious; however, the strategy aspect suggests conscious, intentional activity.

As has been suggested elsewhere in this text, experts do things differently from novices. In the realm of knowledge base, we know that experts have more information, it is better organized, and the experts know they know it. One metacognitive activity that they tend to do, that novices do not, is to analyze a problem in general nonquantitative ways before actually attempting to set the problem up in a quantitative relationship which they will then solve (Chi, Feltovich & Glaser 1981; Larkin, McDermott, Simon & Simon 1980).

Planning, Monitoring, Evaluation

The most common subcategories of metacognition are planning, monitoring, and evaluating. Campione and Brown (1978) noted that such skills are absent in the performance of retarded children.

In some information processing theories, the term executive control is used to label these processes. The idea of conscious intent is indicated rather than some automatic process.

Planning

If you have twelve tasks to accomplish on Saturday and you group them, order them as to when you will do each, predict how long they will take and what the outcomes will be, you have engaged in a typical planning process. The planning involves listing, categorizing, predicting all possible outcomes and their consequences, arranging the activities or events in some order (seriating), and selecting a course of action.

Monitoring

Teachers monitor student learning but may not realize they need to offer students opportunities to monitor their own progress. Questions like "how am I doing?" or "do I understand what I just read (or heard)?" or "can I summarize that?" are monitoring questions. This internal process may be overtly demonstrated if the person sits down and writes out the answers to some of these questions or tells someone else the answer. Because teachers become very adept at assessing the students' comprehension, the students may not learn to monitor their own learning.

Teachers should plan ways to help students get in the habit of checking up on their learning. Markham (1979) looked at monitoring in relation to comprehension. She found that students fail to figure out single sentences and/or they fail to see relationships between ideas. Heuristics for correcting these include looking for other uses of an unfamiliar word in the text or looking it up, looking for restatement of unclear sentences, and being on the lookout for inconsistencies between statements. Failure to recognize conflicting statements is a particularly critical error when students are dealing with real-life situations where there is more information than they need or can use.

One approach to metacognitive activities is to teach students a general set of steps before they start trying to solve a problem (Campione & Brown 1978). To encourage comprehension monitoring, the teacher may insert several questions at the end of each section of the text, ones which require the student to stop and take stock of what the content was.

In cooperative learning groups, each student may be asked to explain and "teach" the other students in the group the content which s/he has read or investigated. This is part of the "jigsaw" activity that is found in almost all cooperative-learning models. Since each student read or investigated a different topic, the group can help each other monitor their learning as one of the group teaches the others. Teachers can ask students to summarize orally or to write a paragraph that summarizes their previous activity. This previous activity could be anything from a trip to the zoo, to a video tape, to an experiment in science, to a play, to any previous event. Not only does such an activity enhance memory and develop writing and/or oral expression skills, but it gives students the opportunity to engage in monitoring. Almost any training program for students in the area of study skills includes the activities of monitoring as well as those of planning and evaluation.

Evaluation

Evaluation is the name given to the reflecting process. Frequently, evaluation of our thinking is not a part of the lesson plan. The pressures of time and content volume push teachers to move rapidly and pace segments of the lesson in a coherent manner. Allowing time for reflection/evaluation is an activity that is often sacrificed because time runs out. Again in the cooperative learning models, evaluation of the group's activity is recommended as part of the process. The groups are asked to talk about how the task went, how

they could have done it better, what they did well, what they need to improve, what they did not do that they should have, what roles needed to be filled that were not, etc.

In Beyer's model (1987) of the direct teaching of a thinking skill, he includes the step of reflecting upon the process. In this evaluation, students consider what they did, how they did, how they could do better, and where they could use this skill in other content areas and in real life. This process of thinking about where one can use a skill or strategy s/he has learned is critical for the process of transfer.

Teaching Metacognition

Teachers are including more and more metacognitive activities in their lessons as they move toward developing higher order thinking in their students at the same time they are teaching content. One purpose of instructing students in metacognitive strategies is to improve their memory. Students remember material that they process more deeply and with more effort. This implies that they should do something with the knowledge in order to understand it thoroughly. Most of us have used underlining, paraphrasing, summarizing, and outlining as techniques to improve our memory. Students need to learn how to do these and know that they are important strategies to improve learning.

The results of various attempts to measure metacognition have not always been satisfactory. The bottom line on metacognition is whether knowledge and process transfer to new situations. This is the way some researchers have tried to measure the persons' development of metacognition as well as any process or content that has been taught. As a result of these experiments, the researchers have raised the question of whether the teacher can actually teach the process of metacognition. The consensus has been that there are developmental characteristics of the learner which limit our ability to measure metacognition. Some point out that the child's ability to verbalize, to handle several dimensions of an event at one time, and to think abstractly suggest that we should not be about the business of trying to teach metacognition. To some degree we would agree, but only to the extent that the teacher not attempt to evaluate formally the process.

Students of all ages should have many opportunities to evaluate, to plan, and to monitor their thinking. Instruction can explicitly encourage transfer. The research on self-regulation, which includes self-monitoring, makes self-management an important part of metacognitive development. As noted in Chapter 3, certain metacognitive activities are part of the four-year-old preschool curriculum developed by the High Scope Foundation. If four-year-olds can do it, all students can. The major emphasis should be on helping students develop the processes of planning, monitoring, and evaluating through the teachers' modeling and the students' participation so that they see these processes as part of effective and efficient thinking.

Reading Comprehension and Metacognition

Reading comprehension will be used as the content to illustrate some of the information we have about our metacognitive abilities. Research studies from first grade to college level demonstrate that metacognitive strategies can be taught to students in developmentally appropriate ways (Dole, Duffy, Roehler & Pearson 1991). Views about what the reading process is have changed in the past 20 years. We no longer believe we can teach reading by teaching a discrete set of skills which are taught to the stage of automaticity; instead, we understand the reading process to be an interactive and constructive process in which the reader brings to the activity his or her prior knowledge, a group of strategies, and some ideas about when and where to use them (Paris, Lipson & Wixson 1983). The strategies are flexible plans the reader consciously uses to construct meaning (Pressley, Johnson, Symons, McGoldrick & Kurita 1989). This suggests that the reader is engaging in metacognitive processes.

To teach students these processes requires that we have students develop a sense of conscious control (metacognition) over strategies they adapt in flexible ways to different kinds of text (Pressley, et al 1989). Five strategies are recommended by Dole, Duffy, Roehler, and Pearson (1991):

1.   Determining importance
2.   Summarizing information
3.   Drawing inferences
4.   Generating questions
5.   Monitoring comprehension

All of these are amenable to instruction; however, each is limited in some way by the developmental level of the learners. Vygotsky (1978) envisioned education as a process of making learning more efficient and effective by the teacher offering the scaffolding which permits the students to engage in activities they would not be able to do independently.

This distinction has been frequently addressed in reading when we talk about instructional reading and independent reading in relation to vocabulary and text structure. The research on the processes listed above indicates that the teacher plays a critical role in the students' reading development. For instance, Hanson and Pearson (1983) recommended giving students visual and kinesthetic reminders of how to integrate prior knowledge and text knowledge.

Mental modeling by the teacher (Herrmann 1988) is a particularly effective method of helping students develop their abilities to monitor their comprehension of what they read and listen to. One of the important values of modeling by the "expert" is that students see that the strategies are flexible and varied and are adapted to different types of text in a variety of applications. They also see that the strategies work.

Teachers have questioned whether to engage students in drawing inferences before one is sure that students are correctly interpreting the literal text. Dole, et al. (1991, p. 246) wrote, "Both basic and applied research supports a strong emphasis on inferential strategies from the beginning of instruction."

One major responsibility of the teacher is to select text material at the appropriate level for his or her students. Another is to verbalize to the students the strategies one might use and to illustrate them with "think aloud" examples. Obviously, students will improve in their strategies with experience and maturity; however, they need to realize early that there are ways to do things that are not chance happenings, but conscious strategies that they can use to complete tasks more effectively and efficiently.

Metacognition is essential to critical and creative thinking. One cannot reason efficiently and effectively without understanding what s/he knows and does not know, how to plan, predict, monitor, deliberate, etc. These strategies will be developed best by modeling by the teacher and planned student activities of reflecting where there is discussion of both the processes and their value. The repertoire of strategies that each student constructs will be of little use if the student cannot think metacognitively about which one will be most likely to work in a given situation. The student also needs to be able to determine whether the one(s) selected seems to be working while the processing is going on. Finally, s/he must decide what the outcomes were and where one goes from here.

* * *

Chapter Five

Problem Solving, Decision Making, and Transfer

Some psychologists separate problem solving, decision making, and transfer as if they were independent of one another. They are not. Each is a part of the other. We use the term problem solving in the broadest sense, not as mathematical problem solving (although that is one kind of problem-solving activity).

In this chapter, we will describe problem solving in more detail than decision making because we view decision making as a specific kind of problem solving, one in which you have to live with the consequences instead of starting back at square one or trying an alternative solution.

In problem solving, if you engage in medical research and you experiment with the effectiveness of one drug on a disease, when the results are not what is needed, you choose another drug to test. This iterative process is a mark of good problem solvers because when they start problem solving, they generate a number of alternative solutions and try first the one they predict is most likely to work. If it does not, they are ready to try some other approach.

On the other hand, decision making results in a relatively permanent solution. For example, when you make the decision to drive a car off the lot of the car dealer, it becomes a used car. Typically, you cannot decide next month that you do not like it and take it back for a full refund. You must live with your decision.

Problem Solving

Objections have been raised to teaching students a 5-step process for problem solving. The opponents argue that teaching students the steps will not assure them of being able to solve a problem. We agree with that general statement. There is value, however, in the student knowing that there are systematic ways to approach problem solving. There are also "rule of thumb" procedures which are called heuristics. They are ways of attacking problems which have good odds of leading to success, but no guarantees. Heuristics will be addressed later in the chapter.

It is helpful if learners are aware that they will be better problem solvers if they spend more time understanding and clarifying the problem and the information available, before trying the first idea that comes to mind. If they can remember to generate as many solutions as they can before they try any of them, and to predict the outcome of each in order to arrive at the best bet to try first, they will be more successful. We believe that students should know there are steps to follow, but that the steps are only guidelines (strategies), not solutions.

One of the best ways to illustrate this is for the teacher to pose a real-life problem with which students are familiar and guide them through the problem-solving process without any reference to steps. When they have completed the process, the teacher asks them to tell what they did first. Then what did they do? After that, what came next? If the answers are written on the board or an overhead, at the end of the reflection (metacognition), the students will have the steps in the problem-solving process.

The scientific method that is introduced or reviewed in every science subject is a variation on the basic problem-solving process. It should be noted that problem solving is a composite of a number of skills and some strategies. Perhaps, we could call it a megastrategy. A verbal map suggesting one possible order in problem solving is shown below.

We may access many procedures and information (declarative knowledge) from our long-term memory. We may have to seek to collect additional data.

Problem solving is, indeed, one of our ultimate challenges, and we do it everyday, from inconsequential decisions, to life threatening or sustaining procedures. One of the areas in which the human brain excels over the computer is in the area of problem solving. Our brains have the ability (1) to adapt heuristics to particular situations, (2) to operate on incomplete information by making inferences that take us beyond the information given, and (3) to be creative in our ability to transfer or to combine information in new ways in order to see additional possibilities. All of these abilities have not yet been simulated by computer programmers.

Those who work with artificial intelligence have made great strides in simulating many of the skill processes, and they may eventually be able to simulate the strategies. Students need to understand the strategies and how they work in order to utilize computer capabilities available to them in the future.

Problem solving as it is usually taught in school does not resemble real-life problem solving according to Paul (1984) and Sternberg (1985a, 1985b). They contend that we typically give students problems to solve that have only one correct solution and are subject specific. These are certainly one type of problem, but most problems have no single right answer and may not have enough information to be solved at all.

Sternberg (1985a, 1985b) also points out the value of using real-life problems with students and allowing them to work on them in groups. He states that few important decisions are made in this world by individuals. Most are group decisions. Reasonably, we should use content-specific problems where appropriate for academic problems. They are one type of problem students need to know how to approach and to solve; however, the concern is that we not stop with this one type of problem.

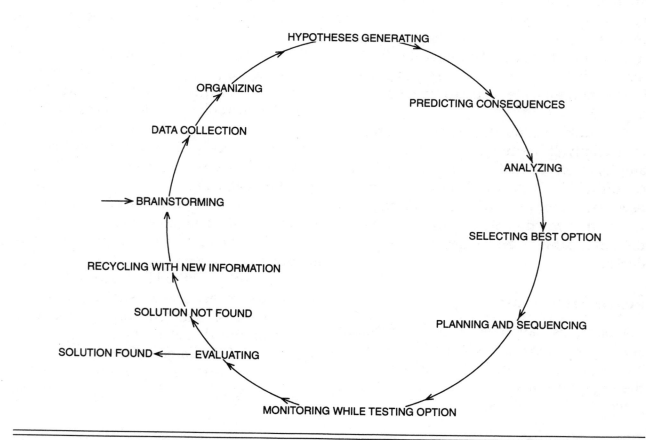

The National Council of the Teachers of Mathematics (1989) and Willoughby (1990) recommend that students be given problems that are "authentic" in that they are "real" math problems that need to be solved, rather than some contrived and artificial ones. A reflection of some of the changes recommended in mathematics is found in the plans for the revised and expanded Scholastic Aptitude Test (1990). It contains a mathematics section requiring students to solve the problems by producing their answer and writing it in grids, instead of choosing an alternative on a multiple-choice item. There are also questions about whether information is needed in order to solve a problem and whether there is information that is irrelevant. In some cases, there may be more than one correct answer!

The introduction of graphic calculators into secondary school mathematics, as well as plans to allow students at and above the sixth grade to use scientific calculators on tests and exams, points to changes and the rethinking of curriculum in mathematics. At the upper grade levels, the emphasis is on the conceptual aspects and problem-solving procedures rather than on the computational component. It is not that computation is unimportant; the mathematics teachers are going to assume that students have the basic computational skills from lower grade-level instruction.

The upper grades will be trying to develop problem solving skills and strategies in order that students in this country will improve their mathematical achievement. Both the National Assessment of Educational Progress and the International Education Assessment have indicated that our curricula are in need of overhaul.

Good problem solvers have been found to operate differently from poor problem solvers (Gagné 1985). Good problem solvers may have more knowledge (declarative) about the circumstances, they may have more experience in solving similar type problems (pattern recognition), and they may be able to distinguish relevant from irrelevant information. One of the major differences is in the time they spend planning before acting. They are more likely to clarify the problem and be able to describe it and its conditions. They are better able then to select what information they have that is needed to solve the problem, as well as what information they still need in order to generate solutions and select a possible solution from among them.

The reflective student who spends time on problem representation (the term for beginning problem-solving strategies) is more successful and can solve increasingly difficult problems. On the other hand, the "fast" problem solver may luck upon the solution or be able to do it intuitively, but will be unable to sustain that performance as the difficulty increases. This is not to say that we should not use intuition; we should. Intuition is not as haphazard as we may think. Some partial information steered us in that direction. It may be a false start, but it may also lead us in the right direction. Part of the problem representation (see below) may be checking out the intuitive solutions we thought of.

The steps in problem solving vary from one writer to the next, depending on how the process is broken down. In general there is

- data gathering
- solutions generated
- selection of operation to try
- evaluation of results
- either exit or try another solution set depending on the evaluation outcome

Another way to say this is input, operation, output; or problem representation, solution set operation, evaluation. Now let us look at the processes, beginning with problem representation, and see what the essential components of these are.

Problem Representation

The most crucial step in problem solving is the problem representation. This includes several processes; all are important. One is *clarifying* the nature of the problem. This is ongoing with other activities such as *data evaluation and collection*. If you collect additional information, it may clarify some aspect of the problem of which you were not aware at the onset. This in turn will clarify the task(s).

Goal setting is where you must assess where you are in relation to the problem and where you want to be when you solve the problem. This may interact with the data collection and evaluation to indicate the need for more or different pieces of data.

Solutions generated involves thinking of as many possible solutions as possible, predicting the consequences of each and the likelihood of the solution working based on an evaluation of the evidence you have. Instead of generating as many plausible solutions as possible (a kind of brainstorming done individually or in groups), one may recognize from the givens that the problem is like one which the individual or group has already solved. In this case, the number of solutions may be few because the likelihood of success is strong. Sometimes one may recognize a pattern which fits a solution s/he has used before. In some cases, it may be an algorithm or formula. These are guaranteed to work if the analysis of the problem is correct (and the steps are followed correctly). If no rule suggests itself to the problem solvers, then the "serving to discover," as Polya (1945) referred to heuristics, comes into play. Some of these approaches will be discussed in this chapter after the examples.

Selection of solution set to try comes next. At this point, the problem has been clarified, the data given has been evaluated and additional information has been sought, the goal has been determined, the solutions generated, and one solution selected to try.

Some researchers separate the hypotheses generating and selection from the problem clarifying and data collection. As you generate solution sets, however, you may find that data collection has to be augmented or that further clarification occurs. If you separate these when you are showing students how to solve problems, they may not see the interre-

lationship of these processes. These processes are the same metacognitive activities described under planning in Chapter 4.

Solution Set Operation

Operation of solution set is where you try out the solution set which you have predicted offers the best chance of solving your problem. During this step, the problem solver must plan how to carry out the operation, sequence actions, and carry out the plan and monitor progress. This involves the metacognitive strategy of monitoring.

Evaluation

Evaluation of solution set occurs after you have tried the solution set you thought would work. This step in problem solving involves the metacognitive strategies of evaluation addressed in the chapter on metacognition (Chapter 4). Now comes the reality test; did it work? In order to complete this step, you must think back to the goal, or what would solve your problem, to see if you have reached the goal and solved the problem. We have all seen cartoons where someone tells you that if you think you know the answer, then you don't understand the problem. In the evaluation, we may find that the solution set worked, but we still have not solved the problem. This may be because we did not understand the problem well enough to plan effectively. Circumstances may have changed during the time it took to try the solution set. If the problem is deemed by the solvers to be solved, then they can move on to other activities and goals.

If the evaluation ends in the decision that the problem has not been solved, then the solver returns to the problem representation stage, adds any new data, selects the next most likely solution set, and continues the process. This iterative process can continue indefinitely until the problem is solved, the solver runs out of solution sets, or drops from exhaustion. Our brains are very persistent once they tackle a problem; most of us hate to admit defeat even with small problems.

PROBLEM-SOLVING PROCESS

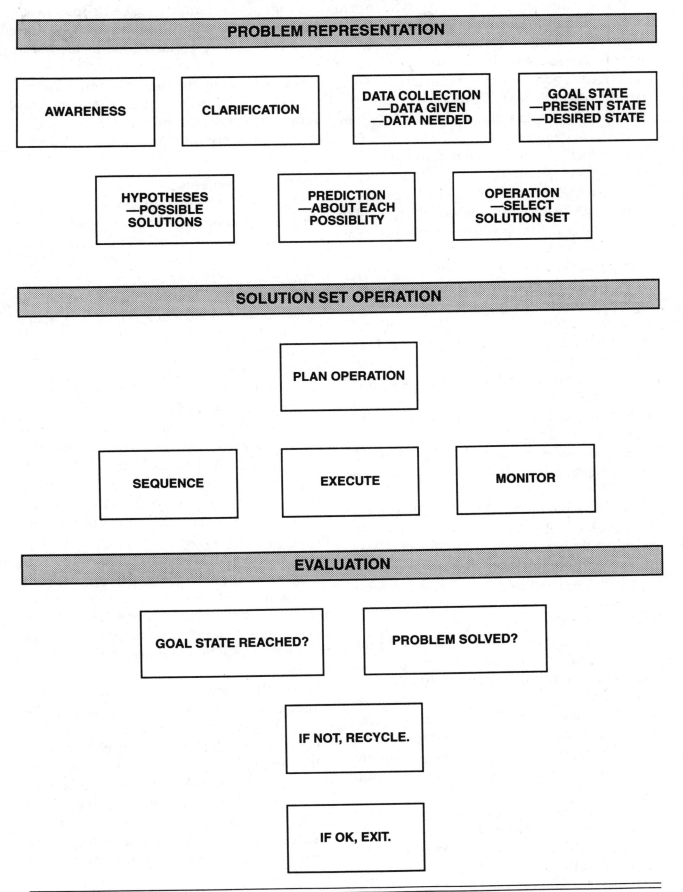

PROBLEM REPRESENTATION

| AWARENESS | CLARIFICATION | DATA COLLECTION —DATA GIVEN —DATA NEEDED | GOAL STATE —PRESENT STATE —DESIRED STATE |

HYPOTHESES —POSSIBLE SOLUTIONS

PREDICTION —ABOUT EACH POSSIBLITY

OPERATION —SELECT SOLUTION SET

SOLUTION SET OPERATION

PLAN OPERATION

SEQUENCE   EXECUTE   MONITOR

EVALUATION

GOAL STATE REACHED?   PROBLEM SOLVED?

IF NOT, RECYCLE.

IF OK, EXIT.

How persistent students are will vary depending on factors such as their confidence in their abilities to solve problems, their self-regulation/motivation to complete a task and complete it successfully, the setting in which they are working, and time constraints. Their confidence in their ability to solve problems is going to be affected directly by whether they believe they have strategies for solving problems effectively and have had many experiences in trying to find solutions.

When the teacher introduces the problem-solving process to students, s/he may want to choose an everyday problem with which most of the students may have coped in the past. Getting locked out of the house, forgetting one's lunch money, having several things to do that are mutually exclusive during the same time span, and choosing how to spend a given amount of money when your wants and needs cost more than you have, are all everyday experiences most students, even young ones, have had. After introducing the problem, brainstorming solutions usually gets enthusiastic participation.

A problem-solving model based on the above explanation would look like the one on page 57.

An example of walking students through the problem-solving processes with a real-life problem (being locked out of one's house) is presented on page 59. Notice that the givens need to be structured to allow students to assess what they know and what they need to know in order to generate solution sets.

Because this is a simulation of a real problem, you will want to push students to generate solutions that they personally might not need. For instance, if there is always a key hidden somewhere in the yard at the student's house, s/he would not have to resort to the other alternatives in real life. Have them pretend the key was not there, then what would they do?

The problem solving worksheet presented on page 60 is a suggested form you can use to give students a format to help them remember to cover all the bases.

Algorithms

Students are frequently asked to solve problems which have only one correct answer. In such cases, it is not unusual for the answer to be obtained by recognizing the type of problem and applying the rule or formula for that type of problem. These are academic problems which may be important for later understanding but are little more than applying a skill that has been taught.

Nonroutine Problems

On the other hand, with nonroutine problems, the teacher may assign a group of five students to write a script for a play (one-act) in which some moral dilemma is showcased. Or perhaps the group is asked to plan a medieval feast for the class. Another assignment might be to plan a space launch for a mock space shuttle. A group or an individual student might be asked to learn as much as possible about a particular country and plan a travel itinerary, brochure, a public presentation of the proposed trip and points of interest.

Ecological problems are excellent opportunities for students to engage in problem solving with real situations. At the elementary school level, students can study and plan for waste collection and recycling. They can devise ways to conserve water, forests, wildlife, marshes, clean air, etc. The proposed work sheet is probably not needed for the one-correct-answer problems which can be solved by looking in the text or applying a rule or algorithm. On the other hand, the second group of problems require more organization and planning; for them, the work sheet could be helpful.

The instructors in creative problem solving generally introduce a "fuzzy mess," and the problem solvers work from there. Whether the students are deciding where to locate their settlement in the wilderness, what to take on their trip to Mars, or how to make ends meet in a new business venture, the use of some guide will make the process more manageable. In using any work sheet or organizer, students need the opportunity to work through

PROBLEM
Locked out of your house

PROBLEM REPRESENTATION	
Awareness:	Student arrives home, no one is home, s/he does not have key.
Clarification:	There is no note to say when someone will be there.
Data—Givens:	It will be dark in one hour. It is cold. There are no signs of any neighbors at home.
—New Data Needed:	Are all the windows that student can reach locked? Is there a ladder available to try windows that are out of reach? Are all the doors locked? Are there any keys hidden anywhere nearby? Check neighbors' houses to be sure no one is there. Does anyone else have a key? Where is the nearest telephone that one can get to? Does the student have money for a pay phone call? Who could one call?
Goal/End State:	Get in the house.
—Present State:	Locked out of house.
Solution Hypotheses (as generated, not yet ordered):	Find window unlocked and climb in window. Find way to get to out-of-reach windows: ladder, tree, stack boxes/lumber, etc. Find door unlocked. Pick lock on door or window. Find key under ledge. Get key from neighbor. Stay with neighbor. Find place to stay warm until someone comes home. Break in door or window. Call someone who has a key. Find phone, find person available.
Prediction:	Take each of the above and predict the outcome. Order them as to which to try first, second, third, etc.

SOLUTION OPERATION
Let us assume that following the discussion, you and the students arrived at this sequence of operation: Look for hidden key (if there is such). Try doors and windows (within reach). Check to see if neighbors are home. Phone someone with key if can find phone. Try to find way to reach inaccessible windows. Try to find place to stay until parents return. If considerable time elapses, break window pane, unlock window, and climb in. The plan and sequence is established. You cannot go much further until you execute one of these and reorder if new information comes to light. Execute solution set one, monitor.

EVALUATION
Are you in the house? If not, do you have any new information that would cause you to reorder the solution sets? If goal not reached and no new information, go to solution set two; try all doors and windows you can reach.

PROBLEM REPRESENTATION	
Awareness:	What do I think the problem is?
Clarification:	Can I clarify this statement? What additional information do I need?
Data: **—Givens:**	
—Data needed, how to obtain:	
Goal or end state:	Where or how do I want to be when I have solved the problem?
—Present state:	Where am I now?
Hypotheses and prediction:	What are some possible solution sets? How likely are they to work?
Operation selection:	Which possible solution should I try first? Why?
SOLUTION OPERATION	
Plan sequence:	
Monitor progress:	Is it working? Can I continue in this direction?
EVALUATION	
Evaluation:	Did it work? Have I solved my problem?

If YES: What did I learn, and how could I have done it better?	If NO: Do I have additional information to add to data? Does it change the solutions I generated before? How? Do I need to modify my understanding of the problem? Do I have new solution sets to add?

the guide with some examples before they try it on their own.

Many teachers may think that problem solving is reserved for middle and secondary school students. One kindergarten teacher was discussing with students popping popcorn for the class, and she asked them what kind she should buy. Was there a brand they liked best? Several brands were mentioned. They talked about how much each cost. Some brands cost considerably more than others. Was the more expensive one that much better than the less costly one? They decided to do a survey of students at their school. They bought two

PROBLEM REPRESENTATION	
Awareness:	What do I think the problem is? —Which popcorn to buy
Clarification:	Can I clarify this statement? What additional information do I need? —What are the brands students like? Orville Redenbacher, Ozark, and Bi-Lo Gourmet How much does each cost? (This was found out later.) Orville Redenbacher $2.53/1 lb. 10 oz.; Ozark $.69/2 lbs.; Bi-Lo Gourmet $.69/2 lbs. How many packages will we need? How much does a package make?
Data: **—Givens:**	—We need to purchase packages of popcorn. We don't know how much different brands cost, but some brands cost more than others. We like brands R, O, and B? The Bi-Lo Store carries all these brands.
—Data needed, how to obtain:	—What brand should we buy? How much does each cost? Buy two, one expensive, one inexpensive, and sample. Maybe we'd like to know which is a better buy. We could buy enough to have other grades sample the popcorn as well as our class.
Goal or end state:	Where or how do I want to be when I have solved the problem? —Buy popcorn for us to pop; test to determine taste; select the best buy.
—Present state:	Where am I now? —Have no popcorn and don't know which to buy.
Hypotheses and prediction:	What are some possible solution sets? How likely are they to work? —Buy one brand based on majority vote of class. Prediction is that some may not be happy and that it may not be the best buy or taste. Probably everyone will enjoy it, and that is good enough. —Find out how much each costs; buy the cheapest. May be OK, but may not have great taste. —Find out how much each costs; buy the most expensive. Will probably taste good, but cost a lot. Don't know for sure about taste. —Buy all the brands. Sample each. Decide what we like best. We don't really need that much popcorn, and it might be hard to select from so many. More trouble to prepare. Hard to keep from knowing which is which. —Buy one of the cheapest and one of the most expensive. Pop each at same time. Sample. Decide what we like best. Is the more expensive one worth the difference? —Prediction will be limited to our class. Do we want to know more? Yes. Let's have other students in school help us decide. *[Continued on next page.]*

PROBLEM REPRESENTATION Continued	
Operation selection:	Which possible solution should I try first? Why? —Students decided on buying one cheap and one expensive. Students decided to have other students sample.

SOLUTION OPERATION	
Plan sequence:	—Teacher will go to store, price packages (check for quantity produced), select one inexpensive and one more expensive kind. Package prices are listed above. —If a package makes two quarts, we will need to have how many packages of each kind in order for the students to sample? If we choose the first lunch period (150 students), and we give each student a small paper cup (party-favor cup) of each kind, we would need 10 packages of each kind (1/2 cup of each would be 75 cups; there are 4 cups in a quart and 2 quarts to a package, 75 ÷ 8 = 9+, so buy 10). Students in kindergarten cannot multiply and divide, but with the use of cups, quarts, and some manipulating, they could conceptualize the process. If the average price is about 75 cents/quart , that will be $15.00. If each of the 30 students will bring 50 cents, we can finance our experiment. —Teacher and delegation of students ask principal for permission to set up in the lunch room. —Children bring money by Thursday. —Teacher purchases popcorn. Teacher borrows poppers from other teachers and friends. Students may volunteer to bring one from home. Teacher purchases paper cups, two colors. —Friday morning the students pop corn. (The teacher has placed all of one brand in an unmarked container and all of the other brand in another container so the students will not know which they are popping.) The poppers will note how many kernels do not pop in each batch. The students will set up a table between ticket taker and cafeteria food line. Put trash can at beginning of lunch line where a student will stand with a clipboard with two columns. S/he will ask each student which s/he liked best and place a mark under the color of the cup. A student will stand beside the table to tell students that they are to choose which brand they like best. Other students will be filling cups (many will be filled prior to lunch), and others will be handing them out. —After the tallying is complete, the teacher and a group of students will count the numbers, and report the results to the class. The number of unpopped kernels will be noted, as well as the volume of corn when popped, and any other observations made during the process. *[Continued on next page.]*

kinds of popcorn, one more expensive than the other. They popped them and then in the lunch line had students from other grades sample each and give their opinion of which they liked best. Of course, the brand name was not visible. Then they tallied their results and ate both kinds themselves. The conclusion, based on the other students' and their own choices, was that the less expensive brand was just as tasty as the more expensive one. While this might not be an earth-shattering finding, look at the higher order thinking going on in those kindergarten students. They solved a problem (found the answer to their question) and developed some systematic ways to go about it. In this case, the process was more important than the content.

The popcorn problem has been used on pages 61–63 to illustrate the use of the problem-solving worksheet. Since the students

SOLUTION OPERATION Continued	
Monitor progress:	Is it working? Can I continue in this direction? —Students will need to work toward being prepared to serve the first lunch sitting. (Of course, if they get behind, they could serve the second sitting.)

EVALUATION	
Evaluation:	Did it work? Have I solved my problem?

If YES: What did I learn, and how could I have done it better?	If NO: Do I have additional information to add to data? Does it change the solutions I generated
—Yes. The students chose one brand consistently over the other. The brand chosen turned out to be the less expensive of the two. —We learned that just because something costs more does not mean that it is necessarily better. —We learned that if you want to solve a problem, you need to have a plan. We developed a plan and it worked. —We learned that in order to handle food, you have to be careful not to touch what others will eat. This is so no one gets sick from germs others might have. —We learned that it takes time to do something well. It also takes a lot of effort. —We learned that it was fun to work in groups to carry out our job in the experiment. Some work harder than others. Everyone needs to do his or her part.	before? How? Do I need to modify my understanding of the problem? Do I have new solution sets to add? —Problem solved.

were nonreaders, the teacher would work with them on the process orally, and she would fill in the information on the board or wall chart.

Although this may seem a lot of effort for a minor question, there was much learned. Obviously, one cannot do activities like this every day, but less complex ones can be done in hands-on science activities that are in all the science texts and supplements; math problems that are real can be solved and social studies dilemmas considered. Problem solving for characters in stories is a good way to have students consider alternative solutions. Sometimes when the rest of the story is revealed, the fact that the character did not use any plan to solve his or her problem and caused the dilemma and its complications may also help students see the value of thoughtful planning.

Heuristics

Earlier the term heuristics was introduced. The phrases "rule of thumb" and "serving to discover" were used. The implication is that there is nothing set in concrete about the problem-solving process. Heuristics are strategies that do not work all of the time but are much better than no strategy at all. A few of these heuristics are frequently named in writings about the problem-solving process: working backwards, means-end analysis, working forward, difference reduction, analogies, and restructuring are some of heuristics (Gagné, E. 1985; Glover, Ronning & Bruning 1990). Some other techniques used in problem solving, which do not rate a name as a full-blown procedure but are means to that end, are restructuring, pattern recognition, and drawing spatial arrays, matrices, outlines, flow charts, etc. A brief description of each follows:

1. *Working backwards* is a strategy where you identify the goal state and then look for procedures which will result in your arriving at your goal. This limits the search to just what will contribute to your getting from point A (present) to point B (goal).

2. *Means-end analysis* is the most frequently seen strategy in the literature. It is a working backward technique. You analyze what subprocesses you can carry out which will lead you to the goal. They are your means to the end (goal).

3. *Working forward* typically is less limiting, may give more opportunities for creative solutions, but may not be as powerful and direct as those above where the goal is constantly being used as the measuring stick for procedures considered.

4. In working forward, one procedure is called *difference reduction*. You assess where you are and where you want to be (goal), but you do not see clearly how to get there, so you choose a process that will change where you are and reduce the difference between it and where you want to be. If you want to reach a certain location and you know in what direction it is, you could start in the right direction with the plan to look for signs or someone to ask. You will not be likely to happen upon the goal, but you will be closer to it and be in a position to see more clearly what it will take to get there. In school, a student may decide s/he wants to improve his or her grade-point average. The student may not know all that needs to be done, but knows that one way to start is to prepare for the test in science on Friday and spend some extra effort on the expository-writing assignment due in English or Language Arts on Monday. The student could also be sure that always hav-

ing one's homework is important to avoid any zeroes, and so s/he will be prepared for any class assignment which might be graded that is based on the homework. All of these result in difference reduction.

5. *Analogies* are also suggested as heuristics which may help you see a solution path. Unlike means-end analysis, which requires the greatest amount of domain specific or declarative knowledge in order to be used, analogies can help with solutions when the problem solver has less knowledge about the domain. It allows the problem solver to transfer a procedure from another domain with which s/he is familiar and use it in a new situation. Actually, most people do not seem to do this very well. Unless the analogy is made explicit, pointed out, the problem solvers seldom see the possibilities (Gick & Holyoak 1980; Terry 1990). Once they have had the relationship pointed out, they can use the strategy in a new situation.

6. *Restructuring* refers to rewording or redescribing the problem. One may decide to oversimplify by dropping out details or making it appear more like a general problem type. This may suggest a solution path.

7. *Pattern recognition* involves looking for similarities between the current problem and some you have dealt with in the past. The pattern may be physical similarities or may be cognitive, procedural similarities. Although much of our time is spent in organizing and categorizing the objects, persons, and events in our lives to bring order out of chaos, we do not recognize patterns that are cognitive nearly as well as we do those that are physically observable. This was illustrated above in reference to the use of an analogy in problem solving.

8. *Verbal and graphic "doodling"* can be par-

particularly useful in clarifying the relationships among the givens of the problem. Such sketches may help correct misconceptions and may help to eliminate irrelevant data. Setting up a matrix to use in reasoning through a complex relationship is particularly effective when there are more parts than can be juggled in one's working memory.

Some of these actions are helpful when the problem is ill-defined. They can help clarify and focus. Providing many opportunities to try problem solving with lots of feedback and discussion may be helpful. If students work many examples of a certain type of problem, they will recognize the pattern and quickly select an algorithm or strategy that they recognize will work. A set of problems of the same type were developed by Luchins (1942).

In Luchins' (1942) set of problems, the subject is given a set of jugs which hold various amounts, and there is unlimited water available. The task is to measure out a specified amount. Five examples from his set are given in the table below.

Capacity of Jug A	Capacity of Jug B	Capacity of Jug C	Desired Amount
21	127	3	100
14	163	25	99
9	42	6	21
20	59	4	31
15	39	3	18

Stop at this point and work the problems above. What was the strategy you used? Could you write it in generic form?

If you wrote down a generic form, it probably looked something like B − A − 2C = desired quantity. If you used this algorithm to work all five problems, it would be a case of functional fixedness . If you look again at the last problem, you will see that it could be solved by A + C = desired quantity, a simpler solution than the one needed for the first four problems.

Humans tend to take advantage of shortcuts. Once we find a way to do something, and it works every time, we tend to gravitate to it. This means that if we give a cursory look at something, and it looks like a common pattern, we activate the response set without fully analyzing the situation. Usually, this results in freeing our working memory for other tasks and allows us to seem to attend to two or more things at once; sometimes it may not be the best or most efficient way to solve a problem. We should have students monitor their problem solving to be alert to this possibility. If a person is given five problems to solve, and the first four are solved in a particular set of steps, then the fifth one, which appears to be the same type of problem, is typically solved by using the same procedure. The problem solver does not look for the best strategy but uses what has worked for the other four.

Decision Making

Decision making is another form of problem solving. The planning phase, or problem representation, is more critical than in many problem-solving situations where you can try and try again. As was mentioned earlier, the critical difference is that you have one chance to make the decision, and then you will have to live with it. This makes the prediction of consequences of various options the key to a good decision.

One of the important parts of the prediction process is the evaluation of the likelihood of that consequence really happening. This evaluation of evidence is a thinking strategy that has been largely neglected in school. In fact, prediction and estimation are frequently overlooked. The difference between fact and opinion is the major topic that is addressed in the evaluation of evidence in most curricula. Estimation, which is in almost every mathematics text, is frequently postponed until the last of the year (although it appears early in the text), and then time runs out and students do not deal with the topic. Actually, it should be a part of most lessons in math. Students should get in the habit of estimating in order to judge the reasonableness of the answer they get when they work problems. Plausibility of math answers is another kind of likelihood of consequence mentioned above.

The planning in decision making is the same as for problem solving. The problem representation follows the same pattern. Writing down or drawing the relationships is particularly useful in decision making when the results are crucial.

One additional step which might follow the prediction of consequences of each choice is the assessing of the predicted result in terms of your likes and dislikes, emotions, feelings, comfortableness, etc. You need to ask yourself how much will it cost me (time, money, heartache, opportunities, etc.) if I choose this option and I am wrong? As it turns out, we may think logically and reasonably about a decision and arrive at the indicated choice only to realize that we cannot live with it. The decision you made is not comfortable or seems to you to be out of character or incompatible with your present status.

If you are buying a house, and you find two you really like with comparable prices, you may decide on the one closer to your work but find that it puts your child in a different school from the one you believe is better. Listen to those ideas and be sure you have resolved them before making the choice.

Most training in decision making recommends a period of waiting between making the decision and declaring it publicly. This is to allow for the settling of these issues in your mind *before* you are bound by them. Obviously, this is not always possible.

The more practice students have had in making decisions by approaching them in a systematic way, the better able they will be when time is a luxury they do not have. They may have to telescope the process into a short time span, yet if they spend some time predicting consequences and their likelihood, they will make better choices in the long run.

A worksheet for decision making is given on page 67. Usually there are only two or three viable alternatives or options. The prediction of the consequences/results is a critical step in the decision-making process. The worksheet might be used by a group in class with an assignment which involves data gathering, organizing, and reporting on a special topic. If they change the "I" to "we," they can use it easily. Decisions about what is needed, where it can be found, what assistance will be needed, who will do what, how we will organize what we find, who will do the organizing, how we will deliver our report (Written? Oral? Skit? Product?), and who will do which of these can be made using the worksheet.

Decision making involves a number of thinking skills and strategies. Some of them are making accurate observations, using reliable sources, engaging in causal inference based on data, predicting consequences and their likelihood, ranking options based on some scheme or qualities, valuing the options, comparing and contrasting, and making the decision. It does not end there, however, as the decision must then be carried out. This involves the rest of the steps in the problem-solving process: operation and evaluation.

The choice to recycle is usually not an option during evaluation, but one may have to decide how to live with the decision that has been made, which may place the person in the problem-solving mode again. One question that should be asked in the problem-representation stage of decision making is, What caused me to need to make this decision? and/or What is responsible for this problem? This is part of the data-gathering task. It may alter our perspective of the situation.

We make hundreds of decisions every day; most are not life-threatening or critical, but

DECISION MAKING REPRESENTATION			
Awareness:	What decision do I need to make?		
Clarification:	Can I clarify this? Is there more than one decision? Does one decision depend on the outcome of another?		
Data collection: **—Givens:**			
—Data needed, how to obtain:			

EVALUATING OPTIONS			
Options	**Consequence/result**	**Likelihood**	**Valuing**
1.			
2.			
3.			
4.			

For each predicted outcome, how likely is it? On what am I basing my determination? How do I feel about that outcome?

SOLUTION OPERATION
Plan for option selected/ sequence:

EVALUATION	
Evaluation:	How good was my decision? Does it require other decisions?

some are. Based on the figures on traffic accidents and the high incidence of alcohol related deaths, we can conclude that many people who drink make a poor decision to drive. Which brand we buy at the store probably will not matter; whether we eat pizza or Chinese food for supper may have temporary effects of indigestion, but no long-lasting outcomes, but we do make important decisions more often than we realize.

Students have to make choices about extracurricular activities, courses of study, accepting responsibilities, work habits, peer group, allocation of money and time, and many others. They will feel more confident if they know they have a way to approach decisions that is not haphazard and irresponsible.

When teachers set up learning centers with a variety of activities and assign the students to complete a certain number of each kind of activity by a certain date, the students are charged with making decisions about which ones to do, when to do them, how many they will have to do per day in order to finish them all by the due date, and other decisions.

The frequently requested decision of what topic on which to write a paper is going to be influenced by what the student knows about certain topics, where information is available, how accessible the information is, how long it will take to collect data, how long it will take to write it, how interested the student is in the topic, how much time the student has available to work on the task, and other related elements. If the student spends a little time considering what is involved, the decision might be easier to live with. A student might know a lot about a particular topic, but not be interested in doing anything with the knowledge. On the other hand, if the student chooses a topic of personal interest on which s/he knows little, a big hunk of time will be spent in gathering data, but the process may be enjoyable.

Which route to take may be determined by how much time is available for the student to devote to the task. If the student is chairperson of the Homecoming celebrations which take place the day the assignment is due, the choice is probably self-evident. Decision making is an important part of "taking charge of your life," and its exercise in some systematic approach can reduce "learned helplessness" and other feelings of being out of control. Goal setting, responsibility acceptance, and positive thinking are other elements in the taking-charge approach.

Transfer

Transfer is an integral part of the learning process as has been mentioned a number of times in this text. Based on *the Nation's Report Card*, Applebee, Langer, and Mullis (1991) recommended that teachers spend more time applying and practicing the processes we are teaching, rather than covering more material. "But transfer does not take care of itself, and conventional schooling pays little heed to the problem" (Perkins & Salomon 1988, p. 22). Beyer (1985) reminded us that transfer must be taught explicitly. He further recommended that the first time after we have taught a process, we should ask students to use it again, and the context should be the same. Only after practice and guidance, with prompting if necessary, should we ask students to transfer the process to a different context.

Perkins and Salomon (1988) referred to low-road (near) transfer and high-road (far) transfer. They pointed out that near transfer occurs when there is considerable perceptual similarity between the original context and the new context. On the other hand, "high road transfer depends on deliberate, mindful abstraction of skill or knowledge from one context for application to another" (p. 24). They suggested that these differences helped to explain why transfer may not occur and why teachers may have to plan deliberately to obtain any transfer other than rather obvious applications to similar context to that in which the process was learned.

Learners may know a process, but not rec-

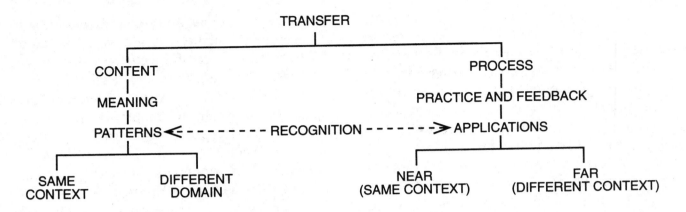

ognize that it would be appropriate to use because it has been stored as "local knowledge" or domain-specific knowledge. Perkins and Salomon (1988) recommended that the teacher intentionally bridge the two contexts, and do it frequently. In addition, they pointed out that helping students engage in metacognitive activities about the processes they use will improve transfer and the recognition of opportunities to transfer.

The transfer of a skill or process is different from the transfer of declarative information. Both are important; declarative knowledge needs intentional meaningfulness; process transfer requires practice, guidance, prompting, and multiple experiences in different contexts. Seeing similarities or relationships between observable, physical kinds of things is a form of pattern recognition. We spend much of our early years learning to do this kind of task. Seeing similarities and relationships between procedures is not so obvious and is more difficult to show and teach. Yet, it is this recognition that separates creative problem solvers from those who have to find a previous problem from which to copy the process they used.

In a workshop on gifted children, James Curry (1981) stated that there were no gifted activities, just gifted responses. Some individuals have the ability to see new and different relationships between the circumstances within a problem. Or they may see a relationship between a problem and some other problem which is not directly similar, but which

uses the same solution processes. Some of us may not be very good at seeing these relationships. Most of us would be a lot better at seeing them, however, if we were familiar with the elements and situation in the problem (declarative knowledge) and had had frequent practice in processes which were explicitly noted at the time (procedural knowledge). All of us can improve with experience.

Thorndike (1906) began investigating transfer at the turn of the century to show the "faculty" psychologists that transfer was much narrower than they believed. These subscribers of the Doctrine of Formal Discipline (Angell 1908) were of the opinion that the teaching of Latin and certain mathematics such as geometry were necessary in education because they trained the mind or taught discipline of the mind. Thorndike (1906) reported that the transfer occurred between these subjects and other schooling only in so far as there were common or identical elements. His view seems too narrow in the other direction based on many studies of cognition in recent years. Students do recognize and transfer skills that have the same logical structure, even with different surface elements, although they may sometimes need hints or clues (Gick & Holyoak 1980, 1983; Terry 1990).

Students do not go to school all of their lives; at some time they enter the work force or become wards of society. The mission of education is to improve their quality of life and make them able to be contributing members of society. Since little of what goes on in the workplace, at home, and in the community closely resembles the experiences students have in school, one of the major tasks of the educational system is to teach for transfer. If we compound this task with the elusiveness of transfer of processes, we can see that activities which foster transfer need to be integral parts of the lessons we teach. If this is the case, why do we not intentionally do more to promote transfer?

Time and lack of emphasis on reflecting after lessons on processes are the major stumbling blocks to more effective teaching for transfer. One way to address this problem is to build in to each unit time for reflecting upon declarative and procedural knowledge the students have learned. If this evaluation by the students makes the learning more meaningful, then it will be possible to reduce the amount of drill and concentrate on practice opportunities which illustrate the use of the processes with different subject material. Meaningfulness of the material and the activity and self-referencing are still the most consistently effective ways to increase remembering. If students generate the transfer possibilities, particularly ones that relate to their own lives, and if the class or groups discuss these ideas, transfer will improve. Practicing a process is always necessary for learning to be permanent; changing the circumstances will broaden the students' scope of their use of the process.

Resnick (1987) surveyed a number of programs claiming to teach thinking skills, learning skills, or higher order cognitive abilities. She reported that the programs which seemed to be the most successful were those that "have features characteristic of out-of-school cognitive performances," involve students in "organized joint accomplishments of tasks," make "usually hidden processes overt," are set up to "encourage student observation and commentary," are "organized around particular bodies of knowledge and interpretation—subject matters, if you will—rather than general abilities," and "engage students in processes of meaning construction and interpretation" (p. 18). These are procedures which also enhance the transfer of knowledge and process. The best insurance for obtaining transfer is to plan for the students to verbalize, orally or in writing, explicit examples of the transfer use of the processes. Since one student's idea may trigger another student's connection, it is recommended that these activities be done in groups or total-class format at the end of lessons in which identifiable processes have been practiced or taught.

The old adage, if something is worth doing, it is worth doing well, might be applied to process skills. The by-product of this will be an increase in transfer. Because the processes are sometimes not a set of x number of steps but are strategies with *if* and *then* statements, not all may be "taught." That is, metacognitive processes may need to be developed by practice opportunities where using the strategies as they are indicated will change from one task to another.

Chapter Six

Creativity

Creativity is one of the most fascinating characteristics of human beings. Other animals may exhibit what one would call creative behavior, but none can compare with the abilities of the human race to be inventive and creative. Our control of our environment, which many would agree has not been in our best interest in the long run, is a result of our creativeness. All the extensions of man—tools, transportation, communications, social institutions, etc.—have been products of our inventing. Creativity is the ultimate problem solving.

With Piaget's theory of cognitive development, some of his followers have pursued the extension of formal operational thought to a substage they have called problem finding. The idea is that some people extend their thinking beyond the problems at hand and enter the realm of the future.

Many inventions were not appreciated at the time they were invented. One example of this is the hologram. When in 1947 the engineer, Dennis Gabor, developed the theory of a three-dimensional projection by using a coherent light, the actual invention had to wait on the development of the laser, another magnificent idea, in 1963. Gabor may have anticipated some of the uses of such an invention. It is doubtful that, in his wildest dreams, he imagined all the ways this creation would be used—to find defects in manufactured products, to assist in delicate surgical procedures, to study slices of tissue for medical research, to project images in the sky such as at Disney World and in TV programs, to simulate all kinds of motion, and to give aesthetic enjoyment to the public through exciting productions. There will be other applications in the future; the potential is awesome. It was not until 1971 that Gabor received the Nobel Prize in Physics for his work.

What is creativity? Webster's Dictionary gives its definition in terms of the verb by saying it is creative ability. The definition of create includes such phrases as "cause to grow," "make; originate," "cause to come into existence, produce; bring about; give rise to." Inherent in all these is the concept of inventing and the extending of what currently exists. These concepts are accepted without difficulty by most people. The problem arises when one tries to measure "creativity" or to identify creative individuals. Obviously, it would be to society's benefit to encourage the pursuit of creative activities.

Identifying Creative Individuals

If we could identify individuals who are unusually creative, we could give them opportunities to create, we could foster such pursuits. Industry has done this when they enlist bright scholars and researchers in "think tanks." How does industry identify these individuals? Previous products or systems invented by an individual are probably the most common way to select a person for such a group. There are no guarantees that such an approach will, in fact, identify the persons with the greatest potential. Some persons may never invent, but by their questioning and probing, serve as a catalyst for someone else. Identification is an imprecise art, not a science.

Education and Creativity

What does this have to do with education and the development of higher order thinking? The connection is that inventing and creating are perhaps the highest level of thinking. They require all of the other processes and something more, but we do not know exactly what that is. Schools can segregate their "gifted" and put them into classes where such activities are encouraged. The problem is that most schools identify their gifted by academic achievement scores. Many creative individuals are not strongly motivated to learn the curriculum of their schools, and in the regular classroom, creative ideas can be very disruptive to the continuity of the lesson in progress.

Education has been accused of killing off any creative ability by the time the student gets to the middle school. There is some evidence of our squelching creative ideas because they do not fit into our scheme of things. One plea that has come from the studies on creativity is that teachers be tolerant, at least, if not supportive of inventive children.

Elements of Creativity

Torrance spent a lifetime working with creativity. He developed a set of tasks (1966) to identify creative individuals. Earlier (Torrance & Palm 1959) he addressed the idea of measuring inventiveness as one important aspect of creativity. His tasks were based on the characteristics he thought comprised creative behavior: originality, flexibility, fluency, and elaboration.

Originality

Originality refers to the unusualness of a response or production. You have to ask, Is the behavior or product unusual and unlikely for this individual at this age in this circumstance? This allows you to recognize rare productions on the part of very young children by putting originality in perspective.

Flexibility

Flexibility is the ability to change directions, accept new and sometimes conflicting views or information, and generate multiple directions and pursue any or all of them. Flexibility is not only a mental approach, but a personality reflection. Some individuals are much more rigid in their thinking than others. They experience difficulty in handling ambiguous information or conflicting ideas. They may have trouble taking risks. This lack of flexibility will reduce the potential for creative thought.

Guilford (1967) proposed that individuals engage in convergent and divergent thinking. The divergent thinking was defined as what would probably be a combination of originality and flexibility as set forth by Torrance. Although one may not be able to teach someone to be flexible, enticing students into being more flexible and taking risks is worthwhile in the developing of their ability to think.

Fluency

Fluency refers to a multiplicity of ideas or thoughts. Some individuals seem to generate streams of ideas, solutions, topics, or whatever. When Thurstone (1938) was developing his theory of intelligence, in which he postulated seven mental abilities that worked together, he proposed that fluency was one of them. He constructed a part of his test of Primary Mental Abilities to include a section where the students wrote as many words as they could think of that began with the letter *s*. When you have students engage in brainstorming, you become aware that some students have many ideas where others have few. This fluency can be developed and enhanced, but probably not created. The stu-

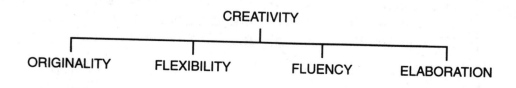

dents will generate more solutions when they have more information at their fingertips and are in a nonthreatening, encouraging atmosphere.

Elaboration

The fourth term Torrance (1966) addressed was what he called elaboration. This is a person's ability to take a topic or idea and expand, extend, rotate, reorganize, and develop it. In creating and inventing, you can see that all of these attributes would be conducive to the development of something new and different.

Creativity as Design

Perkins (1984, 1991) looks at creativity in the light of knowledge as design. He contended that creativity thinking is "thinking patterned in a way that tends to lead to creative results." The general principles he lists were that creative thinking

1. involves aesthetic as much as practical standards;
2. depends on attention to purpose as much as results;
3. depends on mobility more than fluency;
4. depends on working at the edge more than at the center of one's competence;
5. depends as much on being objective and being subjective;
6. depends on intrinsic, more than extrinsic motivation (Perkins 1991, pp. 85-86).

Schools fall short of addressing these aspects of creative development (Perkins 1991). He also pointed out that such a conceptualizing of creativity is broader than most definitions, but that if we viewed knowledge as a product of creative effort and asked four design questions, we would be thinking of creativity in this broader sense. The four questions are

1. What is its purpose?
2. What is the structure?
3. What are some model cases?

4. What are the arguments for or against the design? (Perkins 1984, p. 18)

Who Is Creative?

Are all of us creative or is it reserved for a few? Gardner (1983), in his theory of multiple intelligences, suggests that individuals could be creative in one area and not in another. Even Spearman's theory of intelligence (1927) had, in addition to the general factor (g), a number of specialized factors (s) where specific abilities might manifest themselves. The Japanese, it has been said, hold the belief that each child is creative and gifted; it is the parents' responsibility to discover and nurture these abilities. Some of us seem more creative than others. If you ask the students in your class who has the wildest solutions or ideas, the most off-the-wall suggestions, you will probably identify the student who is most creative. This is not to say that all students cannot be creative and cannot invent. It probably does mean that there are differences in how creative and how inventive one student is when compared with another.

Because creative behavior can be needed in problem solving, particularly real-life problem solving, teachers should want to nurture creativity in each child, even when it may lead to what Hunter called "birdwalking" (straying from the topic at hand to a related or peripheral topic). Sometimes "birdwalking" and the teachable moment may be hard to distinguish from one another.

Stimulating Creativity

Can you teach creating? The answer is probably "no" since, at the least, it is a strategy, a collection of skills organized in some unique way to produce an outcome, product, or idea. Strategies cannot be taught in any lock step fashion since the skills used, and the way they are used, change from one circumstance to another.

Even if you cannot teach creating, you can set up opportunities for students to *try* to invent or create. Here are some examples:

- Ask them to create a new country and write about it.

- Have them invent a new animal which can exist in a certain climate and has some characteristics of animals they have already studied.

- Let them portray some events or situations by a mural or their own drawing.

- Ask them to write a song, poem, story, or other verbal exercise.

- In class discussions, ask them questions like, What would happen if...? or How would things have turned out if ——— had happened? or If you were looking back on the events in the world today 100 years from now, how would you interpret them?

- Have them inductively solve problems without previous instructions in the process. (This would need to be carefully presented because the chance of failure would be greatly increased. Some would take it as a challenge, but others might be afraid to try.)

Some teachers use boundary breakers to stimulate learners to think beyond the conventional. Boundary breakers are activities, usually of short duration, which engage students in thinking beyond the common usage or function of an object or process. Activities which have students use a pair of pliers, a thumb tack, or a brick in ways different from its intended function and activities which we label brain teasers are examples of boundary breakers.

Swartz and Perkins (1990) wrote of "breaking set" as creative thinking. Most students enjoy these exercises even though they may only have been used as "sponge" activities. Classes of students identified as gifted are more likely to have opportunities to work with creative and inventive tasks. All students need to have such opportunities.

With the emphasis on process skills in science, we may see more planned activities to encourage inventing. The science process skills in one curriculum sound much like the thinking activities we have listed; they are observing, predicting, classifying, inferencing, and evaluating. Also included were the processes of manipulating, communicating, and responding. The agreement between these and the various taxonomies in higher order thinking is very close.

Semantics have proved a stumbling block in the higher order thinking programs and efforts. The use of commonly understood terms leads to a variety of interpretations and usages. The use of more esoteric terms, or the inventing of terms, as is done by many theorists when they present their theories, is as much of a problem in the other direction. When selecting a skill or strategy such as creating or inventing, be sure to define and give examples to clarify. This way you can avoid getting into terms such as "proceduralization."

If you dismiss the identification of students who are, or potentially are, inventive and assume that each can be inventive or creative, you can get on with the creative activities in your classroom. After all, you do not want to wait to identify your students who have made contributions to society (one way of identifying creative people) posthumously.

Tolerance of ambiguity and low levels of structure will permit more creative and inventive activities in the classroom. Even if you need every minute of the day organized and formally laid out in a lesson plan, you may still be able to handle ambiguity. In fact, knowing where you want to go and some ways to get there may be just what you need to allow the students the opportunity to engage in some of that "messy stuff" that can result in creative products. It may be hard to allow what appears to be much movement and activity, noise and confusion. You can always bring them back to your plan, however, if you judge that time is being spent unproductively. If the activity has been structured so that students understand the task, you may be surprised at the results.

Although it may not be done often, some teachers have allowed students to dramatize an event, past or present, on the school stage. You may have done this or some other planned creation in an art form that relates to your subject area. Literature, social sciences, art, music, drama, biological and physical sciences all offer opportunities for creativity. Science fairs originated with this idea. Even mathematics can easily be used as a vehicle for creativity. (You may feel that your students are already too creative in their mathematical problem solving.) You could ask students to explain to the rest of the class a theorem such as the Pythagorean theorem. This was used with great success in studies of cognitive development by Bruner (1968). The use of manipulatives in developing mathematical concepts may help students to develop strategies for explaining spatial and number concepts.

In conclusion, creativity is an amorphous, unidentifiable act which needs to be tolerated and nurtured. Because creative productions are strategic thinking, they may require incubation time and stimulation. You may want to design your lessons as you would any metacognitive activity. If your needs for structure and order in the classroom will not let you plan activities designed to produce creative and inventive products, other than writing, then present the students with activities they are asked to do outside of class, individually or in groups. You can encourage originality, flexibility, fluency, and elaboration.

We must remind ourselves that if we want to judge whether something is creative, we need to judge it from the perspective of the student's developmental level and the background experiences and knowledge available to him or her, not by our standards of what would be creative for us.

Chapter Seven

Direct Instruction of Thinking Skills

The teaching *of* thinking means the teacher will instruct the students in a process of higher order thinking. This is different from some of the instruction described later in the book in the chapters on content areas (Chapters 10–13). Those chapters show many activities that engage students in higher order thinking, but contain only a few examples of the direct teaching of a thinking skill or the application of thinking strategies to specific situations. Many teachers will be tempted to skip this present chapter as nice, but not necessary. Unfortunately, nothing could be further from the truth.

One of the major differences in the performance of gifted children and other students is the repertoire of strategies which gifted children develop and use appropriately. Many students will never spontaneously generate a strategy for doing a task more effectively, but they can learn and use a strategy that they are taught.

Many conscientious teachers will ask for a laundry list of strategies. They will proceed to try to work them into their instruction. This is not the best way to proceed. A strategy should be incorporated when it is appropriate for the student to use it with the content and objectives being taught. If you want students to compare and contrast life in the Middle Ages with life today, or to compare two authors or two plays or several passages, you will want to be sure students know how to do analysis. If you remind students of how to go about doing analysis, and they do not seem to know, then this is the time to teach them the process directly.

Higher order thinking strategies used to be a secret that teachers knew and students had to find out; unfortunately, only the better academic students usually figured them out. There are plenty of opportunities to teach higher order thinking strategies. In mathematics you may find that students do not look at their answers to see if they are plausible. Give them instruction in how to estimate and predict. You may have a classroom-management problem which you want students to help you solve. Use this as a vehicle to teach problem solving. The students may need to make decisions about what project to do or what topic to do their paper on. Use this opportunity to teach them decision making. If your students are preparing to debate a topic, give them exercises and instruction on the evaluation of evidence and determining fact and opinion.

You may say you do not know how to teach any of these. You know more than you think you do, but to bolster your confidence, there are many materials available to help you. We will take you through some examples below. Additional techniques are in the commercially available programs discussed later in the book.

Many districts have developed a scope and sequence of strategies and skills so that the teachers in a certain grade level will focus on one or two a year. For instance, classification is a critical skill for primary students. You may think that classification is not a higher order task; however, it depends on the developmental level of the students, on how it is taught, and on how much structure there is. Recognition of something as belonging to a particular group when one has been shown the group with that item in it is not higher level thinking. Determining what the characteristics of a group are, which are critical and which are not, and placing novel objects in the group based on the characteristics is higher order thinking.

Observation is not necessarily a higher order skill. Observing accurately, however, is the hallmark of data collection. Without making careful observations, one may have no data base to build on. Thus, one might give students activities where they must make accurate and detailed observations, which then lead to classification, which in turn can lead to some other process involving that class of objects, people, or events.

There is ample evidence that we can teach students some thinking skills (i.e., specific thinking processes). The use of these at appropriate times, and the selection of which ones to use, involve metacognitive strategies (managing one's thinking). If we teach the skills in context and engage students in practicing and reflecting upon them, they will build up a repertoire of skills from which to select a set when the context is different.

It is probably not necessary to get hung up on whether something is a skill or a strategy. The more practice your students have in various process skills or strategies, the better they will be able to use them.

Creating a Thinking Environment

Before giving some specific examples of teaching thinking skills directly, we will review some of the desirable characteristics of the environment that will promote and support these activities.

The first point is that the environment should be nonthreatening. This involves several aspects of teacher behavior. First, the students must know that if they try to do this skill, they will not be graded while they are learning it. Second, they need support from the teacher and the peer group. This can best be attained by having the students work in groups or at least in pairs. Third, the teacher needs to encourage the attempts without judging the results. If the teacher wishes to give feedback to assist the students in being successful, it probably should be done individually and in the form of hints or cues.

The teacher must transmit to the students his or her confidence in the students' ability to do the activity. If the teacher presents the students with a situation like the one s/he wishes to have them work on, walks through it with them, models what s/he is thinking, including false starts and irrelevant notes, and solicits ideas from them about how to proceed, the students will learn that exploring a problem with false starts and wrong directions is not making errors and is not wrong, but is the way we use our minds to figure things out. Fear of error increases with grade level, so a nonthreatening approach is particularly important in secondary classes. If the personality of the teacher has already established a nonthreatening atmosphere, s/he can concentrate on getting the students interested and motivated.

Time must be allocated for student thinking. Rushing students through a series of steps and concluding that they are now able to perform this skill, and will do so in the future, is not going to work. Anytime you place students in the position of interacting with the content and carrying out processes, more time is needed than if you only lecture to them about the content and the process. Students are not as adept as you at thinking; they will stumble and flounder and make false starts. This is the only way they can learn and improve; you cannot do it for them or tell them what to do when they try it on their own.

Teachers will have to be tolerant, willing to change, and flexible in order to bring this off. Reduced structure and teacher control in such activities can be, but should not be, threatening to a teacher. The noise and seeming disarray appear necessary in order for students to learn, particularly to learn processes.

Teaching Content and Thinking

Students may have trouble learning content at the same time they are trying to learn a skill or strategy. Although one is declarative knowledge (content) and the other is procedural knowledge (skill or strategy), there can be interference in learning. The lesson should focus on the process when you are teaching a skill directly. The easiest way to avoid the overload is to use material students have already learned and have them carry out the process on the knowledge base, that is, do something new with old information, the new process being the skill you are teaching.

If you want to teach them an organizational strategy, and they have just recently studied the sources of energy in science, they could be shown how to use a cognitive map, a matrix, a verbal outline, or some spatial array (like Ausubel). Then, they could work together to organize the material. The groups could share their outlines with other groups in the class. A discussion could follow in which the steps they used are enumerated on the board and then generalized to a model for organizing material. This activity could be followed by having all the students write an individual expository paper.

The writing process, modeled after the Bay City model, could be taught to students if they have not already been instructed in process. There are several processes involved here—interpreting, rewriting, and correcting. Pairs of students could work on their drafts, and eventually each student will hand in a paper for your review and comment. You probably should not introduce more than one new process in a lesson.

Be sure you label a process when you teach it and when you reference it and its uses at other times. If you do not follow a lesson with others which allow the practice and feedback of the process, you will probably be unhappy with the results.

How you introduce the teaching of a process is going to make a difference in how the students do the activities and what they remember from them. You might say, "We're going to learn a way to make good decisions, and we'll see how it works for you. There are many times you have to make decisions both here and when you're not in school. Wouldn't it be great if you knew a way to improve your decision making? And it can even be fun at the same time." Such a positive lead in is bound to help with motivation. It assures them that this skill is worth learning because they will have lots of chances to use it. It doesn't promise any miracle cures, but it says, You can do it.

The direct teaching of a thinking skill follows the general deductive model described in Chapter 3. The steps are outlined on p. 80.

Since these skills are processes, the teaching of them follows the same procedure as for teaching an operation in mathematics (addition), science (the scientific method), language arts (the writing process), or any other content area. The teaching of a process, in order to be effective, must include opportunities for students to use the process in a variety of contexts, feedback from an "expert" and fellow pupils, and the generation of ideas for applications. A worksheet which might be helpful in planning to teach a thinking skill is provided on p. 82.

Once the students have mastered the particular skill you are teaching, this skill should be combined with as many other thinking skills as you or the students can produce. With practice, these more complex combinations of skills can be combined into thinking strategies and will become available to your students.

The idea with strategies is that you are aware of the elements (skills) you can use or combine, and you decide which combination will be best for the task at hand (metacognition). Thus, automaticity, which is a characteristic of a well-mastered skill, is not really desirable when it comes to thinking strategies. In order for us to remain flexible, we need to think consciously about the best way to put together our solution. When a pilot lands a jetliner, you, as a passenger, want him or her to go through all of the sets of prescribed procedures, but you also want him or her to be monitoring the airfield, the weather, the airport traffic, etc. in order to modify and combine procedures differently if the circumstances warrant.

Steps in Teaching Thinking Skills Directly

  I. Teacher presents introductory set

    A. Names and describes the skill

    B. Explains the purpose of the skill

    C. Gives examples of when it can be used

        1. content areas

        2. real-life situations

 II. Teacher demonstrates the skill

    A. Models the skill for students

    B. Works through an example with them

    C. Discusses the process, generalizes the skill

III. Students practice the skill

    A. Students work in groups (or pairs) on example(s)

    B. Students discuss outcomes, process, and problems

 IV. Students evaluate process in relation to when they could use it both at school and outside of school

    A. Students generate examples of when the skill could be used appropriately in the current content and in other subjects as well as outside of school now and in the future. (This is best done in small groups or total class to maximize ideas.)

    B. Teacher suggests other times they might use the skill

  V. Teacher follows up lesson within the next several days with opportunities for students to practice and refine the skill. They may need a prompt and/or a review of the steps. The teacher needs to give them as much support as possible to encourage them to try the skill. Letting them work in groups or pairs will usually help.

Example: Analysis

In the following sixth grade social studies example, the number of the steps in the outline on p. 80 for teaching a thinking skill (or any other process skill) are in parentheses within the lesson description.

1. Objectives and definition (I)

Teacher dialogue: "Students, during the past several days you have been studying the characteristics of a tribe in Kenya. Each group has studied a different tribe. You have discovered, through references, artifacts, presentations, community resource people, and other sources, the characteristics of your people. You now know what they live in, what kind of work they do, the role of various members of the tribe, their habitat, the climate, the terrain, what animals are nearby, and their customs and habits. Now you are going to take two of those tribes and work on the process of analysis.

"Analysis permits us to see relationships between parts and between two or more groups. There are two basic activities in analysis: one is breaking something into its parts in an organized way, and the other is comparing/contrasting. You will also be learning about tribes other than the one you have been studying. These are our objectives—to learn about the tribes and to learn to make comparisons and draw inferences from data."

2. Modelling/walking students through process (II)

Teacher dialogue: "First, we will setup a matrix to put our information in. On the left side we will put the two tribes, and across the top we will label the information we have. I am going to put labels on this matrix, and you can decide whether we need to change them afterward. The chart will look like the one below.

"Other tribes can be added later. We might want to make several other entries under the columns. In fact, we might want to add more columns and enter food, clothing, family structure, religion, vegetation, division of labor, tools/weapons, number in tribe, language, and other information. We might also want to make the cells larger so we could include more facts. For instance, the El Moro fish on Lake Turkana, a huge saline lake formed when the Rift Valley separated water from the Nile and encompassed it with land. The El Moro live on islands in the lake. On the other hand, the Masai live on and around the Masai Mara game preserve. Game is abundant in the area, and there are large forests as well as savannas. This information can be condensed and added to the matrix.

"Now, we have organized the material and broken it into parts. We are ready to compare and contrast. I am going to look at what we have in the chart and tell you some similarities and differences I see. Then, you can help me add to those with other observations. First, I know the tribes are alike in that they are natives of central eastern Africa, in particular, Kenya. They have the same kind of governance, and the climate is similar. Both are carnivorous.

"As to differences, they subsist with different occupations. Where the Masai herd their cattle and thus have a diet of much meat, mainly their cattle, the El Moro fish and eat mainly the fish and some wild animals. Both live in tropical climates, but the rainfall is different. The Masai live in a much wetter

Tribe	Location	Occupation	Governance	Shelter	Customs	Climate	Animal
Masai	south central	cattle	tribal chief	mud/stick	dance	tropic	elephant
El Molo	north Rift Valley	fish	tribal chief	acacia/ palm leaf	jewelry & rafts	tropic	oryx & topi

DIRECT TEACHING OF A THINKING SKILL

1.   Set (name, describe, explain purpose, give examples)

2.   Teacher demonstrates skill (models, works through)

3.   Students practice skill (groups, also discussion)

4.   Students evaluate process and generate example of transfer

5.   Follow-up activities you plan for practice and refining

region. Because the El Moro live on the lake in almost desert conditions, their huts have to withstand the 40+ m.p.h. winds that blow without ceasing on the lake. Their customs are different. The Masai are known as warriors and are noted for their dances. The El Moro wear different jewelry—strings of ostrich eggs and glass beads. They also have pottery made from clay which is dug nearby."

3. Expand/relate (III)

Teacher dialogue: "Let us now go back to our matrix and expand the information on the Masai and the El Moro, and then let's add the Turkana, Samburu, and Kikuyu tribes. The recorder for each group can come up and add their tribe."

4. Practice process/summarize content (III)

When the five tribes are all on the chart, the teacher will have the students find similarities and differences between them. They will discuss these first in their groups and then summarize for the class.

5. Evaluation (IV)

When the students have done the comparing and contrasting, the groups of students will discuss the process of analysis, how they went about doing it, how they could have been more efficient, and where they could use analysis in their studies and outside of school.

6. Follow-up Activities (V)

As the students study other countries, they could engage in analysis between countries. The science teacher could arrange for them to compare and contrast different plants (or animals). The language arts teacher could have them compare and contrast two stories. In each case, it is important that the students be reminded of the process by name and review how to do the process before they begin.

Students learned some content as well as process during the above lesson since each group had only studied one tribe. It would probably be better if all the information was familiar at the start.

If your students have read two stories, you could set up a matrix where the story titles are on the left and characteristics such as plot, main characters, mood, set, author's point of view, etc. would be the labels across the top. (See example below.)

Modeling by the teacher, think-aloud examples, and other overt demonstrations of the teacher's thinking are valuable to students who may feel they are clumsy and inept at the process. They will be, until they have had some practice. Seeing the teacher make false starts or abandon a direction when more information is obtained or back up and try again reassures the student that the process is not something they should be able to do without struggling.

In the chapter on problem solving (Chapter 5), the process of problem representation was discussed. One way to help students gather and organize information for analysis is to show them good data-gathering techniques. In the case of problem solving, the data gathering becomes the basis for generating solutions and predicting their consequences.

Everyone has a different set of skills and strategies. It is not necessary to teach students all of them and certainly not advisable to teach them more than a few a year. The important thing to do is to teach them well; offer students the direct teaching of the skill and follow it with many opportunities to use the skill.

In the case of a combination of skills which involves the metacognitive process of planning, sequencing, etc., the students need to be

Title	Plot	Main Characters	Mood	Setting	Author's Point of View
Story A					
Story B					

given novel tasks which involve the skills learned but allow them to decide which skills to use and in what combination and sequence. Creative problem solving is just such a process.

Coordinating Efforts

It would be helpful if you and other teachers who work with the same students you teach could agree on which processes to work on during the year. For instance, you might select data gathering (observing), describing and classifying, and conceptualizing as the skills on which you will concentrate. These need to be addressed at all grade levels in at least a review mode, but these are particularly appropriate for the primary and upper elementary grades. Under each of these are subskills which you may want to teach one at a time or you may want to group as a whole process.

Through grade-level or subject-area meetings, you could coordinate the introduction and the practice across subject/grade. If you have at least one other teacher who is willing to work with you in the exchange of ideas and results, you will feel more confident. Without a support system, such efforts can be difficult to sustain. This has been particularly noted by teachers who have tried to introduce cooperative learning into their teaching. There are ups and downs, successes and not-so-successful trials, in any effort to deviate from the standard operating procedures. The support of the principal is also needed.

What goes on in the classroom when you close the door is your responsibility. Many teachers survive a situation in which they and their principal have different philosophical views of how children learn best by telling themselves that. However, winning-over the principal or finding that the principal already supports your efforts is well worth exploring.

If your school has a pull-out program for gifted students, you may want to talk with the gifted teacher about materials and ideas. Most gifted teachers have been working with their students in the areas of strategies and higher order thinking skills as their basic curricula.

The exception to this is in districts where gifted curriculum means acceleration only. These districts simply place the students identified as gifted in the texts and subjects of the next grade level up until high school, where they enter Advanced Placement courses in several areas. Many would question whether that is a gifted curriculum, and most who work with gifted would say it is not.

Deciding What to Teach

When you select the skills and strategies upon which you will focus at your grade level, you do not omit having the students engage in other processes in the taxonomy. It is impossible to avoid students making decisions and solving problems, for instance, and you would not want to. Inferring is an integral part of most units of study. Analysis is also. Whenever these processes are being used, you can guide students and give them cues about doing the activity and suggest that they start to develop their own way of attacking such tasks. A suggested taxonomy of higher order thinking skills and strategies was presented earlier in this book. It is presented again on p. 85 for ease of reference. Some of the important skills/strategies you could address are shown in this taxonomy.

This is not an exhaustive list; persuasive argument, for instance is not named, but you may find it is appropriate for your subject area and the developmental level of your students. You could analyze the processes in developing skill in persuasive argument. It would be a problem-solving process in which the outcome is to persuade someone to take your point of view. Synthesizing all the arguments into a persuasive oral or written presentation would be the product. But before this could be carried out, data would need to be collected and evaluated as to their usefulness, reliability, likelihood, etc., and much inferring would go on. Organizing and planning would be critical strategies in putting it all together.

A TAXONOMY OF THINKING SKILLS AND STRATEGIES (O'Tuel and Bullard)		
Category	**Processes**	**Applications**
Collecting Data	Observing	senses—appearances, materials, origins; feelings—emotions, value, personal significance; recording—preciseness, recall, reliability
Relating/Clarifying Data	Describing	physical properties; functions; relationships; analogies
	Classifying	critical attributes; compare/contrast; class inclusion; hierarchaical
	Pattern Recognizing	processes; events; objects; persons
Conceptualizing	Evaluating Data/Relations	data source, authority, reliability; data/relations; cause/effect; fact/opinion; reliability/likelihood; valuing; relevance
Using Processes on Data/Concepts/ Relations	Summarizing	concluding, annotating
	Inferencing	generalizing, if…then; estimating; predicting consequences/likelihood
	Organizing/Planning	developing frameworks, scaffolds; relating pieces to whole
	Analyzing	breaking whole into parts; relating parts to each other; compare/contrast
	Hypothesizing	generating solutions, ideas; what if
Using Multiprocesses on Data/Concepts/ Relations	Problem Solving	using processes above to clarify problem, generate solutions, test hypotheses, evaluate
	Decision Making	using processes above to weigh choices, predict consequences, evaluate, decide
	Valuing	evaluating how comfortable one's actions and/or choices are with one's value system
	Synthesizing	abstracting/combining bodies of knowledge and/or series of procedures into coherent wholes
	Creating/Inventing	generating new products and/or procedures which go beyond what is already known and understood

The skills and strategies in this taxonomy are overseen by metacognitive processes of planning, monitoring, and evaluating at all levels.

Even though persuading is a process and is not on the list by name, it is a higher order thinking procedure which includes many skills in the taxonomy.

The scientific method is not in the taxonomy, but again, it is an example of problem solving in the fullest meaning of the term. Many teachers may want to use the scientific approach as the vehicle to present problem solving to their students.

All of the procedures you ask students to perform in class can probably be placed under one or a combination of the skills and strategies in the taxonomy. The taxonomy is generic in that it is not adapted to any particular subject or content area. As you feel more comfortable with the meanings of the terms, you will begin to analyze the tasks you are planning in terms of the skills and strategies shown here. When you do that, you will know whether your students have had experience with the necessary processes, whether you need to present one or more of them directly, or whether you want to build in guidance at this time with the idea of presenting them later.

In deciding what you want to teach your students, you need to remember that the lower on the hierarchy the process is, the easier and more explicitly it can be taught. As the processes move from data collection to using processes on the data, you shift from what one might call skills to those that would be considered strategies.

Since strategies are combinations of skills used in variable ways depending on the current situation, there is no way to teach a one-method (single-strategy) approach. Thus, practice and feedback on trying the strategies becomes the *modus operandi*. You still need to define, describe, and illustrate the strategy. You still need to model it, and you still need to walk students through a situation where they deal with the options and choose the particular combination of skills they will use for the specific situation. Then, there probably need to be situations which require different combinations offered close together in time and characteristics. This is to keep the students flexible in their approaches; remember the Luchins jars (p. 65)!

Since there may be no single solution that is most effective for a given situation, you must be willing to have students generate their own combinations and try them out. What they need to conclude from such strategy lessons is not steps set in concrete, but a sense of selecting from their repertoire of skills a combination to solve a particular problem, and the realization that the next problem may require a different combination. This is why metacognitive activities may not be "teachable" but "practice-able."

Other Examples

The higher levels on the taxonomy subsume that individuals can carry out any of the processes in the taxonomy below them. Evidence evaluating and organizing will be addressed as examples.

Evaluation of Evidence

When students try to conceptualize the data they have collected, there are several processes you need to address. First, you will want to be sure that they can observe (gather data) accurately and sufficiently, and you will need to ascertain that they are able to describe and classify what they have collected. These are the processes beneath evaluating and relating evidence on the taxonomy.

There are two major parts to working with evidence: the evidence itself and the source of the evidence. There may be some overlap in the two and in the data gathering that has preceded them. For instance, in brainstorming, all suggestions, no matter how impractical, are kept until all ideas have been elicited. The next step is to select those to be maintained as problem solution sets. When the weeding out is taking place, students may throw out an idea because the source is unreliable, and therefore, the idea may be false.

The source of the data is very important. Are you not more likely to believe something you have seen with your own eyes than something you are told by a stranger on the street?

What are the questions one should ask about the source of the evidence or data?

The table below lists questions to consider when evaluating evidence.

Such a sheet could be put on the overhead when students are practicing evaluating evidence, so they will be reminded of the questions they need to ask and the judgments they need to make.

Fact and opinion exercises are frequently found in reading lessons. One of the most interesting ways to treat the evaluation of evidence is in analyzing advertisements and propaganda examples. You might want to introduce the types of propaganda to show students that they must be alert to a number of devices when they evaluate evidence.

EVALUATING EVIDENCE		
General Questions to Ask	Where did the evidence come from? How reliable is it? How do you know?	
Source	First Hand (Primary Source)	Five senses—Are they reliable? Frequency of observation? Equipment accuracy? Replicated? State of mind, bias?
	Secondary Source	An expert on the topic? How do you know s/he is an expert? Hearsay? Date? Printed evidence? Previous performance? Corroboration? Background, qulaifications, bias? Conditions of person, event?
	Printed Document	Author, editor? Publication bias? Factual or opinion? Date recorded?
	Observer (Primary or Secondary Source)	Any way to verify? Why should you believe him or her?
	Evidence or Data	Is there a cause-effect relationship? If there are several possible causes, how can you select? Most likely? Is it verifiable, factual, or is it opinion? Check source (see above), reliable? How likely does it seem? Does it relate to other information in noncontradictive way? What is its relation to what is already known? What is its use and its value? How do you know? If it doesn't fit, which do you believe? Why?

Organizing

If you want to teach your students "organizing," you might want to consider the entire process. It would involve collecting data, relating and clarifying the data, conceptualizing groups of data, making inferences about the groups, analyzing, and organizing. Thus, at the point of organizing, one has considerable information. If you decide that your students can perform all these steps, then you could work with them on setting up relationships and on techniques for graphically representing the relationships. Relationships include part-whole, such as superordinate and subordinate, and part-part, which are usually coordinate relations. If these relationships are too confusing for students, you may want to have them work on whether two sets of data are equal to one another or whether one is a part of the other. Some data need to be ordered chronologically, such as events in history; some need to be ranked by size or prioritized by importance.

Once these ideas have been inferred, the students need to choose a technique for displaying the relationships. During previous chapters we have suggested some techniques to use.

- Verbal outlining is a useful way to relate data. Choosing the main idea with its subsets is a variation on the verbal outline.

- Summarizing condenses the data to the major ideas and their relationships to each other.

- A taxonomy is a verbal outline of a fashion.

- Not to be forgotten are the spatial arrays described and used previously.

- The cognitive map may be used in place of the verbal outline. It may not be quite as precise in indicating the relationships, but it can be used easily and does show major and minor components.

- A graph may summarize a set of data in a very interpretable manner.

- The matrix has been used several times in this book to organize bodies of information into some treatable form.

- Students may be asked to draw an illustration which shows the relationships. Murals are wonderful examples of this.

- Maps may be used to place data in perspective. Charts may also be used.

- Auditory renditions and motoric performances may illustrate relationships in meaningful ways. Rapping, calypsos, ballads, plays, operas, ballets, contemporary dances, and musical compositions without words are all expressions of relationships.

The important aspect of organization is that it helps the student to place the data in some meaningful configuration that s/he can use to understand better the components. Since organizing is at the strategic level, you may want to expose the students to as many techniques as you feel are appropriate, and then have them choose the one they want to use. This can be particularly helpful where students' learning styles are varied. The students could group themselves according to which technique they wished to employ, and then each group could present their outcome to the class. Imagine how exciting this could be!

The chart on p. 89 provides a brief outline of the information to be presented to students in a lesson on the process of organizing.

When this information is presented, it may be put on an overhead or the board so that the students can refer to it as they begin relating and displaying the body of information with which they are working. In presenting this to the students, you need to define, illustrate, and model. When you "think out loud" about which technique to use, you might want to select one and then change to another to illustrate the flexibleness of the organizing. As soon as the students have watched (and perhaps helped) you organize some data, ask them to work in groups to organize some other data to which they have already been exposed, but which they have not had presented to them as a coherent whole.

The writing process offers many opportunities to work with organization. It may be easier for students to learn to organize their own ideas before they try to organize various content areas. This is a decision which you can best make.

Subject Specific Processes

There are processes which are subject specific. These should be taught in the same direct manner as the outline for directly teaching a process illustrated on p. 80. The difference is that you will need to show when and where the process is used in your subject. If it is not generalizable to other areas, you should explain why. If it is usable in another area, you may want to suggest that.

Many math teachers in middle and high schools are teaching students the process of using a graphic calculator. It has many uses within the subject of mathematics. Since it could also be useful in sciences, you might want to alert both the teachers of the sciences as well as your students about its use. To make the best use of the skills and strategies your students are learning, you need to improve communications between you and other teachers. Many schools are working in this direction in their restructuring plans.

Students need to know the name of a skill or strategy, how to go about doing it, and how it may be used in a variety of settings. This repertoire will last them a lifetime while the declarative knowledge we teach them will be replaced rapidly by new findings. Again, this is not to say that declarative knowledge is unimportant. Students cannot operate in a vacuum; they need to learn and organize their schemes in the content areas. The more information they have, the better it is organized, the more they bring to the problem-solving process. And they achieve more confidence in their abilities when they know they have a set of procedures to try. The direct teaching of the skill, or the opportunities to engage in a strategy, and the continued offerings of situations where they can apply them are necessary for students to develop thinking strategies and the awareness that they have them.

ORGANIZING PROCESS		
Relationships	Part-Whole	Superordinate Subordinate
	Part-Part	Coordinate
	Ordering	Chronological Ranked/Sequential Magnitude Prioritizing
Techniques	Verbal Outlines	Outlining, Main Idea, Summarizing, Taxonomy
	Graphic Organizers	Cognitive Map, Spatial Array, Graph, Matrix, Drawing, Mural, Chart, Map
	Auditory Organizers	Rap, Calypso, Ballad, Opera, Play, Musical Composition
	Motoric Organizers	Ballet, Contemporary Dance, Games, Simulations

Chapter Eight

Evaluation of Higher Order Thinking

Measurement experts assure educators that they can construct assessment instruments which will measure how well individual students perform on higher order thinking, as well as ones which will evaluate programs of higher order thinking. In fact, they can point to lists of available instruments which they say will do these two tasks. These measurement experts also caution educators not to just order an instrument from such a list.

Curriculum (what students should learn and be taught) should drive instruction (what and how students are taught) which in turn should drive evaluation (determination of what was learned and not learned). Information from evaluation should then assist in the fine-tuning of instruction. As with instruction, planning evaluation is determined by the goals and objectives of instruction. If these assumptions are correct, the decision about how to evaluate higher order thinking will need thoughtful planning.

There is no consensus on what a higher order thinking (HOT) program should be. Some are designed to develop philosophical reasoning, some to train formal logic, some to improve inductive reasoning, some to focus on problem solving, others on decision making; some are subject specific, some are generic, some are generic skills and strategies embedded in content areas but are designed to be transferred deliberately to other content. Is it no wonder that choosing an instrument or constructing one to evaluate higher order thinking is a complicated task!

Student or Skill Evaluation

This chapter will focus on classroom evaluation. Commercially available tests will be briefly discussed in the program evaluation section at the end of this chapter. If a formal evaluation of a program designed to develop higher order thinking is planned, these commercially available instruments should be studied to see if any have the potential to measure what your program is designed to do. These commercially available instruments are not likely to serve the needs of the instructor who wishes to measure what the learner has learned in a specific situation.

Evaluation and assessment are frequently used interchangeably. They are not the same to psychological measurers. Assessment usually refers to whether someone can perform a task or knows something or does not. The National Assessment of Educational Progress reports what percentage of a certain age group know or can do certain things. On the other hand, evaluation means that the outcome or student performance is being compared with some standard to see if it meets that standard. There are criteria that have been established against which someone's performance or knowledge may be compared. The distinction between the two has become fuzzier with the use of rubrics to score various student products. If a writing sample has four scoring levels, which is the standard or criteria? how do we say a score of 3 indicates the student "knows" that? For this reason the technical aspects of the differences between the two will be ignored in this chapter. Either term may be used.

Most teachers who are working with their students on the development of higher order thinking are interested more in how they can measure their students' successes and progress. This interest may translate into how well an individual student is performing, or it may focus on how the class as a whole performs on a particular task designed to measure the HOT skill or strategy with which they have been working.

Measuring Student Success

You can use two basic approaches to measuring student success in higher order thinking skills and strategies—evaluate the product or evaluate the process. In fact, the ASCD's *Update* article on national standards (1992) talks of the three *p*'s of assessment—performance tasks, projects, and portfolios.

Articles on assessment are also making great pleas for the use of "authentic" assessment (for example the *Educational Leadership* special issue on "Using Performance Assessment," May 1992). The term authentic has been used differently by various authors. Universally, it seems to mean that the problems and tasks are not contrived. Some authors would allow the task to be authentic for the subject matter at a given point in time, such as carrying out a laboratory experiment that illustrates a principle or concept. Others would insist that the task should have real-life implications or applications. Therefore, if the subject area is mathematics, the problems would deal with situations in which the student might find him or herself or which s/he could relate to as "real." In foreign language, for instance, the students would listen to a radio broadcast by a native speaker on current topics, instead of some passage invented by the teacher to cover that day's vocabulary words. It is obvious that transfer to real life from school activities is going to be facilitated by the use of such tasks or problems.

You may be using performance tasks, projects, and portfolios frequently in measuring student success in or mastery of basic or academic skills. Most teachers have used tasks and projects; portfolios have been more often used in the arts.

Recommendations about the use and handling of portfolios are available (see *Educa-tional Leadership*, May 1992). Many authors recommend that the portfolio show progress and development; therefore, it must have beginning samples and later samples. Some portfolios are "showcases" and only have the students' best works.

One clear message from users of portfolios is that students must have a great deal to say about what is included and to whom the materials belong. Whether the portfolio will go with the student to the next grade or all through school is a decision that must be made. If it is cumulative, as the present cumulative records are, then where to store these collections must be considered. The subject and the nature of the specimens will determine how the portfolio may be stored. In some cases, laser disks and computers can be used to store portfolios.

In order to judge student competency in higher order thinking, we recommend that you choose several approaches. You could evaluate the students' mastery of a higher order thinking skill by having them demonstrate that skill on novel material. This would be a performance measure.

Sometimes you will examine a product (or answer) obtained when the student engaged in a particular higher order thinking skill or strategy. An invention could be evaluated to determine the student's ability to analyze and synthesize as well as create. A solution derived by the student could be evaluated to assess problem solving. There is a caution here, however. Sometimes we arrive at an acceptable answer by reasoning erroneously. If you only look at the product, you may not always be sure about the competency of the student on the process that was believed to produce the product. Products are usual outcomes of units of instruction, and you can learn much from evaluating them. They reveal the content mastery of a series of lessons, and you may infer certain skills and strategies from the tasks completed.

Note that if tasks have been done over a period of time, both in and out of school, you may be evaluating a parent's competency on certain processes. Just reminding yourself of such possibilities will help you to reduce them. Gathering several assessment measures will insure against undue affects from such possibilities.

Collecting data on the student's thinking processes is a desirable approach; however, it is impossible to observe mental processes directly. You will have to make some inferences. The approaches most often used are

- Observations of students' efforts in multistep processes (checklists are often constructed to help) to see that they properly sequence the segments or complete the situational test
- Think-aloud observations done with videotaping or audio taping or a transcriber (other than the student)
- Observations of a student's response to prompts designed to elicit certain processes
- Interviews (particularly immediately after a process is completed)
- Oral or written self-reports about the process

You do not want to ask students to think about what they are doing while they are doing it; this interferes with the students' mental processes for the task. If you use the think-aloud technique, ask the students to say out loud what they are thinking (like a stream of consciousness), rather than how or why they are thinking what they are. Thinking aloud still seems to interfere with some students' task thinking; they may need to practice before you use it to gather performance data. If you think about how difficult it was for you to model mentally for students the first time you did it, you will be able to identify with the students' difficulties.

Some of the techniques above are hard to carry out, such as observing individual student's performances when you need observations on your entire class. It may be possible to observe more than one student at a time, or it may be that you can observe a group-assigned task and judge the adequacy of the performance.

Pencil-and-paper tests are frequently not available to measure a particular skill. Some computer programs are designed to assess student performance on language arts tasks that may involve inferring, generalizing, summarizing, etc. Using such a program can permit you to look at the results when the student has gone home or is in another activity.

Beyer (1987) has some excellent guiding directions for constructing an evaluation of the students' abilities to perform a higher order thinking skill. He recommends items which ask the students to define, to identify and give examples, to execute the skill (at least 3 situations), and to explain how they did it.

One of the advantages of observational data is it does not confine the student to one correct answer. This is particularly important in problem solving, decision making, and strategy assessment, where there is no single set of skills that must be executed in any one particular fashion. The evaluation then can be planned just as you planned the practice sessions for the HOT instruction or the follow-up practice afterward. The difference is that you may evaluate and record this in terms of student mastery or competence and/or diagnosis for further instruction.

If you are interested in whether a student in auto mechanics has learned to change the oil in a car properly, you do not want him or her to write about it; you want the student to perform the task and have someone check to see that all the steps are done correctly. This is because it is a process, not a set of facts that the student can give you back. This holds true for all processes; the best way to determine mastery or competence is to see each individual perform the task under typical circumstances. You may be able to have students check one another, using criteria you have established. You may also collect a product which you can examine later that is a result of the process. This will help you to keep the checkers accurate. Do not evaluate a student's competency until there has been ample opportunity for practice and feedback. Formative checkups are helpful to give the student feedback. Steps in evaluation planning may be found on p. 95.

Formative and Summative Evaluation

Formative evaluation is when you and the students check up on how they are doing. It is a form of monitoring (a metacognitive strategy discussed in Chapter 4). Students perform a task, answer questions orally or in writing, and check their own work. This way you and they know whether they need further practice, and you can give them feedback about what they need to work on. You can use the techniques from mastery learning and/or cooperative learning where students who have mastered one part help another student on that part.

Formative evaluations should be an integral part of instruction; they assure you that you do not take students too fast or too far before you and the students know how they are doing. You do not record grades on formative evaluations. You do not expect mastery when you are just introducing a skill, but you do need to know how they are comprehending your instruction. Because some students are disinclined to take risks, you need to reassure them that these checkups are for diagnosis and adjusting, not for showing them up as incompetent.

Summative evaluation, on the other hand, comes at the end of a unit of instruction and has as its purpose the determination of students' success with the objectives of the unit. If you taught content facts, concepts, and principles, you will want to assess what the students have learned. By the same token, if you have taught processes, you will want to assess the students' performances on them. At this point, you do evaluate their knowledge, both declarative and procedural, against the criteria you have set for success. In some cases, you may not want to grade the processes but concentrate on grading the content.

As standardized tests are revised, all of them are including items in various content areas that require higher level thinking processes. Your state or district can have a subscale of these items scored for higher order thinking on several standardized tests now. The clinker in this is that there is currently no evidence that supports the validity of these subscales to measure higher order thinking. These items seem to require the use of higher order thinking skills and strategies; however, whether a collection of them measures HOT is not known. At present there is no measuring stick to place each instrument against and say whether it does or does not measure higher order thinking. This is partially due to the different definitions of HOT, and partially because validity of current standardized measures depends upon the nature of the validity studies.

For summative evaluation of a HOT process, you will probably be safest if you have the students perform the process on new material in a similar situation to the one in which they learned it. At some future date, you may want to look at how well they select and sequence skills from their repertoire. That is a tougher task but an interesting one.

Qualitative and Quantitative Evaluations

Data that score how many responses are acceptable out of a total number are quantitative data. They may be averaged, assigned grades, etc. Qualitative data are more subjective in that there are not necessarily numbers associated with them. Checklists used in observations are subjective, but you can count how many of the items the student performed, for instance, and assign a score. Therefore, they are considered quantitative. Interviews are qualitative; you may design a set of questions to use which will help to assure you of collecting similar data from each student, but you must make judgments based on your skills and knowledge as to whether the student does something, believes something, is

Steps in Planning to Assess Student Learning
1. Determine the educational outcomes of the instruction.
2. Examine content outcomes and how the students will learn them.
3. Select one or more ways to measure the content. Test? Kind? Demonstration? Presentation? (individual or group?) Product?
4. Examine the process outcomes of the instruction.
5. Decide what methods you will use to assess the students' competence on the processes. Are you going to measure product or process? or both? Do you need to develop a list of criteria?
6. How will you measure progress during instruction? How will you give feedback to students about how they are doing? Have you built in practice for the processes? How will you plan correctives or additional assistance during the instructional sequence?
7. Are your examples, problems, and demonstrations related to real types of questions and/or problems? Would they be considered authentic?
8. How can you manage the logistics of collecting the various kinds of data? Will you use portfolios?

disposed to use HOT skills and strategies, knows how to approach a particular kind of problem, etc. Qualitative data are enriching and informing, but are difficult to summarize. Typically, in qualitative research the investigator gathers copious "field" notes which s/he then studies for extended periods of time in order to discern individual's behavior patterns as well as interactive dynamics.

If you are trying to discover how students solve particular types of problems, you may want to interview them immediately after their performance. Although time consuming and subjective, such data are fascinating to analyze. For example, fifth grade students explained their reason for choosing a particular pair in a deductive logic problem as being that the information did not say anything about the pair, so they assumed (incorrectly) that this pair must be the right answer (O'Tuel & Bullard 1988). If this had been mentioned by only one student in the rationales that they wrote down immediately after working the problem, the faulty reasoning would probably have been dismissed, but five of the seven who missed the problem had listed this as their reason for choosing the particular pair.

In skill and strategy teaching, sometimes you need to undo faulty reasoning by helping students to reason "logically" toward their answers. First, you must realize what is steering them toward unproductive responses. In a class of 20–35, one way to manage the gathering of this type of data is to present the task, preferably on the board, overhead, or top of the sheet of paper they will turn in, and as soon as they finish, have them bring their response paper, with their name on it, to you. At this time, you give them a sheet of paper which asks for their name at the top and below asks the student to describe how s/he arrived at the answer s/he has turned in. Interestingly, during this process in the research referenced above, two students recognized their errors, noted them, then explained how they arrived at their new answer.

Another aid that students used in the deductive logic problem above was graphic organizers. Several students sketched or made a chart of the relationships as they read the information; all of these students successfully arrived at the correct pair.

You can teach students to use matrices and spatial arrays as techniques for helping them to work complex problems or tasks. They are organizational tools. Students learn these readily, but some of them still will not use them when faced with similar problems (O'Tuel & Bullard 1988, 1990). This is why Norris and Ennis (1989) talk about assessing students' dispositions to think critically. It is one thing to know a skill or strategy; it is another to use it appropriately on subsequent occasions. For a more thorough treatment of evaluation issues written for teachers, see Norris and Ennis (1989), *Evaluating Critical Thinking*.

Measurement Issues

Measurements must meet the criteria of being objective, reliable, and valid. Although you may not want to establish formally your criteria for measuring students' learning, you will want to safeguard as well as you can your measures' adherence to these criteria.

Objectivity

To determine a measure's objectivity, ask yourself if someone else scores or observes this, will they arrive at the same data you have. If the answer is uncertain, think about how you might modify the measure to make it more objective. For instance, you plan to observe the performance of students, but you do not have a list of behaviors you will use to determine that the students can perform the task adequately. Deciding what is critical to an adequate performance and training someone in what to look for are steps that would increase objectivity. Putting these down in checklist form will help. If you are the only one observing, it is still worth making a checklist because it helps you to focus on the critical elements in the performance.

Reliability

Reliability refers to the consistency of the measurement. Lack of consistency can come from several sources. One source of inconsistency is the student; the younger the students are, the more this source must be considered. Are their attitudes, knowledge, health, and comfort status about the same as during previous assessments? Another source of variation may be the environment. Are the testing conditions the same? Another source of inconsistency may lie in the instrument you use. Is the task as similar as you can make it to previous measures—same amount of time, same type of performance requested, similar directions and format, same time of day, etc.? In the case of multiple choice tests, if you add more similar items to the test, you will usually get a higher reliability coefficient.

The question being asked when you consider reliability is, How well am I measuring these students' performance? If I gave this over and over and they did not learn anything in between or improve from practice, would they score about the same each time? If you have reasons to answer this yes, then your instrument is probably reliable. In the case of observers, if they all get almost the same results from observing the same individuals performing the same tasks, then the interrater reliability (consistency) is acceptable. If your results are to be used to make critical decisions about your students, you will need to establish reliability statistically.

Validity

Validity means the instrument measures what it is suppose to measure. In the case of higher order thinking this is tricky. As mentioned above, there is no yardstick by which instruments can be measured. There are several kinds of validity—content validity, construct validity, and predictive ability.

The final test of any instrument of this type is whether it predicts performance. If you could follow your students five years down their academic road and find that they were consistently performing skills or strategies as they had on your measure, and there had been no intervening instructions, you could arrive at a correlation coefficient for your measure's predictive validity. Obviously, that is not likely.

If there were other instruments available which had established validity, you could give your students one of these along with your measure. If the performance of your students on the two measures were similar, that is, when a student scored high on one, s/he scored high on the other and each student's performance ranked similarly on the two instruments, then it would establish criterion-related validity for your measure. Unfortunately, such instruments are not available. A few commercially-available standardized tests measure particular types of thinking, such as formal logic, but most measure other things. Since you cannot establish criterion-related validity and do not have data for five years down the line, you can look at the content and the construct validity.

Content validity is usually dependent upon expert judgment. If you have a group of teachers trained in developing higher order thinking in their classes and they are familiar with the particular skill or strategy you wish to measure, you could have each of them judge whether your measure's content will determine student performance on the skill. If you do not have a group of experts available, you can give your measure a careful analysis to make a determination yourself.

Construct validity has to do with whether your instrument measures the underlying abilities or processes. The more the instrument is a product, the harder this is to judge. The instrument might measure what you want it to measure, but the students do not perform well on it. If you conclude that the poor performance is because it is a poor instrument, you might be wrong. It may be that the students were not disposed to respond, rather than that they did not know how to respond. This leaves you with an unanswered question concerning its constructs. Again, you want to weigh the arguments for yourself to determine whether the measure will give you data from which you can infer that you have measured the underlying constructs.

Variety of Data

Because of the measurement issues mentioned above and because you may have several HOT objectives you want your students to attain, collecting a variety of data makes sense. If you evaluate some products, measure some processes, and collect information on attitudes, dispositions, and interests, your conclusions about the development of your students as effective and efficient learners will be more defensible.

Efforts to change testing at the macrolevel are very much in evidence today. California, North Carolina, Colorado, Maryland, Arizona, Connecticut, Vermont, and other states, as well as the New Standards Project, are changing the face of large-scale testing to performance tasks and products which allow for a variety of answers, more authentic problems to solve, multiprocess dilemmas to investigate, and scoring that varies from analytical to wholistic with the use of rubrics to designate which kinds of performance or product yield what scores within a given range.

Instruments referenced elsewhere in this chapter are as follows:

1. Structured (with criteria for evaluation)
    - situational tasks
    - product evaluation
    - objective instruments (i.e., multiple choice)
    - observation checklists
2. Open-ended
    - think-aloud recording
    - interviews, class discussions
    - prompts and student responses
    - self-report, written or oral performance/ presentation

- unstructured observation
- product assessments, no preset criteria—essay (particularly argumentative), theme, report, story, poem, physical structure, invention, etc.

For example, a situational task to evaluate organizing might ask students to read a previously unread section about a topic they had been studying and then to organize the content in an appropriate way. This would be looking at a strategy since any of a number of organizational techniques might be employed. In addition, immediately after the task, students could write down what they thought about when they chose the technique to use, how they went about doing it, whether they thought their choice was a good one and why, and whether there were other techniques that would have worked.

Statistical vs. Educational Significance

If you have good measures and you collect a set of data which is used as the basis for statistical tests, how do you know whether the results are significant? There are differences between statistical significance and educational significance. More often than not what is statistically significant is also educationally significant and visa versa, but there are times when these relationships do not hold.

If you have a large sample of students in your study (1000s) and you get statistically significant results on a measure of higher order thinking skills, you may decide that one point difference between students who received the HOT training and those who did not is not educationally significant. On the other hand, if your sample is very small and the comparison between the two groups, those treated and those not treated, is not statistically significant, yet on every measure the treated group outperformed the nontreated group, you may decide the trend is educationally significant. Such judgments are reasoned decisions based on the best data you have available. There is much about the interpretation of statistics outside the laboratories which is more art than science.

Program Evaluation

Differences between program evaluation and individual evaluation are primarily in scope and long-range planning needed. If your school or district decides to purchase and implement a commercially available program, the school or district must provide the material support, as well as the staff development required, and typically an evaluation of the effectiveness of the program. The expenditure of time, effort, and funds must be defended to the community, school board, professional staff of teachers and administrators, parents, and students. In some states, such as South Carolina, where the schools have been mandated to develop students' higher order thinking skills and strategies, the legislature must also receive information as to the efficacy of a program selected.

The HOT program to be implemented, whether commercial or locally developed, should have an evaluation design in place before the implementation begins. Evaluations are usually designed to answer one or more of the following questions (Callahan 1989):

1. Why implement this program in the first place?

2. What makes you believe it will work?

3. What makes you believe that, given available resources, the program can be implemented as intended?

4. Does the program exist in fact as well as on paper?

5. What parts of the program *appear* to be working and what parts *appear* not to be working?

6. What needs to be changed and what are some alternative ways of changing it?

7. What are the effects of the program?

8. Can this program work in other settings? Was this program worth the money?

An evaluation plan builds in the ability to answer the questions deemed important. Certainly, 7 and 8 above are likely to be questions all programs need to have asked about them. Linnemeyer (1989) listed 10 functions a good evaluation should perform. These are given here as another facet of evaluation planning.

1. Evaluation should be devised upon implementation of the program.

2. Evaluation should assess the degree to which the goals are met.

3. Evaluation should be sensitive to all strengths and weaknesses of the program.

4. Evaluation of a program...should assess those program components that are distinct and unique from program components of a regular...program.

5. Evaluation should be both formative and summative.

6. Evaluation should consist of both qualitative and quantitative research.

7. Evaluation should be multidimensional.

8. A time line must be established for the collection of data and individuals responsible for data collection designated.

9. Evaluation results should be made available to all concerned individuals. In addition, results should be presented in an appropriate format for each audience by a knowledgeable individual who holds significance for that audience.

10. Evaluation must be utilized by decision makers to implement appropriate program modifications.

These procedures for sound evaluation were first presented in relation to programs for the gifted and talented because gifted and talented programs have focused on higher order thinking components in their curricula since the 1970s. Evaluation has been difficult because the evaluators have been trail blazers in the realm of higher order thinking.

One state-level committee studying assessment of higher order thinking cautioned that "all aspects of higher order thinking cannot be assessed with traditional objective evaluation instruments. In fact, some aspects of higher order thinking may require performance-based evaluation instruments" (Higher Order Thinking Assessment Committee 1990, p. 14). The report goes on to state that more than one type of assessment must be used, tasks should reflect real-life situations, results should not be reported at the student level, and assessment should be used for improvement and staff development, not accountability.

In states with high-stakes testing programs where reforms, funding, and teacher, school, and district incentive money are all based on test results, using the results of higher order thinking assessments for improvement rather than accountability will be hard to sell.

One reason for designing evaluation of a program before you implement is that many designs involve collecting pre- and postdata on the group receiving the program (treatment) and a comparable group who is not receiving the program. These groups are generally called experimental and control groups.

It is getting more and more difficult to establish control groups. There are so many reform programs involving higher order thinking going on that the results from your control group may be confounded by some other treatment those students are receiving.

You also need to be aware that people in general will try harder if they know they are part of an experimental group. Because this was clearly established years ago at an industrial plant called Hawthorne, it is called the Hawthorne effect. If the students in your program know they are part of an experimental (translated, special) group, their improved performance may be a result of extra effort, rather than the program itself. It may take a year or more for this to level off. To offset this, some researchers recommend that the control group also be part of a special group, but the intervention be something unrelated to the objectives of the program in the original experimental group. This way both groups may be affected by the desire to do better because they are special.

The following is an outline of the steps in planning the evaluation of a program:

1. Determine what the goals and objectives of the program are. Decide the purpose of the evaluation.

2. Decide on the technical approach. Select or construct measurements to evaluate each of those objectives.

3. Develop a management document/time line for the collection of data, implementation points, staff development, material ordering dates, and distribution dates. Every aspect of the program should be on the time line with a beginning date and a completion date, a brief description of the task, and who is responsible for its implementation and completion. Although this planning may seem too detailed, it is required on most state, federal, or privately funded projects, and it is the only way to guard against delays in testing, training, and implementing.

4. Develop budget with line items for each expenditure. Prepare the budget along with the design for approval.

5. Get approval of the design, costs, contracts, etc. from those responsible.

In working with evaluation, you may want to obtain the *Evaluator's Handbook* (Herman, Morris & Fitz-Gibbon 1987) from the UCLA Center for the Study of Evaluation's *Program Evaluation Kit*.

Some districts will purchase a commercial higher order thinking program which has materials, staff development, implementation procedures, and other components of the program. Some of these have suggested evaluation designs which the district may adopt.

There are two reasons a district might not want to use such an evaluation plan; one is that researchers tend to take a suspicious view of instruments designed by the program authors to measure a program that they, the developers, are selling for a profit. The other reason may be cost. Of course, some programs do not have any prescribed evaluation plans and evaluation of them must be planned from scratch. Hopefully, the objectives of the purchased program and those of the district are the same.

Other districts will develop their own program. It is generally advisable to obtain the services of an outside evaluator to design and carry out the evaluation. This is to eliminate the possibility of anyone questioning the results on the grounds of vested interest.

The instruments which meet the criteria of measurements—objectivity, reliability, and validity—are not numerous in the areas of higher order thinking. Even those which appear to meet these standards will still have to be considered on the validity issue for your local program. An instrument may be valid for one use and not for another.

Commercially Available Instruments

The annotated list below is from Norris and Ennis (1989), Arter and Salmon (1987), and Baron and Sternberg (1987). Arter and Salmon divide their characteristics matrix into instruments for critical thinking and problem solving, developmental tests, creativity tests, and achievement tests. The instrument's focus, grade levels, subject specificity, forms, levels, items, item type, and administration time are given where available. Also given are scoring procedures, norms, reliability and validity status, comments, and information about where each is available.

Cornell Critical Thinking Test **Forms X, Z (1985)**—These tests are for grade 4-adult with the Z form directed toward gifted and adults. Sections include induction, credibility, observation, deduction, and assumption identification. Multiple choice. Pacific Grove, CA: Critical Thinking Press & Software (formerly Midwest Publications).

Ennis-Weir Critical Thinking Essay Test **(1985)**—This instrument for grade 7 and up is designed to measure students' ability to analyze logical weaknesses in arguments by responding to a fictional letter. Pacific Grove, CA: Critical Thinking Press & Software (formerly Midwest Publications).

Judgment: Deductive Logic and Assumptions Recognition **(1971)**—This test is for students in grades 7–12 and has as its purpose to assess students' logical ability. Multiple choice. Los Angeles: Instructional Objectives Exchange.

New Jersey Test of Reasoning Skills **(1983)**—The test is for students grade 4–college. Sections on syllogism (heavily represented), assumption identification, induction, good reasons, and kind and degree. Reading level grade 5 or below. Multiple choice. Montclair, NJ: Institute for the Advancement of Philosophy for Children, Montclair State College.

Purdue Elementary Problem Solving Inventory **(1972)**—This inventory is for students in grades 2–6 and tests their ability to solve common sense real-life problems. Multiple choice. West Lafayette, IN: Gifted Education Resource Institute, Purdue University.

Ross Test of Higher Cognitive Processes **(1976)**—This test is for measuring higher level thinking skills of students in grades 4–6. Multiple choice. Novato, CA: Academic Therapy Publications.

Test on Appraising Observations **(1983)**—This test is designed to assess students' ability to appraise the reliability of observational statements. It is for junior, senior high school. Multiple choice. This is to be one of a series of critical thinking tests being developed. St.

John's, Newfoundland, Canada: Memorial University of Newfoundland.

Watson-Glaser Critical Thinking Appraisal (1980)—This test is designed for use with grade 9 to adult. Real-life situations are used. Inference, recognition of assumptions, deduction, interpretation, and evaluation of arguments are the subtests. Hand or machine scoring. San Antonio, TX: The Psychological Corporation.

For additional listings, see Arter and Salmon (1987).

In order for a test to be valid for your program, the purpose of the test must match the objective(s) of your program.

The educators who implement any higher order thinking program intend that it will have sustained effects (mastery, competency), transfer, positive side effects, and the development of metacognitive abilities. "We are interested in observing how students produce knowledge rather than how they reproduce knowledge" (Costa & Lowery 1989, p. 89).

PART II
Content Integrated Instruction

Chapter Nine

Planning an Integrated Instructional Unit and Lessons

This part is designed to take you through the process of developing a unit, including the direct teaching of a thinking skill or the experience of working with a higher order thinking strategy (a combination of skills). There will be examples and suggestions for teaching higher order thinking within various subject areas and at various grade levels. Not every lesson will include the teaching of a thinking skill because it may have been taught in a previous lesson. In such cases, the teacher's reminder to students and the request that they recall the process either as a total-class activity or as a small-group review suffices as a prompt and as a checkup on whether they remember the process well enough to use it. If a teacher in another subject area has taught the skill needed for the lesson at hand, the request that the students recall the process and tell how they can use it in the current lesson should be part of the recall of prior knowledge, which is recommended for the beginning of all content-area lessons.

You want the students to bring forth their prior knowledge, both declarative and procedural, so they will have a place to store the new knowledge and so it will be presented in a meaningful context of past learning. If the content is to be completely novel (difficult to achieve in present-day times), you do not want to introduce any new processes. You will want to build on ones they have practiced and developed on familiar material.

Unit Planning

The next sections deal with the step-by-step planning of a unit. If you place the outline for a unit (p. 104) and the forms for lessons (p. 110) where they are side by side, you will be able to fill in your plan as you go through this section. Blank forms are provided for photocopying.

Select a Topic

The topic may be determined by your teaching assignment; however, you might want to plan a unit that integrates more than one subject. For example, the language arts unit in Chapter 11 on *The Upstairs Room* incorporates history, literature, writing, and reading assignments with learning a higher order thinking skill. The topic can often be the chapter heading in your textbook. If you are planning an in-depth study, the topic may be one for which you know there are resources available and that will be motivating, but the topic is only mentioned in your text. If the topic can serve as a vehicle for developing students' research skills, for developing their conceptual knowledge of a field, time, or process, or for integrating across subject areas, the topic may be legitimately selected, even when your text does not focus on it.

Select Approach Appropriate for the Grade Level and Development of Learners

Even though the grade level or group may be a given, not all of the students in the same

GENERIC UNIT PLAN

TOPIC: SUBJECT

Grade level or group: Primary:

Estimated time (hours or 50-minute periods):   Others:

EDUCATIONAL OUTCOMES OF UNIT

Content:

Process:

Products:

RATIONALE:

ASSESSMENT PLAN

Purpose:

How?   _____ Observation   _____ Checklist   _____ Informal Questions   _____ Product

        _____ Written assignment   _____ Demonstration   _____ Test   _____ Other

Test?   _____ Multiple choice   _____ Completion   _____ Short essay   _____ Long essay

        _____ Combination

SPECIAL NEEDS FOR UNIT (IF ANY)

Materials: Time:

Resource persons: Space:

LESSON TOPICS/TITLES

1. _____

2. _____

3. _____

4. _____

5. _____

6. _____

7. _____

8. _____

9. _____

10. _____

11. _____

12. _____

13. _____

14. _____

15. _____

Activities: In lesson plans and in unit "Extension Activities."

Bibliography

grade or group are developmentally ready for certain kinds of tasks and assignments. The variability increases when groups are heterogeneously placed; adult learners may be the most diverse because their experiences outside of school may be so different. The age range is likely to be greater.

Estimate the Time the Unit Will Take

Most of the examples in this book are geared to class periods of roughly 50 minutes. It goes without saying that elementary school teachers who have self-contained classes will enjoy much greater flexibility than teachers at other levels. Tech centers and vocational training centers may operate on class periods that vary depending on what day of the week they are taught. Some teachers may have block scheduling which allows them to have at least two consecutive periods. The transfer to your time constraints is something most teachers are accustomed to doing. In order to deal with a topic in any depth, you probably will need about 10–15 periods. This length allows you to introduce new material and have the students build an information base at the same time that they carry out activities with the material. This amount of time also offers you the opportunity to teach or review one of the higher order thinking skills or strategies and let the students practice it.

Select Content Objectives or Outcomes

The development of the unit depends on what the content and process outcomes are that you have selected for your students. Outcomes are always expressed in terms of what the students know or can do. You will have one or more general student outcomes in your unit plan; more specific objectives will be listed in the individual lesson plans. For the more general outcomes, you may want to use verbs like appreciate or conceptualize or understand. The more precise, however, you can be about the learning, the easier it will be to design assessments.

The selection of an instructional model can be made once you have determined your content and process outcomes. This will have a strong bearing on what activities your students will carry out in your lessons.

Select Process Outcomes or Objectives

These outcomes may be more general in the unit plan than in the lesson plans. You might say the student will be able to analyze in the unit plan, but when you write your outcomes for a lesson, you may want to use compare and contrast, break into parts, or organize into an outline. It is at this point that you might consult the list of critical and creative thinking processes in the taxonomy (Chapter 3) which is reproduced here for your convenience (p. 106). You may see a skill or strategy that fits into the activities you will be having the students do. If none seems to jump out at you, you may want to delay the completing of this section until you have studied the resources available.

Because an example can sometimes make it easier to see how something fits into your plans, we have developed the chart on page 107. The major skills and strategies are shown on the left and different groupings of learners head the columns across the page. Any of the activities might be used at any other level if done in a developmentally appropriate way.

Scope and Sequence

The question always arises when planning instruction, particularly where processes are concerned, as to what order the processes should be taught. There is no single order that is correct or necessary across age levels. You might, however, want to focus on particular skills and strategies more at some levels than at others. The chart on page 108 is suggested as a general guide, but by no means a checklist.

What Products Will You Want the Students to Develop?

Again, you may add to these as you flesh out your lessons and decide how students will show you that they comprehend something or can do some process.

Develop a Rationale for Teaching the Unit

When you selected the topic, you probably thought about why this would be a good unit

A TAXONOMY OF THINKING SKILLS AND STRATEGIES (O'Tuel and Bullard)		
Category	**Processes**	**Applications**
Collecting Data	Observing	senses—appearances, materials, origins; feelings—emotions, value, personal significance; recording—preciseness, recall, reliability
Relating/Clarifying Data	Describing	physical properties; functions; relationships; analogies
	Classifying	critical attributes; compare/contrast; class inclusion; hierarchaical
	Pattern Recognizing	processes; events; objects; persons
Conceptualizing	Evaluating Data/Relations	data source, authority, reliability; data/relations; cause/effect; fact/opinion; reliability/likelihood; valuing; relevance
Using Processes on Data/Concepts/ Relations	Summarizing	concluding, annotating
	Inferencing	generalizing, if…then; estimating; predicting consequences/likelihood
	Organizing/Planning	developing frameworks, scaffolds; relating pieces to whole
	Analyzing	breaking whole into parts; relating parts to each other; compare/contrast
	Hypothesizing	generating solutions, ideas; what if
Using Multiprocesses on Data/Concepts/ Relations	Problem Solving	using processes above to clarify problem, generate solutions, test hypotheses, evaluate
	Decision Making	using processes above to weigh choices, predict consequences, evaluate, decide
	Valuing	evaluating how comfortable one's actions and/or choices are with one's value system
	Synthesizing	abstracting/combining bodies of knowledge and/or series of procedures into coherent wholes
	Creating/Inventing	generating new products and/or procedures which go beyond what is already known and understood

NOTE: The skills and strategies in this taxonomy are overseen by metacognitive processes of planning, monitoring, and evaluating at all levels.

EXAMPLE ACTIVITIES FOR EACH SKILL/STRATEGY BY AGE GROUP				
Skills/Strategies	K–3	4–7	8–12	Adult
COLLECTING DATA observing (senses) feeling/valuing recording	Students collect leaves in fall; study each for color, texture, shape, size. Share information. Students collect pictures that represent different feelings. Discuss. Students collect measurements in classroom, size, furniture, equipment.	Students work in groups, collect information on a particular country (political, social, economic, and physical characteristics). Prepare list of facts (tell where found). Students check one another for accuracy.	Students will conduct research on given topic. They will collect data from multiple sources in room, library, community, and possibly write for other information. They will keep record of sources.	Learners will collect samples of rocks from various sites in specified areas. They will write a report of their collection process and what they collected. Learners will be given problem to solve.
RELATING/ CLARIFYING describing classifying pattern recognition	Students write or orally describe leaves, pictures. Students classify leaves or pictures according to type. Students look for pattern of similarity in leaves, pictures. Students look for geometric patterns in room.	Students classify country in terms of political structure, social customs and religion, economic system, and physical characteristics. Students write their descriptions with supporting references.	Students will classify data into categories with descriptive labels.	Learners will study geological materials, classify rocks by type. They will write a description of each sample and categorize by text. Problem is presented; learner will describe, look for pattern, classify.
CONCEPTUALIZING relating evaluating data —source —fact/opinion —cause/effect —reliability —likelihood —relevance —value	Teacher will read two stories to class: one fact, one fantasy. Discuss fact/opinion, cause/effect, likelihood. Students collect ads from magazines, newspapers. Students will distinguish fact and opinion, evaluate reliability, likelihood, relevance, and sources.	Groups swap material. Each will evaluate accuracy, reliability, likelihood, relevance, sources, etc. Students will relate other groups' findings to their category.	Students will evaluate the reliability of their sources. They will search for relationships among their categories of data.	Learners will examine each others' samples, classify them. If there are differences, learner will evaluate his/her reasoning/sources and retain or change. Learner will relate problem to other info, evaluate sources and resources, look for analogy.
USING PROCESSES AND MULTI-PROCESSES ON DATA, CONCEPTS, RELATIONS inferring —generalizing —predicting —summarizing —hypothesizing analyzing organizing/planning problem solving/decision making evaluating synthesizing creating/inventing	Students are given nonroutine problems to solve that require them to predict, hypothesize, plan, organize solutions. Students will test some of the solutions and evaluate the results. Students will each create another problem and propose solutions.	Students will take info on country and compare with that of another country already studied. They will analyze by categories, find similarities and differences. Students will organize their material using verbal or graphic organizer. Students will decide where they would rather live and why. Students will predict future for their country, support predictions.	Students will organize data, prepare outline of paper, decide what to include, write draft of paper (synthesizing), edit draft for interpretation (inferencing). Rewrite and prepare references.	Learners will write paper about samples. For each sample, the learner will hypothesize about how it got where it was, analyze the characteristics of the area that might explain its presence. What is its function in its locale? How else might it be used? Learner will organize data, hypothesize solutions, predict, test best option, evaluate.
METACOGNITIVE PROCESSES planning monitoring evaluating	Students will set up design for project (planning), carry out, and monitor; evaluate. Ask how to do it better.	Groups will plan how they will set up their comparisons, carry out their plan, evaluate results.	Student plans where and how to collect data, carries out plan, monitors the collection. Student evaluates paper.	Learner will plan collection, monitor it. Learner will evaluate classification, plan paper, write. Learner has represented problem, planned solutions, monitored testing, evaluated result.

SUGGESTED FOCUS FOR VARIOUS LEVELS OF LEARNERS	
K–3 **Acquisition Stage**	Young children are making order out of their world and are learning to classify what they observe into manageable groups. Thus, observing (collecting data), describing, and classifying are very important. They also need to plan, monitor, and evaluate the choices they are given.
4–7 **Achieving Stage**	Children at this age are developing the work and study habits which will last a lifetime. They need to be conceptualizing, inferring, analyzing, organizing, problem solving, and evaluating their decisions. The context needs to be social as well as cognitve.
8–12 **Expanding, Applying Stage**	Adolescents are developing the abilities to deal with abstract ideas. They need to focus on expanding their abilities to conceptualize, infer, analyze, create, organize, and evaluate. They need numerous opportunities to solve problems and make decisions in a broadening context. They are capable of developing their metacognitive strategies in more complex ways. They have an increasing awareness of their own mental functioning.
Adult **Extending, Improving in Larger Context**	The focus for adults is on interpersonal relations, occupational problem solving, quality of life. Since problem solving has steps, but no clear order of options, adults need to focus on how to become better problem solvers and decision makers in all phases of their lives. Since they may not have been taught skills and strategies previously, they may need instruction/practice in all levels of the taxonomy.

to teach for this group of students. That can be your rationale.

Plan How You Will Assess Student Learning

This does not mean that you have to make out a test at this point. The consideration of assessment needs to be thought about early on because some of the students' activities will constitute assessment. It may be that the learners are producing a product which will assess how well the students did on your objectives/outcomes; it may be that you will observe them executing a process, and you will make an evaluation of their abilities to carry out one of your process outcomes.

Gather a List of Resources Which are Available and Collect All You Can Use in Planning Your Unit

By checking the school library, the local libraries, the community organizations, individual resource people, text material, your personal materials, and materials from other teachers, you will be able to list the resources you have for students to use and the ones you need to plan the unit. If there is enough lead time, you may want to order some particular resource material.

Determine If There Are Limitations or Special Needs for Space or Time

If you are planning a medieval feast, on the day it occurs, you will need some additional time and probably a place outside of your classroom. If you are planning for the students to enact a play, you will need rehearsal time on a stage as well as a time for the performance. Note any of these special needs. You will have to evaluate whether you can overcome the limitations you find for these special needs.

Plan the Lesson Titles and Place Them by the Lesson Number on the Unit Planning Page

These titles will give you a sense of how the unit will develop. You may want to list major activities instead of topic headings if they will help you to think through the sequence. You may want to set up a reading schedule for students as you list these heading for your lessons, or if this is premature at this junction, wait until you plan each lesson.

Plan the Major Activities Students Will Do

By listing the major activities, you will be able to space out the other tasks and fit in some of the supporting tasks. You might also be thinking at this point about who will perform these—groups, individuals, pairs, or total class.

Set up Time Schedule for Projects and Activities

Because it is helpful to give students some structure to assist them in their planning, you may want to develop a list of all activities, indicating which are required, which they can choose from, and you may want to develop a calendar which you can give them which shows due dates for various tasks. Again, if some of this is still not clear to you because you have not planned the individual lessons, you can return to this later.

Plan Each Lesson in the Unit

Although you do not have to use the lesson plan form which we have included, it can help you to plan your lessons systematically. As you plan each lesson, collect or develop any handouts. You can obtain these before you start the unit so you will have everything on hand. Sometimes our estimated times for various activities do not come out as planned; if you have the handouts on hand, you can move on to the next lesson without a problem. We will walk through lesson planning after the next paragraph, which is the unit final check.

Look Again at the Outcomes and Assessment

At this point, you may want to revise your outcomes. You may have expanded the students' tasks and products. Ask yourself, "If a teacher who teaches in this area were handed this unit with its lesson plans, would he or she be able to teach this unit? Do I have everything one would need to do a good job with this topic?" If the answer is yes, then your unit planning is complete.

LESSON PLAN FOR LESSON:

TITLE:

OBJECTIVES

Content:

Process:

Products (if any):

MATERIALS AND RESOURCES:

TIME ESTIMATED:

INTRODUCTION OF LESSON (PROMPTS)

Objectives stated? _____ yes _____ no

If no, how is interest to be raised?

Students recall prior knowledge?

Students make self-reference?

Points essential to set forth?

ACTIVITIES/SEQUENCE

1.

2.

3.

4.

5.

ASSESSMENT

Student's metacognitive questions:

Teacher assessment of students:

FOLLOW-UP

Content:

Process:

Notes (student grouping, prompts, spatial organizers, verbal outlines, etc.):

Lesson Planning

The headings below refer to the lesson plan form provided on page 110.

Lesson Number and Heading

It is easy to forget to number a lesson because you are focused on that particular set of activities, but for the overall continuity of the unit, it is a good idea to number as you go along. If a lesson takes more than one class period, you can mark that in the space provided. The heading of the lesson may be the topic for that lesson, the title of a chapter in the text, or the name of a literary unit or publication. It is helpful to use a topic that is descriptive of the lesson. As you look back at your unit outline, you will see the headings you have chosen. As you develop the activities in a particular lesson, you may want to edit the title you have given in the unit in order to make it more descriptive.

Objectives

Almost every lesson has a *content* objective. Not every lesson has a process objective. We suggest that you turn to the verb chart (p. 112) that was described in Chapter 3 to select appropriate verbs to describe what your students will be doing. You may also find it helpful to refer to the taxonomy of skills and strategies on p. 106.

One advantage of referring to these charts is that you are likely to select higher level verbs when you see the many choices you have. Usually these higher level verbs lead to activities that involve students more with the material, which should increase student retention and interest.

Process objectives focus on what skills and strategies the students will learn or practice. By writing these in your lesson plan, you are more likely to remember to call students attention to what processes they are using and can use in this and other lessons. If you are introducing a skill for the first time, you may want to review the steps recommended for teaching a higher order thinking skill in Chapter 7. The activities that you develop for your lesson should include describing the skill, giving examples, modeling, and working through an application before you ask students to practice it. If you have taught the skill in a previous lesson, you need to give students an opportunity to recall what they did when the skill was introduced (with prompts if needed) before you ask them to carry it out in the current lesson.

Your content and process objectives often imply that the students will produce some tangible outcome. These frequently become *products* used in your assessment of student learning.

Materials and Resources

You have probably collected most of what you will need in the way of materials and resources as you planned the outline of your lesson in the unit plan. The task now is to decide what you will use in which lessons and to arrange to obtain any resources you do not have on hand. You may need to call a resource person and ask them to come on a specific day. You may need to order specific materials (in the unit outline on space travel in Chapter 13, there were excellent materials available from NASA). The media center may need to be alerted about a particular activity.

Time Estimated

This is where you note if you think the lesson will take more than one class period.

Introduction of the Lesson

Several prompts have been listed in this section of the lesson plan. You may not want to put anything here. The purpose was to assist in the anticipatory set planning, and to remind you about having students recall prior knowledge and engaging in self-referencing. These will assist students in encoding the material and processes into their long-term memory in a meaningful manner. You may believe that you need an object of art, a hands-on activity, a video, or just the simple statement of the objectives. The line labeled "points essential to set forth" is where you can highlight what you want to stress.

Taxonomy

LEARNING/PROCESS VERBS

EVALUATION

interpret
judge
justify
criticize
solve
decide
infer
verify
conclude
appraise
evaluate
rate
compare
value
revise
select
choose
assess
estimate

SYNTHESIS

add to
predict
assume
translate
extend
hypothesize
design
reconstruct
rename
reorganize
regroup
restate
systematize
symbolize
vary
formulate
substitute
modify
minimize
maximize
alter
connect
compose
plan
propose
arrange
assemble
collect
construct
create
set up
organize
manage
prepare

ANALYSIS

take apart
part of...
fill in
take away
put away
combine
differentiate
divide
isolate
order
separate
distinguish
dissect
subtract
associate
relate
pattern
analyze
apraise
calculate
experiment
test
compare
contrast
criticize
diagram
inspect
debate
inventory
question
solve

APPLICATION

organize
group
collect
apply
summarize
order
classify
model
construct
relate
code
translate
interpret
use
demonstrate
dramatize
practice
illustrate
operate
schedule
shop
sketch

COMPREHENSION

explain
translate
group
conclude
summarize
describe
restate
discuss
describe
express
identify
locate
report
review
call

KNOWLEDGE

explain
show
list
observe
demonstrate
uncover
recognize
discover
experiment
define
memorize
repear
record
recall
name
relate

Activities/Sequence

The heart of a lesson is the activities the students do. Students will remember material longer and better if they do something to or with it. It takes longer to ask groups of students to discuss and report on a task, but the likelihood of retention and understanding is measurably enhanced. Sequence can make a difference. In the language arts unit on *The Upstairs Room*, there is a lesson on prediction. The key to that lesson is reading selected portions of the story in order, stopping after each reading, and having students predict what they think will come next (and why).

Assessment

Under assessment, there is a prompt to ask students to engage in metacognitive questioning. Since teaching metacognitive strategies is in question, experience with this type of thinking is probably the best way to build expertise. You may find that you add this type of questioning into the activities as the lesson unfolds.

You may have already designated assessment of your objectives by observing students' products and activities. Listing them here is helpful if someone else is looking at your lesson, and it reminds you of what you need to collect or observe. Observation or processes, projects, demonstrations, written and oral expression, and other student products may constitute elements of your assessment. Chapter 8 suggests a variety of assessment procedures.

Follow-up

Homework, announced tests, plans for future practice of processes, and other related activities are listed here; for example, a "near transfer" follow-up activity or reminders of long-term assignments.

Notes

This section was included for miscellaneous information or reminders you may want to note. You may want to jot down where you located some particular information. Another note might be about what worked really well and what needs to be modified.

Lessons are usually planned in order of presentation, but there may be times when there is one key lesson that is so important, you will want to plan it completely before filling in some lessons which precede it. Teachers' personalities and styles play a part in how lessons are planned. The important note is that they be planned!

Model Units and Lessons

It is probably presumptuous to use the term model units and lessons for the examples which follow in the next four chapters. The term model means "ideal" to some. These units are examples. You could improve on each of them. We did want to offer you some developed topics, and we hope you can use them as you plan your units and lessons.

There will be a few introductory comments in each chapter followed by unit-plan outlines at different levels. In the areas of social studies, language arts, and mathematics, you will find one unit in each with all of the lesson plans developed and included. The unit/lesson plans will use the format presented in this chapter.

Over and over in these examples you will see the emphasis on student participation, student construction, student inferring, concluding, summarizing, reporting, cooperating, etc. Whether content or process, educational outcomes should always state what students will be able to do when the lesson or unit is completed.

Score Sheets

In addition to the unit and lesson formats included in this chapter, here are two score sheets which are used in the model unit on Africa (Chapter 10), but which you might want to adapt for other purposes.

The first form is for scoring oral presentations; the second is for written presentations. Note that we do not include grammar and mechanics in scoring the written presentation. We believe that is a separate assignment although the same sample may be used for it.

CLASS PRESENTATION SCORE SHEET
Student Name or Group Members:
Presentation Topic:
Date:
CONTENT ACCURACY (50 points) =
Notes:
DELIVERY (50 points) =
Visuals:
Originality:
Quality:
Use of time:
Contributions from everyone (if group):
Notes:
TOTAL POINTS =
Notes:

WRITTEN REPORT SCORE SHEET
Student Name:
Report Topic:
Date:
TITLE PAGE (5 points) =
TABLE OF CONTENTS (10 points) =
NEATNESS (15 points) =
BIBLIOGRAPHY (30 points) =
CONTENT (40 points) =
Illustrations:
Maps:
Information:
Organization:
TOTAL POINTS =
Notes:

Chapter Ten

Social Studies

Nowhere is it more apparent than in social studies that students need to be able to evaluate evidence, make inferences, and interpret what they read, see, and experience. Many of the first efforts at developing higher order thinking took place in classes in social studies or language arts.

The unit that follows is an example of one you might develop about any country, region, or continent. After this unit and its lessons, which focus on middle school grades, there will be a suggested unit plan (without the lessons developed) for an elementary unit and another for secondary students.

UNIT PLAN

TOPIC: Africa

Grade level or group: Grades 6–7

Estimated time: 15 periods

SUBJECT

Primary: Social Studies

Others:

EDUCATIONAL OUTCOMES OF UNIT

Content: Students will have an understanding of geography, climate, resources, people and cultures, history, and wildlife of parts of Africa.

Process: Compare and contrast, inferencing, research, note taking, map reading, synthesis, problem solving

Products: Presentations, class matrix, cognitive maps, maps

RATIONALE: In order for students to have an appreciation of the contributions of Africans and their current life-styles and problems, they will study African history, general characteristics of Africa, and focus on specific groups. In the concluding activities of this unit, the students will be involved in comparing and contrasting different tribes of Kenya. Teachers could choose to use different countries instead of different tribes.

ASSESSMENT PLAN

Purpose: Demonstrate learning

How? √ Observation   ___ Checklist   √ Informal Questions   √ Product

√ Written assignment   √ Demonstration   ___ Test   ___ Other

Test? ___ Multiple choice   ___ Completion   ___ Short essay   ___ Long essay

___ Combination

SPECIAL NEEDS FOR UNIT (IF ANY)

Materials: Cloth for kangas, shelter materials, classroom reading materials, any authentic objects available, resource books, maps

Time: For projects and independent study

Resource persons: Anyone who has lived in or visited Africa

Space: At home or after-school work space

[Continued on next page.]

LESSON TOPICS/TITLES

1. Introduce unit, give overview, expectations, requirements

2. Assumptions, groups research truth of these assumptions

3. Geography and resources

4. Ancient Africa

5. Ancient West African empires

6. Ancient history/slave trade

7. European exploration/exploitation of Africa

8. Modern Africa

9. Africa today—problems and promise

10. Tribes of Kenya

11. Research on chosen tribe, prepare presentation

12. Presentations, entries on chart

EXTENSION ACTIVITIES

One extension activity below which you could use is a list of questions at the various levels of Bloom's Taxonomy, or you could have students generate other questions by using these as samples. These are looking at just two of the Kenyan tribes. Earlier in Chapter 7, analysis was taught directly using this general body of information. You might want to review that in terms of teaching analysis. A few activities that might be used as extensions or file folder activities are listed after the Bloom questions. You will probably think of many others.

QUESTIONS
KNOWLEDGE
- What do the Masai eat?
- What is the main occupation of the El Molo tribesmen?

COMPREHENSION
- Describe what the huts of the Masai look like.
- Why does the Masai's diet consist mainly of meat?

APPLICATION
- If you were a member of the El Molo tribe, how would you spend most of your day?
- If you were living with the Masai, what would you find the most difficult chore to do?

ANALYSIS
- How are the Masai and El Molo alike? How are they different?

SYNTHESIS
- If a Masai tribesman were to find himself transplanted to Columbia, South Carolina, what job interviews would the employment agency be likely to send him on?
- Write a story about life among the El Molo children.

EVALUATION
- If you were going to join an African tribe, which one would you choose and why?
- Why do the Masai consider the El Molo to be "Poor Beggars"? What is their justification? Do you agree with them? Why or why not?

OTHER EXTENSION ACTIVITIES

1. Find articles about current archaeological explorations in Africa. Report to the class on where these are being carried out and what has been discovered thus far.

2. Gold is a precious metal and continues to carry high value. What about salt? Do you think you could trade salt for gold today? Why or why not? What are some other things people consider valuable? What

determines how valuable something is?

3. Research the topic of mining, trading, and valuing salt. Write a report. Include information about the ancient North African salt-mining city of Taghaza, methods of salt production in the United States today, and/or salt's role in cooking, food preservation, and health.

4. Find out about camels. How do they survive the heat and dryness of the desert? How are they trained and used in caravans? Create a poster presenting this information.

5. Find out about the African journeys of David Livingston. Use an outline map of Africa to label the regions he visited and identify when he visited each. What were the purposes of these trips?

BIBLIOGRAPHY

NOTE: Since many African names are spelled phonetically, variations in spelling occur among sources, for example, Masai and Maasai.

Amin, M., and Eames, J., eds. 1989. *Kenya* (Insight Guide.) Singapore: APA Productions.

Amin, M.; Willetts, D.; and Tetley, B. 1988. *Kenya: The Magicland.* Nairobi, Kenya: Westlands Sundries (PO Box 14107, Nairobi).

Bartlett, D., and Bartlett, J. 1992. "Africa's Skeleton Coast." *National Geographic* 181 (1) (Jan.): 54–85.

Beckwith, C., and Fisher, A. 1991. "The Eloquent Surma of Ethiopia." *National Geographic* 179 (2) (Feb.): 76–99.

Chadwick, D. H. 1991. "Elephant out of Time, out of Space. *National Geographic* 179 (5) (May): 2–58.

Consolata Fathers. (no date) *El Molo.* Nairobi, Kenya: Text Book Centre (Box 47540, Nairobi, Kenya).

———. *Kikuyu.* Nairobi (see above).

———. *Maasai.* Nairobi (see above).

———. *Samburu.* Nairobi (see above).

———. *Turkana.* Nairobi (see above).

Crowther, G. 1987. *East Africa: A Travel Survival Kit.* Berkeley, CA (PO Box 2001A): Lonely Planet Publications.

Davidson, B. 1974. *Africa in History: Themes and Outlines.* rev ed. Macmillan.

———. 1971. *African Kingdoms.* Time-Life Books.

Gordon, Rene. 1981. *Africa: A Continent Revealed.* St. Martins Press.

HBJ Social Studies 1985. *The World Past and Present.* Orlando, FL: Harcourt Brace Jovanovich.

Hamby, J., and Bygott, D. 1984. *Kangas: 101 Uses.* Nairobi, Kenya: Lino Typesetters (PO Box 44876, Nairobi, Kenya).

Harris, J. 1987. *Africans and Their History.* New York: Mentor Books.

Joubert, D. 1991. "Eyewitness to an Elephant Wake." *National Geographic* 179 (5) (May): 39–49.

Kaputo, R. 1991. "Zaire River." *National Geographic* 180, (5) (Nov.): 5–35.

Kendall, T. 1990. "Sudan's Kingdom of Kush." *National Geographic* 178 (5) (Nov.): 96–125.

Kirtley, M., and Kirtley, A. 1982. "The Ivory Coast—African Success Story." *National Geographic* July: 94–125.

Packer, C. 1992. "Captives in the Wild." *National Geographic* 181 (4) (April): 122–36.

Palmer, C. 1992. "African Slave Trade: The Cruelest Commerce." *National Geographic* 182 (3) (Sept.): 63–91.

Palumbo, J. 1991. *Mansa Musa: African King of Gold.* Los Angeles: National Center for History in the Schools (UCLA, Moore Hall 231, 405 Hilgard Ave., Los Angeles, CA 90024–1521).

Rake, A. ed. 1986. *Travelers Guide to East Africa and the Indian Ocean.* New York: IC Publications Ltd (Room 1121, 122 E. 42nd St., NY 10168).

Rand McNally 1992. *Kenya Safari.* Skokie, IL: Rand McNally.

Scott, J. P. 1984. *Know Kenya's Animals.* Milan, Italy: Kina Italia.

Severy, M. 1992. "Portugal's Sea Road to the East." *National Geographic* 182 (5) (Nov.): 56–93.

Zich, A. 1990. "Modern Botswana: The Adopted Land." *National Geographic* 178 (6) (Dec.) 70-97.

LESSON PLAN FOR LESSON: 1

TITLE: Introduction, Overview, Requirements

OBJECTIVES

Content: Students will know the general outline of topics and requirements for this unit on Africa.

Process: Students will assist in constructing a cognitive map (semantic map) about Africa.

Products: Cognitive map

MATERIALS AND RESOURCES: Textbook and classroom library books

TIME ESTIMATED: 1 period

INTRODUCTION OF LESSON (PROMPTS)

Objectives stated?　　　　　_____√_____　yes　　　　　_____　no

If no, how is interest to be raised?

Students recall prior knowledge? Through cognitive map

Students make self-reference? Students are asked to recall any personal experiences with Africa—visits, friends from there, African objects, foods, books, movies, etc.

Points essential to set forth?

ACTIVITIES/SEQUENCE

1. Teacher puts word AFRICA on board. S/he asks students what they would want to know about Africa.

2. Teacher fills in a cognitive map with the responses students give. For example, students might say, "Animals, safari, tribes, wild animals, endangered species."

3. The teacher informs students that they will be studying these areas and others. Add additional items to cognitive map.

4. Students are given a check sheet of the unit. The check sheet lists the requirements and lets the students know about independent work and the dates on which the work will be due. Since this is going to vary from one teacher to another, the requirements are not given here. Students will be expected to enter the dates on their planning calendars. The planning calendar is distributed. (See notes below for blank forms to copy.)

5. Students are asked to keep a list of questions that come to mind as they are studying. These are to be used to investigate further the topics in other lessons.

6. If the teacher has a display of African objects, s/he will discuss these at this time.

7. Students are shown the classroom resources that will help them in their assignments. Resources in the library should be suggested also.

ASSESSMENT

Student's metacognitive questions: How would you find information on...? How could you best collect information and store it so you will have it later in a useful form?

Teacher assessment of students:

[Continued on next page.]

FOLLOW-UP

Content: Ask students to set up a calendar for the next four weeks. Here they will record assignments as they arise, in order to budget their time.

Process:

Notes: Cognitive map (below), calendar (p. 123), check sheet (p. 124), and sample check sheet (p. 125) included

Cognitive Map

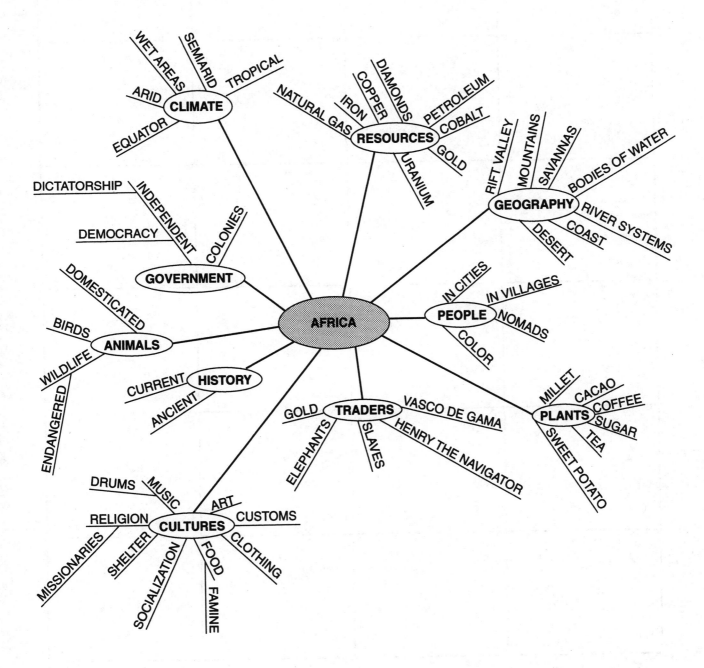

SUNDAY	MONDAY	TUESDAY	WEDNESDAY	THURSDAY	FRIDAY	SATURDAY

UNIT:

NAME: _____

DUE DATE: _____

Activity	Due Date	Student √	Teacher √

UNIT:

AFRICA

NAME: _____

DUE DATE: _____

Activity	Due Date	Student √	Teacher √
Cognitive map on Africa			
Cognitive map on tribe			
Map			
Story on African family			
Strategy paper on "Improving Conditions"			
Skit			
Matrix information for tribe			
Additional reading done—			
Additional activities done—			

LESSON PLAN FOR LESSON: 2

TITLE: Assumptions about Africa

OBJECTIVES

Content: Students will recall information they believe to be true about Africa.

Process: Individually students will make a list of ten already-known "facts" about Africa. Then students will work in groups cooperatively. Five or less students will be in each group. Groups will select ten to twelve of their facts and combine them on a sheet of chart paper to display in the classroom.

Products: Chart from each group

MATERIALS AND RESOURCES: Large sheets of chart paper, markers

TIME ESTIMATED: 1 period

INTRODUCTION OF LESSON (PROMPTS)

Objectives stated?   √   yes   no

If no, how is interest to be raised?

Students recall prior knowledge? Through remembering what they believe to be true facts and discussing their information in their groups

Students make self-reference?

Points essential to set forth? Not everything we remember or have heard is true. We may find that some of our "facts" are true and some are not.

ACTIVITIES/SEQUENCE

1. Each student constructs a list of ten "facts" s/he believes to be true about Africa.

2. Students work in groups of five or less to combine their information into a list of ten to twelve "facts."

3. Students will make the list on chart paper using markers. They will place these charts on the wall.

4. Each group will share their "facts" with the class in an oral discussion.

5. Each group is told that they will be alert to find verification for their facts. When they do, they will mark the source in the margin of their chart with a different color marker from the one the fact is written in. If they find their fact is not true, they will correct the chart and list their source.

ASSESSMENT

Student's metacognitive questions: Do I feel my group was effective in reaching our goal of coming up with 10–12 facts? What could I do to make it better? Did I do my best work? If not, what can I do next time to improve?

Teacher assessment of students: Informal observation of how students work in their groups

FOLLOW-UP

Content: Corrections to chart facts

Process: Students make corrections and verifications on their chart

Notes:

LESSON PLAN FOR LESSON: 3

TITLE: Geography of Africa

OBJECTIVES

Content: Students will identify physical features and their importance. Students will identify major regions and the countries in them. Students will name important resources found in Africa.

Process:

Products:

MATERIALS AND RESOURCES: Maps, textbooks, atlases, encyclopedia

TIME ESTIMATED: 2 periods

INTRODUCTION OF LESSON (PROMPTS)

Objectives stated? _____√_____ yes _____ no

If no, how is interest to be raised?

Students recall prior knowledge? Students are asked what they know about Africa.

Students make self-reference? Ask, "Has anyone visited Africa?"

Points essential to set forth? Five geographical regions, deserts, rivers

ACTIVITIES/SEQUENCE

1. Teachers will give students a list of information about the five regions of Africa they will be studying.

2. Students will locate information and place it in their notes. They may work alone or in pairs, but both must have the notes.

3. Teacher will ask questions orally about the topics. Students will respond.

ASSESSMENT

Student's metacognitive questions: How and where can I find this information? Am I taking good notes? How do I know?

Teacher assessment of students: Teacher will skim students' notes for evidence of topic coverage.

FOLLOW-UP

Content: May ask students to construct a physical, political, or product map

Process:

Notes: Topic sheet (see p. 128) and Africa outline map (see p. 129) included

Topic Sheet on Five Regions

1. Geography. Type of land, vegetation, products.

2. Climate. How are regions different? Cause of variation—nearness to equator, rainfall, altitude?

3. Resources. Are particular resources associated with different geographical regions? What important minerals have been mined in Africa? Are they concentrated in certain regions? Has petroleum played an important part in Africa's geographical story? Why or why not?

4. Rivers. What is the importance of the Congo (Zaire) and Nile Rivers? How important are the rivers to transportation in Africa?

5. Agriculture. Is Africa able to provide for her people with her own crops? Why are some areas unable to raise livestock or crops? How does this affect those regions? What methods of farming are used throughout Africa? Is truck farming a major "industry" in Africa?

6. Patterns. Do you see any patterns in the topic information? If so, what?

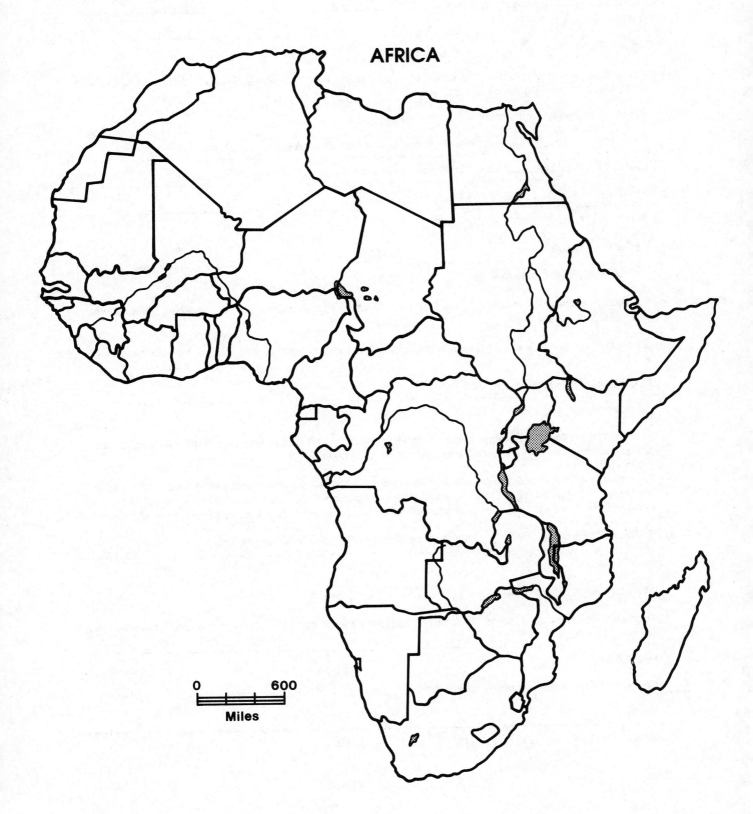

AFRICA

0   600
Miles

LESSON PLAN FOR LESSON: 4

TITLE: Ancient Africa

OBJECTIVES

Content: Students will examine the advantages of tools and trade, how the tools and trade helped bring about bartering, and how they affected cultures.

Process: Students will list contributions of various groups.

Products: Paragraph on the use of camels and horses, list of contributions by cultures

MATERIALS AND RESOURCES: Textbooks and classroom library

TIME ESTIMATED: 1 period

INTRODUCTION OF LESSON (PROMPTS)

Objectives stated?   √   yes   no

If no, how is interest to be raised?

Students recall prior knowledge? In small groups, the students discuss trying to do something without tools and needing to invent them.

Students make self-reference? Students talk about times they have bartered or "traded" for something they wanted.

Points essential to set forth?

ACTIVITIES/SEQUENCE

1. Students will discuss the objectives and read information on the topic, if available. If not available, teacher will give information from fact sheet, and students will take notes.

2. Students will break into groups and discuss the fact that all of these events happened back in time and that the impact is still being felt in the world today. They will develop a concept of how the use of camels and horses allowed trade to advance. Each student will write a paragraph about the use of camels and horses.

3. Students will make one list per culture of the lasting contribution made by this culture.

ASSESSMENT

Student's metacognitive questions:

Teacher assessment of students: Teacher will scan the paragraphs on the use of camels and horses and the list of contributions.

FOLLOW-UP

Content: Continue reading about ancient Africa

Process:

Notes: Fact sheet included on p. 131

African Fact Sheet #1—Ancient Cultures

West Africa

Nok Culture (900 B.C.–200 A.D.)

- 300 B.C.—They heated and shaped iron. They used the iron for hunting and protection and for farm tools. They lived in the area now known as Nigeria.

Sonikes (300 B.C.–900 A.D.)

- They lived in houses in rows in town with a wall circling the town. They farmed and developed an irrigation system. Products were millet and rice. Traders (Muslims) came for elephant tusks, gold. Camels became known as "ships of the desert." They mined for gold by hand. They controlled trade and were known as good barterers (traders).

Ghana (700 A.D.–1087 A.D.)

- This was the first West African empire. It gained control over the area in about 700 A.D. The Sonikes who lived there developed the trade and offered the resources to support it. They continued their farming also. The rulers were called Ghana (war chief), thus the name Ghana. The empire covered a large land area, and they had a large trading center. Their messengers rode horses, and their camels were used to carry merchandise for their trade caravans. One of their scarce items was salt, which was important for good health. The empire had a monopoly on the gold trade. They traded gold for salt. They also traded ivory tusks and cotton. Their homes were of clay, thatch, and wood. The king controlled the trade through tariffs. There were police and judges who carried out the laws. The king maintained a big army. By 1087 the nation had lost its power.

LESSON PLAN FOR LESSON: 5

TITLE: Ancient West African Empires

OBJECTIVES

Content: Students will be able to name two famous rulers of ancient West African territory and their contributions to the development of this portion of Africa.

Process: Students will assess their small group and their individual efforts in the group process.

Products: Presentations of group findings

MATERIALS AND RESOURCES: Fact sheet, textbook, classroom and school libraries (have as many resources as possible available in the classroom)

TIME ESTIMATED: 3 periods

INTRODUCTION OF LESSON (PROMPTS)

Objectives stated?   √   yes   no

If no, how is interest to be raised?

Students recall prior knowledge?

Students make self-reference?

Points essential to set forth? Use of money and credit, reading and writing, profesional army

ACTIVITIES/SEQUENCE

1. Students will work in small groups. Two groups will research Mansa Musa, two will research Askia Muhammed, and the other group will research the empire of Benin. Each group will organize and prepare presentation. (2 periods)

2. Each group will present its report (with visuals, if appropriate) to the class. (1 period)

ASSESSMENT

Student's metacognitive questions: Students will critique each presentation by writing three positive comments. Students in each group need to review the comments about their presentation. This can also be done orally as a total-group activity. Students will evaluate their group's and their own efforts at cooperative learning.

Teacher assessment of students: Appraise the accuracy of the content. Monitor the cooperative-group activities.

FOLLOW-UP

Content: Begin reading on slave trade

Process:

Notes: Fact sheet included on p. 133

African Fact Sheet #2

West Africa

Mansa Musa

- Mali was a great West African grassland empire which in 1324 was the second largest empire in the world. The people were called Mandinkas, and they were related to the Sonikes of Ghana. The land was fertile. Their main occupation was trading; they liked to travel. When the Ghana empire weakened, they took over that part of Africa (1235 A.D.). Their wealth came mostly from trade. They had a system of laws that was considered to be good. It was a peaceful place to live.

  Mansa Musa was the ruler. He wanted the people to use Muslim ways. Few people changed their religion, however. They just learned to combine the new and old ways and teach others in different parts of Africa how to get along. Muslims showed them how to use money and credit instead of bartering. The people learned to read and write. The centers for law and study were Timbuktu and Jenne. The empire flourished until Mansa Musa's death; then it declined.

Askia Muhammad

- Songhais gained strength after Mali's declined. They were primarily farmers and fishermen. In 1464 they began conquering the land of Mali, and they took over the trading centers.

  Askia Muhammad combined the African and Muslim ideas and supported a large university in Timbuktu. He divided the kingdom into provinces with a governor over each. The army was composed of professionals who were well trained and paid to bear arms full time. Muhammad also had a navy. For over 100 years the empire prospered. In 1591 Morocco sent an army of 4000 soldiers who successfully reduced the empire and its power.

Benin

- Benin was an empire in the rain forest area of the West Africa coast. Around 1500 the capitol city (Benin) had broad streets and tidy, orderly houses. The people were called Edo; they lived at the mouth of the Niger river (area known as Nigeria now). They traded pepper, cotton cloth, and animal skins. They were noted for their art work—brass and bronze sculptures. The government was strong and controlled the trade in the area.

LESSON PLAN FOR LESSON: 6

TITLE: Ancient History/Slave Trade

OBJECTIVES

Content: Students will examine the increased demand for slaves from Africa and how this demand affected everyone involved.

Process: Students will compare and contrast slave trade of West Africa and East Africa.

Products: See follow-up activity

MATERIALS AND RESOURCES: Fact sheet, textbook, classroom and school libraries

TIME ESTIMATED: 1 period

INTRODUCTION OF LESSON (PROMPTS)

Objectives stated?   √   yes   no

If no, how is interest to be raised?

Students recall prior knowledge? Ask them to remember what they know about slavery.

Students make self-reference?

Points essential to set forth? Effects on villages as well as individuals who were taken as slaves.

ACTIVITIES/SEQUENCE

1. Students will recall what they remember about slavery from other sources.

2. Students will read materials on West African slave trade and discuss the material as a whole-class activity, with particular emphasis on the effects on individuals and their villages.

3. Students will read materials on East African slave trade and discuss the material as a whole-class activity.

4. Students will compare and contrast the effects of slavery on the two areas, West and East Africa.

ASSESSMENT

Student's metacognitive questions: Students will determine if they have a strategy or organizer to assist them in the analysis activity.

Teacher assessment of students: Compare and contrast product

FOLLOW-UP

Content:

Process: Each student will write a fictional account of an African family whose father/husband does not come home one night and is never seen again.

Notes: Fact sheet included on p. 135

African Fact Sheet #3

Slave Trade

When we think of slaves, we think of Africa. Most of the slaves who came to America were from Africa. We may not realize that the Africans used slaves also. They sold prisoners of war and criminals to traders. Slavery was not a big business until 1600 when the need for labor in North, Central, and South America created a demand for workers. The Europeans were not willing to work in the hot climates on plantations and in mines. Slaves, since they were owned, did not have a choice and did not have to be paid.

By the late 1700s, the attitudes of Europeans toward slavery began to change. Religious leaders in Great Britain preached against the injustices of slavery. Both Britain and France took a stand against slavery. The slave trade stopped about 1870.

Treatment of slaves was a major concern of those who spoke out against it. Most of the slaves were taken from West Africa. They were torn from their families and marched to the coast where they were crammed into ships. During the Atlantic passage, many died on the ship; more died after they began to work. Over 12 million West Africans became slaves during this period.

Europeans began to get slaves from East Africa about 1750. This slave trade helped rebuild the Swahili cities after Portugal nearly destroyed them. Zanzibar was a big slave-trade city. By 1880 trade in slavery in East Africa ended.

East Africa

The major events in the development of East Africa are related to traders and explorers/exploiters. In 300 A.D. Indonesians sailed across the Indian Ocean to East Africa, bringing yams and other plants. Arab traders came to trade for ivory, coconuts, gold, animal skins, and slaves. Many of these traders married African women. By 900 A.D. a culture which combined these two groups arose. Swahili was the name given to this cultural group, a blend of Arab and African.

LESSON PLAN FOR LESSON: 7

TITLE: European Exploration/Exploitation of Africa

OBJECTIVES

Content: Students will read and discuss the explorations of Europeans such as De Gama and the sailors of Prince Henry the Navigator's vessels. Students will investigate the 1884 meeting in Berlin, with close attention paid to the European point of view. Students will explain the difference between direct and indirect rule.

Process:

Products:

MATERIALS AND RESOURCES: Fact sheet, textbook, classroom and school libraries

TIME ESTIMATED: 1 period

INTRODUCTION OF LESSON (PROMPTS)

Objectives stated?　　　　√　　　　yes　　　　　　　　　　　　　　　no

If no, how is interest to be raised?

Students recall prior knowledge? Ask them what they remember about explorers and whether they know what imperialism is.

Students make self-reference?

Points essential to set forth? Imperialism

ACTIVITIES/SEQUENCE

1. Students will read what they have available on the early European explorers of Africa. They will discuss this information in class.

2. Students will discuss the term "imperialism" and what it means in relation to Europe and Africa.

3. Students will read and discuss the Berlin meeting of 1884. Have students consider the points of view and whether it was legitimate and moral to make decisions about another people without those people being represented in the proceedings.

4. Students will determine the difference between direct and indirect rule as it applies to this period of time.

ASSESSMENT

Student's metacognitive questions: Do you see any parallels between what occurred in Africa due to European influence (exploring/exploitation by Europeans, Berlin meeting) and any other events in history?

Teacher assessment of students: Monitor student discussions

FOLLOW-UP

Content:

Process: Begin to look for articles on modern Africa in newspapers and magazines

Notes: Fact sheet included on p. 137

African Fact Sheet #4—European Exploration/Exploitation of Africa

Exploration

Vasco da Gama, representing Portugal, sailed into Quelimane on Africa's East Coast for a peaceful visit. In 1505, however, a fleet of Portuguese attacked the town of Kilwa. Portugal's trade had prospered under Prince Henry the Navigator. He had hired navigators to improve instruments and engineers to improve vessels. He had sent ships to buy goods and spices. Henry died in 1460, but the Portuguese ships continued to sail to various trade markets, and, frequently, they took what they wanted by force.

By 1600 England, France, Spain, and the Netherlands came to Africa to help the Africans retaliate against the Portuguese, who were cruel and forceful. Portugal no longer had control over African countries by 1650.

During the 1800s, Africa's trade with Europe had grown tremendously. During the middle of the century, Dr. David Livingston, a Scottish doctor, spent 25 years in the less-travelled areas of Africa. He kept a journal of his experiences. Not only did he treat the sick, he tried to convert the natives to Christianity, and he tried to stop the slave trade. The famous expression "Dr. Livingston, I presume" comes from the meeting of Livingston with Henry Stanley who had been searching for him for months. When Stanley came upon him in the rain forest, he is reported to have said "Dr. Livingston, I presume" as if he had run into Livingston casually on the streets of London.

Imperialism

Imperialism by the European countries grew rapidly. In about 1870, the countries began to build empires to protect their trade. Each country felt that it was its responsibility to spread its government to other places. These European countries competed with each other for parts of Africa. Finally, in 1884, fourteen nations of Europe met in Germany to work out a plan to divide Africa among the major European countries. Each received the parts of the continent where they already had settlements. Africans were never considered for attendance at the meeting; their culture, language, and compatibility were never considered in making these divisions. Some tribes were separated into different countries and some warring tribes were placed in the same country.

For the most part, Europeans controlled what happened in Africa until the 1950s. Many changes took place; some were good for the Africans and some were not. Different countries ruled their colonies in different styles. For instance, Britain allowed the Africans to keep some of their own leaders, and the Africans could participate in their own governance. This type of rule was called *indirect*. Germany, on the other hand, had a strong control and a *direct* rule. Some countries forced the Africans to work in the mines for them. Positive actions by Europeans included the establishing of schools and the building of railroads. Ethiopia and Liberia were the only places in Africa that did not belong to a European government by 1900.

LESSON PLAN FOR LESSON: 8

TITLE: Modern Africa

OBJECTIVES

Content: Students will be aware of the important issues and problems of Africa since World War II.

Process: Students will take notes on their reading.

Products: Student notes

MATERIALS AND RESOURCES: Textbook, encyclopedia, class and school libraries, current periodicals

TIME ESTIMATED: 1 period

INTRODUCTION OF LESSON (PROMPTS)

Objectives stated?   √   yes   no

If no, how is interest to be raised?

Students recall prior knowledge?

Students make self-reference?

Points essential to set forth? Population movement, conflict between and within countries, independence

ACTIVITIES/SEQUENCE

1. Teacher will lecture or students will read fact sheet.

2. Students will read other materials on some of the issues, such as poor soil, disease, drought, overpopulation, famine, conflicts between and within countries, transportation, decline in the lands available to animals, endangered species, and struggles to set up independent nations. Each student will take notes on his or her readings.

3. In groups, students will discuss their findings.

ASSESSMENT

Student's metacognitive questions: Have I put all the important information in my notes?

Teacher assessment of students:

FOLLOW-UP

Content: Students will look at an old political map of Africa (prior to 1960) and note the differences between it and a current map of Africa.

Process:

Notes: Fact sheet included on p. 139

African Fact Sheet #5

Only Liberia and Ethiopia were independent of European control in 1911. Forty-six years passed before the next African country became independent. Ghana won its independence from Great Britain in 1957. As of 1993, there are 51 independent nations.

After World War II a large portion of the African population was seeking work and moved from the villages to the large cities. The part of the large cities to which these villagers moved was temporary housing made out of tin or discarded materials. These became known as "tin can" cities. Many of the migrating natives were unable to find work; some deserted their wives and children in the "tin can" shanties.

The African countries warred between and within their boundaries, and, in fact, the boundaries constituted part of the disputes. In order to reduce the quarreling and bloodshed, the Organization for African Unity (OAU) was formed in 1963.

Conflicts among tribes within countries has been a continuing problem. As one group has gained control over others, they have established a government which lasts only until the next group overthrows it and forms another. For example, in 1989 the warring tribes of the northern and eastern parts of Ethiopia overthrew the ruling government after years of civil war.

Many countries accept aid from other countries, but they are wary of accepting anything that might carry with it any restrictions on their independence.

LESSON PLAN FOR LESSON: 9

TITLE: Africa, Problems and Promise

OBJECTIVES

Content: Students will work in groups on one of the major issues and/or problems listed under activity 2 in Lesson 8 (see p. 138). The teacher may want to specify which issues, depending on the materials available and relevancy to current news.

Process: Students will consider data and generate strategies to improve the problem studied.

Products: Strategy papers

MATERIALS AND RESOURCES: Current publications (newspapers, magazines, and books)

TIME ESTIMATED: 1 period

INTRODUCTION OF LESSON (PROMPTS)

Objectives stated?   √   yes   no

If no, how is interest to be raised?

Students recall prior knowledge? Notes from previous lesson

Students make self-reference?

Points essential to set forth?

ACTIVITIES/SEQUENCE

1. Students will discuss their notes and read additional information in order to generate strategies to improve the conditions of their chosen problem.

2. Students will discuss with the class their group's issues and strategies or will prepare a skit or a visual display which they will exhibit the next class period.

ASSESSMENT

Student's metacognitive questions: Did I gather all the pertinent data to learn about my problem? Did I generate plausible strategies? Did I plan, monitor, and evaluate my results and my thinking?

Teacher assessment of students: Monitor the discussion, skit, or display.

FOLLOW-UP

Content: Complete presentation for next day.

Process: Practice, if skit.

Notes:

LESSON PLAN FOR LESSON: 10

TITLE: Tribes of Kenya

OBJECTIVES

Content: Students will remember what they know about Kenya's tribes.

Process: Students will brainstorm to determine what interests them about Kenyan tribes, and these areas of interest will be placed on a cognitive map. Students will select a tribe for their group to study.

Products: Cognitive map

MATERIALS AND RESOURCES: See listings in unit bibliography. Students will need current information on these tribes. The "Insight Guide to Kenya" is an excellent source.

TIME ESTIMATED: 1 period

INTRODUCTION OF LESSON (PROMPTS)

Objectives stated?   √   yes   _____ no

If no, how is interest to be raised?

Students recall prior knowledge? See objective—brainstorming

Students make self-reference?

Points essential to set forth? See cognitive map on p. 142

ACTIVITIES/SEQUENCE

1. Students will brainstorm about what they would like to know about Kenyan tribes.

2. Teacher will place the areas of interest on a cognitive map.

3. Students will divide into 5 groups. Each group will select a Kenyan tribe to research (Kikuyu, Masai, Turkana, El Molo, Samburu, or Gabbra). Teacher may need to assign specific tribes to groups.

4. Students in each group will plan to research their tribe in the areas of interest designated on the cognitive map.

ASSESSMENT

Student's metacognitive questions:

Teacher assessment of students: Presentations

FOLLOW-UP

Content: Look for information on tribe.

Process: Begin to research tribe.

Notes:

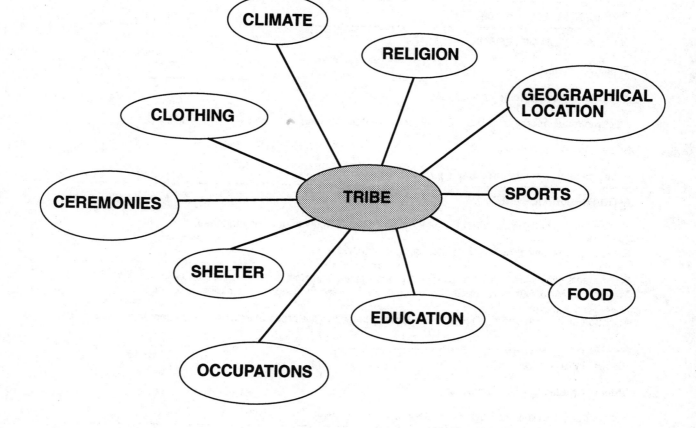

LESSON PLAN FOR LESSON: 11

TITLE: Research on Tribes

OBJECTIVES

Content: Students will collect data on their tribe.

Process: Students will engage in research on tribes. The students will prepare their presentation to the class as well as their entries in the matrix.

Products: Data for chart and presentation

MATERIALS AND RESOURCES: Textbooks, objects, artifacts, books, periodicals, and any other available resources

TIME ESTIMATED: 3 periods

INTRODUCTION OF LESSON (PROMPTS)

Objectives stated?   √   yes   no

If no, how is interest to be raised?

Students recall prior knowledge?

Students make self-reference?

Points essential to set forth?

ACTIVITIES/SEQUENCE

1. Students will work individually and in groups to gather the data on their tribe.

2. Student groups will prepare their entries for the matrix.

3. Student groups will prepare their presentations.

ASSESSMENT

Student's metacognitive questions: Where can I find what I need to know? Do I have the right information for the matrix? How can we present this to the other students in an interesting manner? What can I do to make my group successful?

Teacher assessment of students:

FOLLOW-UP

Content: Data for chart organized

Process: Presentation planned and prepared

Notes:

LESSON PLAN FOR LESSON: 12

TITLE: Presentations, Matrix Entries

OBJECTIVES

Content: At the end of two days, students will be able to give general information about all the tribes.

Process: Students will demonstrate their knowledge about their tribe by a class presentation. They will fill in the matrix cells for their tribe. Students will make inferences and compare and contrast the tribes.

Products: Matrix, presentations

MATERIALS AND RESOURCES: Matrix and students' research findings

TIME ESTIMATED: 2 periods

INTRODUCTION OF LESSON (PROMPTS)

Objectives stated?　　　　　√　　　　yes　　　　　　　　　　　　　　no

If no, how is interest to be raised?

Students recall prior knowledge?

Students make self-reference?

Points essential to set forth?

ACTIVITIES/SEQUENCE

1. Students will gather information on the categories in the matrix. The teacher may want to select which categories to use if information is limited. If there is much data available, the teacher may let the students choose which headings to use. The basic choices might be food, shelter, clothing/adornments, customs/ceremonies/religion, education, occupation, government, locale (climate, geographic location, animals and plants which share habitat), tools/weapons, number in tribe, and language. A matrix which uses column headings of locale, occupation, customs/ceremonies/religion, food, clothing/adornments, and shelter is included. Although there are many other items which could be entered under each column (and many other columns you could have), these will give you an example.

2. Students will enter the tribe's information in the appropriate matrix cells in conjunction with their presentation to the class about their tribe.

3. Students will make inferences from individual cells, then from rows or columns of cells. Students will compare and contrast tribes. Students will generalize about tribes in Kenya.

ASSESSMENT

Student's metacognitive questions: Before presentation: Are we prepared?
After presentation: Did we do a good job on our presentation? Did students understand our points? Do I need to look again at the information on the matrix? How could we have done a better job?

Teacher assessment of students: Critique presentations, entries, and inferences. Suggested checklists to use in scoring are on pp. 146–47.

FOLLOW-UP

Content:

Process:

Notes: Matrix sample is on p. 145, checklists are on pp. 146–47.

TRIBE	LOCATION	CLOTHING	PRODUCTS	OCCUPATION	CUSTOMS & RELIGION	FOOD	SHELTER
TURKANA	north-west Kenya between Lake Turkana and Uganda, mountainous	women wear elaborate beaded necklaces, cattle hides are used for sandals, spears are 8-feet long, leaf shaped	millet, gourds, timber, leather, implements of metal, bone, and ivory, beaded jewelry, sandals	nomadic, women farm men collect timber, tan hides; collect metal, bones, ivory, make iron tools; cattle herders, camels, goats, sheep	patriarchal clans (sons stay), witch doctors, aggressive (cattle raiding is a sport), dowery is cattle, marriage is 3-year ceremony	women raise millet and gourds; meat, blood, and milk are main diet; butter, camel milk for babies	hides used to cover thatched huts and to make mats for sleeping
KIKUYU	central Kenya near Mt. Kenya, mountainous, high rainfall	sandals and straps made from hides	pottery, vegetables, sandals (hides), woven baskets, trays, iron implements	agricultural, marketers, vegetables, livestock, coffee, tea, cattle raisers, vegetable farmers	council of elders, more than one wife, one god, witch doctor, ceremonial dance, sheep and goats, use religion, sacrifice, politically active, Mau Mau Rebellion	coffee, tea, bananas, sugar cane, yams, beans, millet, maize, sweet potatoes, other vegetables, livestock	thatched huts of elephant grass, animal hides for bedding
MASAI	throughout Kenya, but mostly south of Mt. Kenya, grasslands	boys naked, girls fully clothed, bead and feather jewelry	feather headpiece, beaded collars, blankets, woven materials, shields, spears	pastoral, cattle herders, sell meat to Meat Commission, women raise millet	sacrifice cows to god, dance by jumping, warrior ceremony is 4 days, mother shaves head, he selects wife, powerful, ferocious warriors	beef only eaten at ceremonials, sheep and goats are eaten other times, blood and milk, eland and buffalo (no other wild)	huts have thorny shrub for frame, covered with manure, mud, and grass, dome shaped, thorn fence surrounds 10–20 huts
EL MOLO	north-west Kenya, two islands in Lake Turkana, winds blow all the time—40 mph, very dry	ornaments, scant clothing, multiple strings of ostrich eggs or glass beads, men and women wear wrist and elbow bracelets	fish ornaments	harpoon hippos and crocodiles, fish by harpoon, net, hook and line, women build huts, no cows, make doum palm rafts to fish	one god, wedding dowery, no chief, bury dead in stone cairns	have no cattle, fish—fresh and dried, Loka (palm dates), crocodile, turtle, hippo, wild game	huts of acacia (thorny) covered with doum palm leaves, reeds, grasses, anchored by stones (to resist winds), dome shaped, circular, doum palm for bedding

CLASS PRESENTATION SCORE SHEET
Student Name or Group Members:
Presentation Topic:
Date:
CONTENT ACCURACY (50 points) =
Notes:
DELIVERY (50 points) =
Visuals:
Originality:
Quality:
Use of time:
Contributions from everyone (if group):
Notes:
TOTAL POINTS =
Notes:

WRITTEN REPORT SCORE SHEET
Student Name:
Report Topic:
Date:
TITLE PAGE (5 points) =
TABLE OF CONTENTS (10 points) =
NEATNESS (15 points) =
BIBLIOGRAPHY (30 points) =
CONTENT (40 points) =
Illustrations:
Maps:
Information:
Organization:
TOTAL POINTS =
Notes:

NOTE: Some teachers wish to include grammar/mechanics under content, we believe that to be a separate assignment.

Other Social Studies Unit Plans

Native American Unit

The next section presents the unit plan only for an elementary school unit on Native Americans developed by Marty Santiago. With the aid of textbooks and the bibliography listed, a teacher should be able to plan a unit of study that would be both interesting and challenging to his or her students. Some suggested processes have been listed under process objectives.

UNIT PLAN

TOPIC: Native Americans   SUBJECT

Grade level or group: Grades 3–5   Primary: Social Studies

Estimated time: 12 periods   Others:

EDUCATIONAL OUTCOMES OF UNIT

Content: Students will develop an understanding of the culture, including diet, rituals, crafts, literature, and contributions of Native Americans.

Process: Students will engage in research, compare and contrast, draw inferences.

Products: Recipe, presentation of research

RATIONALE: Our country is a reflection of its past history. Its heritage is a combination of the customs, beliefs, and traditions of many groups of people. One of these groups is the Native Americans. The goal of this unit is to promote awareness of the history and the contributions of Native Americans to our culture.

ASSESSMENT PLAN

Purpose: Measure the outcomes

How?	_____ Observation	_____ Checklist	√ Informal Questions	_____ Product
	_____ Written assignment	√ Demonstration	_____ Test	_____ Other
Test?	_____ Multiple choice	_____ Completion	_____ Short essay	_____ Long essay
	_____ Combination			

SPECIAL NEEDS FOR UNIT (IF ANY)

Materials: Authentic recipes, any authentic objects available, and classroom reading materials

Time: For craft work, craft research, presentation

Resource persons: Space:

[Continued on next page.]

LESSON TOPICS/TITLES

1. Introduce unit

2. Stereotypes/assumptions, discussion

3. Preliminary research—formulate questions, make chart, examine sources

4. Literature, modern stories of Indians—compare and contrast

5. Native American cures

6. Rituals, traditions, customs, symbols

7. Customs—learn a dance

8. Food—research, make food for tasting party

9. Legends—dramatize the story

10. Crafts—examine samples, pick a craft to make, make it

11. Research on contributions of chosen people (several historical time periods)

12. Presentations

Activities: In lesson plans

BIBLIOGRAPHY

Amon, Aline. 1968. *Talking Hands: Indian Sign Language*. Doubleday.

Anderson, LaVere. 1970. *Quannah Parker: Indian Warrior for Peace*. Garrard.

Baker, Betty. 1962. *Little Runner of the Longhouse*. Harper & Row.

Balch, Glenn. 1969. *Indian Saddle-Up*. T. Y. Crowell.

Bannon, Laura. 1953. *When the Noon Is New*. Albert Whitman & Co.

Baylor, Byrd. 1976. *Hawk, I'm Your Brother*. Scribner.

Benchley, Nathaniel. 1964. *Red Fox and His Canoe*. Harper & Row.

Bierhorst, Donald J. 1975. *In the Trail of the Winds: American Indian Poems and Ritual Orations*. Farrar, Straus & Giroux.

Burchand, Marshall. 1973. *Sports Hero: Johnny Bench*. Putnam.

Cherry, Lynne. 1992. *A River Ran Wild*. San Diego, CA: Harcourt Brace Jovanovich.

D'Aulaire, Ingri and D'Aulaire Edgar P. 1946. *Pocahontas*. New York: Doubleday.

Fall, Thomas. 1970. *Jim Thorpe*. T. Y. Crowell.

Goble, Paul. 1978. *Girl Who Loved Wild Horses*. Bradbury.

Jeffers, Susan. 1992. *Brother Eagle, Sister Sky*. New York: Penguin.

Mason, B. S. 1974. *How To Make Drums, Tom-toms, and Rattles*. Dover.

Martin, Rafe. 1992. *The Rough-Face Girl*. New York: Putnam.

Economics Unit

The next section will present the outline for a unit at the secondary level on economics.

Directions for the *Free Enterprise Market Game* and the stock portfolio assignment can be found following the unit plan on p. 152.

UNIT PLAN

TOPIC: Basic Economics

Grade level or group: Secondary

Estimated time: 3 weeks plus follow-up one month later (stock portfolios)

SUBJECT

Primary: Economics

Others:

EDUCATIONAL OUTCOMES OF UNIT

Content: Students will be able to define basic terms in economics. Students will understand the relationships among the terms.

Process: Students will be able to use basic information to draw relationships and make economic decisions. Students will be able to compare and contrast and make thoughtful decisions.

Products: Graphs, stock portfolios, game results, matrices

RATIONALE: Students need to see relationships between the national economy and their personal finances. Students need to understand why economists talk about various aspects of business and the stock market which affect their quality of life.

ASSESSMENT PLAN

Purpose:

How?	√ Observation	____ Checklist	√ Informal Questions	√ Product
	√ Written assignment	____ Demonstration	√ Test	____ Other

Test?	____ Multiple choice	____ Completion	____ Short essay	____ Long essay
	√ Combination			

SPECIAL NEEDS FOR UNIT (IF ANY)

Materials: Text, library resources, newspapers, "Wall Street Journal"

Time:

Resource persons: Economist

Space:

LESSON TOPICS/TITLES

1. Introduce the major concepts in economics

2. Relationship of economics to personal budget

3. Three types of economics—traditional, market, command

4. Compare and contrast three economies and relate to present-day countries

5. Develop a national economic plan

6. Businesses, three types—single proprietorship, partnership, corporation

[Continued on next page.]

7. Compare and contrast the three types of businesses

8. Effects of depressions and recessions on businesses and markets

9. Stock market—bull and bear

10. Free Enterprise Market Game (see p. 152) and stock portfolio assignment—3 periods with follow-up one month later

11. Test on content

Activities: In lesson plans

Economics Handout

Free Enterprise Market Game

Each student becomes a buyer or a seller. Together, buyers and sellers will decide the price at which wheat can be sold and bought. Each buyer will be given a buyer's card and sellers will be given a seller's card. The buyer's cards tell the buyers how much they can afford to pay for bushels of wheat. The seller's cards tell the sellers the lowest prices at which they can afford to sell wheat. Neither the sellers nor the buyers should tell anyone the information written on their card. When the teacher says "start," sellers and buyers meet and try to agree on a price for 30,000 bushels of wheat. As soon as a buyer and seller agree on a price, each goes to the teacher's desk and reports the agreement, and the teacher will record the deals on the board. There will be 2 five-minute rounds. After the game, have students record the prices from the board and complete an analysis worksheet.

(John Jay Bonstingl, *Introduction to the Social Sciences*, 1985: Allyn & Bacon).

Stock Portfolios

Students will each be given an investor's portfolio of $50,000 of stock listed on the exchange. S/he must keep records of values listed, make decisions as to whether to sell or buy, and try to improve the investor's market worth at the end of 30 days. The student must engage in at least one transaction and justify it.

Chapter Eleven

Language Arts

Sample unit plans for incorporating thinking skills into the Language Arts curriculum may be found in this chapter. Each unit plan presented follows the format given in Chapter 9. The primary unit on bears and the secondary unit on the book *All Quiet on the Western Front* provide just the unit plan; the middle school unit on the book *The Upstairs Room* includes all lesson plans in addition to the unit plan.

UNIT PLAN

TOPIC: Bears

Grade level or group: Primary grades

Estimated time: 15 hours

SUBJECT

Primary: Literature

Others: Science

EDUCATIONAL OUTCOMES OF UNIT

Content: Students will be able to tell about bears—the different kinds, their habits, and how they are alike and different.

Process: Students will analyze, predict, look at causal explanation, and compare and contrast characteristics.

Products: Rewritten stories, other compositions, matrix, cognitive map, Venn diagram

---

RATIONALE: The students will increase their interest in literature and in bears by the study of these animals. The emphasis on real and fictional bear characters will help them distinguish fact from fantasy.

ASSESSMENT PLAN

Purpose: To measure objectives

How?	√ Observation	___ Checklist	√ Informal Questions	√ Product
	√ Written assignment	√ Demonstration	___ Test	___ Other

Test?	___ Multiple choice	___ Completion	___ Short essay	___ Long essay
	___ Combination			

SPECIAL NEEDS FOR UNIT (IF ANY)

Materials: Books, magazines, dictionaries, encyclopedia, picnic supplies

Resource persons:

Time:

Space:

[Continued on next page.]

NOTE: Ideas for this unit on bears came from projects developed by primary teachers Lori Gibbs and Cindy Sommer.

LESSON TOPICS/TITLES

1. Introduce unit—talk about the information available.

2. "Goldilocks and the Three Bears"—rewrite the story (prediction).

3. Retell "Ira Sleeps Over" from the bears point of view.

4. Write probable causes for the rip in Winnie-the-Pooh's ear.

5. Causal explanation of Sister Bear's trouble with a friend in "The Berenstain Bears' Trouble with Friends"

6. Differences between real and fictional bears

7. "Blueberries for Sal"—descriptive writing of frozen blueberries

8. Use Venn diagram to compare Little Sal and Little Bear.

9. Locate and collect information on bears.

10. Write facts found in research and organize them.

11. Write final draft on bear research.

12. Write and illustrate an original bear story.

13. Fill in Taba Retrieval Chart on different kinds of bears. Play game, "Which Bear Am I?"

14. History of teddy bears

15. Teddy bear picnic

Activities: In lesson plans

BIBLIOGRAPHY

Berenstain, S., and Berenstain, J. *The Berenstain Bears* series. New York: Random House.

Freeman, D. 1968. *Corduroy*. New York: Penguin.

———. 1978. *A Pocket for Corduroy*. New York: Penguin.

Graham, A., and Graham, F. 1981. *Bears in the Wild*. New York: Delacorte.

Kennedy, J. 1983. *Teddy Bears' Picnic*. Green Tiger Press.

Leach, M. 1990. *Bears*. Kewadin, MI: Mallard.

Marshall, J. 1988. *Goldilocks and the Three Bears*. Dial.

Martin, B., Jr. 1970. *Brown Bear, Brown Bear, What Do You See?* Holt.

McCloskey, R. 1987. *Blueberries for Sal*. Puffin.

Milne, A. A. 1970. *Winnie-the-Pooh*. New York: Dell.

———. 1970. *The House at Pooh Corner*. New York: Dell.

Minarik, E. H. *Little Bear* series. HarperCollins.

Nentl, J. 1984. *The Grizzly*. Mankato, MN: Crestwood House.

Patent, D. H. 1980. *Bears of the Wild*. New York: Holiday House.

Rosen, M. 1989. *We're Going on a Bear Hunt*. Riverside, NJ: Macmillan.

Steiner, B. 1972. *Biographies of a Polar Bear*. New York: Putnam.

Van Wormer, J. 1966. *The World of the Black Bear*. Philadelphia: Lippincott.

Waber, B. 1972. *Ira Sleeps Over*. New York: Scholastic.

Ward, L. 1952. *The Biggest Bear*. Boston: Houghton Mifflin.

The Upstairs Room

The next unit is designed for middle school students, and it contains the unit outline and the lesson plans for all the lessons.

UNIT PLAN

TOPIC: The Upstairs Room

SUBJECT

Grade level or group: 8th grade

Primary: Language Arts

Estimated time: 15 hours

Others: History

EDUCATIONAL OUTCOMES OF UNIT

Content: Students will understand the plight of the Jews in Germany during World War II and will understand the conflict they faced and the decisions these individuals had to make.

Process: Students will engage in prediction, drawing conclusions, comparing/contrasting, analysis, making inferences, decision making, and preparing a Taba Retrieval Chart.

Products: World War II time line, paragraph on changing your appearance, letter to Uncle Bram, list of activities to do while in hiding, diary entry from Sini's point of view, current-events list, paragraph on courage, autobiographical sketch

RATIONALE: Students need to understand the extreme hardships of many people during World War II and how terrible war is. They need to see how accounts of individuals can enrich our understanding and how valuable they are as literary works.

ASSESSMENT PLAN

Purpose: Measure outcomes

How?	_____ Observation	_____ Checklist	√ Informal Questions	_____ Product
	√ Written assignment	_____ Demonstration	√ Test	_____ Other

Test?	√ Multiple choice	_____ Completion	_____ Short essay	_____ Long essay
	_____ Combination			

SPECIAL NEEDS FOR UNIT (IF ANY)

Materials: "The Upstairs Room" by Johanna Reiss

Time:

Resource persons:

Space:

LESSON TOPICS/TITLES

1. Introduction

2. Point of view

3. Prejudice and fear

4. Making big decisions

5. Citizenship—Jewish and non-Jewish

6. Families

[Continued on next page.]

7. Characters	
8. Tme of conflict	
9. Personal conflict	
10. Relate a current world conflict to World War II	
11. Prediction	
12. Courage	
13. Reflection	
14. Post writing	
15. Rationale for writing; the author, Johanna Reiss	

Activities: In lesson plans

BIBLIOGRAPHY

Arnothy, Christine 1966. *I am Fifteen—and I Don't Want to Die*. New York: Scholastic.

Atkinson, Linda 1985. *Inkindling Flame: The Story of Hannah Senesh, 1921–1944*. New York: Lothrop, Lees & Shepard.

Atwell, Nancy 1987. *In the Middle*. Portsmouth, NH: Heinemann.

Bernhaum, Israel 1985. *My Brother's Keeper: The Holocaust through the Eyes of an Artist*. New York: Putnams.

Chaiken, Miriam 1987. *A Nightmare in History: The Holocaust, 1933–1945*. New York: Clarion.

Frank, Anne 1985. *Anne Frank: Diary of a Young Girl*. New York: Simon & Schuster.

Heuck, Sigrid 1988. *The Hideout*. New York: Orchard Books.

Laird, Christa 1990. *Shadow of the Wall*. Greenwellon.

McSwagan, Marie 1958. *Snow Treasure*. New York: Scholastic.

Meltzer, Milton 1976. *Never to Forget: The Jews of the Holocaust*. New York: Harper & Row.

Meltzer, Milton 1988. *Rescue: The Story of How Gentiles Saved Jews in the Holocaust*. New York: Harper & Row.

Reiss, Johanna 1972. *The Upstairs Room*. New York: HarperCollins.

Reiss, Johanna 1987. *The Journey Back*. New York: Harper & Row.

Rogasky, Barbara 1988. *Smoke and Ashes: The Story of the Holocaust*. New York: Holiday House.

Serraillier, Ian 1963. *Escape from Warsaw*. New York: Scholastic.

Shirer, William L. 1961. *The Rise and Fall of Adolf Hitler*. New York: Scholastic.

Siegal, Aranka 1983. *Upon the Head of the Goat: A Childhood in Hungary, 1939–1944*. New York: New American Library of Canada.

Stamper, Judith Bauer 1991. *Innovations: Experiencing Literature in the Classroom—The Upstairs Room*. New York: Scholastic.

Stein, R. Conrad 1985. *Hitler Youth*. Chicago: Children's Press.

Vos, Ida 1991. *Hide and Seek*. Boston: Houghton Mifflin.

LESSON PLAN FOR LESSON: 1

TITLE: Introduction

OBJECTIVES

Content: Students will be able to explain the term prejudice. Students will locate major countries of Europe and the city of Rotterdam. Students will be able to define historical fiction and autobiography. Students will place events of World War II in sequence.

Process: Students will classify the book and defend their classification. Students will construct a time line of World War II. Students will select a topic to research.

Products: Time line, paper on hiding

MATERIALS AND RESOURCES: "The Upstairs Room," butcher paper for time lines

TIME ESTIMATED: 1 period

INTRODUCTION OF LESSON (PROMPTS)

Objectives stated?   √   yes   no

If no, how is interest to be raised?

Students recall prior knowledge? Students study maps and recall what they know about World War II and prejudice.

Students make self-reference?

Points essential to set forth? Terms of prejudice, Jews, Hitler, and major events

ACTIVITIES/SEQUENCE

1. Students discuss prejudice. Why does it come about?

2. Students write about where they would want to go or what they would want to do if they had to be locked up or in hiding for a long period of time.

3. Map work: Students look at the map of Europe. They identify Germany, the Netherlands, Poland, France, Austria. Students locate Rotterdam.

4. Students discuss historical fiction and autobiography. They read the page before the introduction. Some libraries classify this book as fiction, some as biography. Teacher asks students, "Where would you put it and why?"

5. Students select topic for research. Each student will choose one of the following: What were Hitler's "ideals?" How did Hitler come to power? What kind of person was Hitler? What was Hitler's downfall? How do most people view Hitler today? Can you think of any contemporary individuals who are like Hitler?

6. Students make a World War II time line for 1930–1945. They are to limit their entries to 15 major events. Students are able to say what events were important and why.

[Continued on next page.]

ASSESSMENT

Student's metacognitive questions: How would you find information on...? How could you best collect information and store it so you will have it later in a useful form?

Teacher assessment of students:

FOLLOW-UP

Content:

Process: Read Chapter 1; begin research.

Notes:

LESSON PLAN FOR LESSON: 2

TITLE: Point of View

OBJECTIVES

Content: Students will develop a concept of "point of view." Students will study character traits of main characters.

Process: Students will begin literature logs, enter character traits of main characters.

Products: Logs

MATERIALS AND RESOURCES: "The Upstairs Room," logs

TIME ESTIMATED: 1 period

INTRODUCTION OF LESSON (PROMPTS)

Objectives stated?   ___√___ yes   _____ no

If no, how is interest to be raised?

Students recall prior knowledge? Students recall what they read in Chapter 1.

Students make self-reference? See question about moving to another country—you and your family.

Points essential to set forth? Point of view, character traits

ACTIVITIES/SEQUENCE

1. Teacher reads first two pages of Chapter 1 aloud to class. Who is telling the story? (Annie de Leeuw—first person point of view)

2. Students will discuss point of view of the story, age of the main character at the opening of the book, setting of the story, mother's characterization, and changes that came about because the family was Jewish.

3. Students record discussion in logs about Annie and Sini. They are to list charcter traits and why they feel the person is this way (through specific details of their actions—include age, appearance, and feelings about other people).

4. Teacher gives students the following questions to consider: From whose point of view is the story told? What did the people on the radio always talk about? What is the setting of this story? In what line of work is the father? Where did Uncle Bram and his family go? What would it be like if you and your family were to move to another country? How is the mother characterized? What does Father start to build? What do you think is going to happen? Who was Marie and why did she leave? What other changes came about because the family was Jewish? When Annie went into the 4th grade, what change took place? How would you feel if this happened to you? What event closed Chapter 1?

ASSESSMENT

Student's metacognitive questions: How do you think the war will change Annie's life?

Teacher assessment of students:

FOLLOW-UP

Content:

Process: Read Chapter 2; begin to look for details on Hitler's use of prejudice and fear against the Jewish people.

Notes: In each chapter the questions may be used a variety of ways—small group discussion, total class discussion, written assignments, pop quizzes, pair assignments.

LESSON PLAN FOR LESSON: 3

TITLE: Prejudice and Fear

OBJECTIVES

Content: Students will understand a child's perception of war by reading about the events from Annie's perspective.

Process: Students will draw conclusions.

Products: Log entries

MATERIALS AND RESOURCES: "The Upstairs Room," logs

TIME ESTIMATED: 1 period

INTRODUCTION OF LESSON (PROMPTS)

Objectives stated?   _____√_____ yes   _____ no

If no, how is interest to be raised?

Students recall prior knowledge? Students talk about what has gone on in Chapter 2.

Students make self-reference?

Points essential to set forth?

ACTIVITIES/SEQUENCE

1. Students record in their logs the details of how Hitler used prejudice and fear against Jewish people in the Netherlands. How did Hitler turn the people of the Netherlands against the Jews?

2. Questions to consider: How does Annie compare her family to the Droppers' family? What has happened back in Winterswijk? When the letter to the Ganses' boy comes back stamped "unknown," what do you think has happened? Is this a foreshadowing ploy on the part of the author? Explain Dad's trip to Switzerland. Why did he pick Switzerland? Explain the irony for Annie to be wearing the Jewish star. What other restrictions were put on Jews? Who notified them of the new rules? What object is personified by Annie? Explain what happens to Mother. All the people are leaving; even Bobbie the dog was taken to a farmer. What does this foreshadow?

ASSESSMENT

Student's metacognitive questions: See homework assignment and questions above on what you would do.

Teacher assessment of students:

FOLLOW-UP

Content:

Process: Read Chapter 3.

Notes:

LESSON PLAN FOR LESSON: 4

TITLE: Making Big Decisions

OBJECTIVES

Content: Students will interpret the physical and psychological characteristics of the individuals in the story.

Process: Students will infer a character's point of view. Students will discuss decision making in relation to the story.

Products: Paragraph on disguise

MATERIALS AND RESOURCES: "The Upstairs Room," Chapter 3

TIME ESTIMATED: 1 period

INTRODUCTION OF LESSON (PROMPTS)

Objectives stated? _____√_____ yes _____ no

If no, how is interest to be raised?

Students recall prior knowledge? Students recall events in Chapter 3.

Students make self-reference? See activities.

Points essential to set forth?

ACTIVITIES/SEQUENCE

1. Students write a detailed description of how they would change their appearance if they were to be incognito. The description should be one paragraph long and contain good adjectives.

2. Teacher divides the class into groups. Each group will take the posiion of a different family member. They are asked to consider the following: What action would that family member want the whole family to do during these years? What in the story supports that action? Would the story be different if it were written from the point of view of someone in your family?

3. Students are asked to consider the decision the father had to make about leaving his ill wife behind. Did he have other alternatives?

4. Questions to consider: How do they get places for all the family members to hide? Why do the girls take great care in disguising themselves when they go into their hiding place? What measures did they take to change their appearances? Who tells Annie her mother will probably die? How would you feel if you had to go into hiding and leave your dying mother behind? Rachel is staying behind; would you stay or go into hiding? Some decisions are made on the basis of intellect, while others are made on emotions; discuss this in light of the decisions people are making in the book.

ASSESSMENT

Student's metacognitive questions:

Teacher assessment of students:

FOLLOW-UP

Content:

Process: Read Chapter 4.

Notes:

LESSON PLAN FOR LESSON: 5

TITLE: Citizenship—Jewish and non-Jewish

OBJECTIVES

Content: Students will hypothesize about choices the characters in the book could have made. Defend the choice made by Sini when confronted with a situation that goes against her personal religious beliefs.

Process: See above.

Products: Taba Retrieval Chart or other type of chart

MATERIALS AND RESOURCES: "The Upstairs Room," Chapter 4

TIME ESTIMATED: 1 period

INTRODUCTION OF LESSON (PROMPTS)

Objectives stated? _____√_____ yes _____ no

If no, how is interest to be raised?

Students recall prior knowledge? Students recall what they read for homework.

Students make self-reference?

Points essential to set forth?

ACTIVITIES/SEQUENCE

1. As a class, students discuss the choices people had to make if they were Jewish or if they were non-Jewish.

2. Teacher reads the chapter aloud to the class.

3. Students are asked to consider the thoughts and feelings of the major characters in the book other than Annie. They are asked to keep these in mind for the next several chapters. Students are told that they may want to set up a chart, such as a Taba Retrieval Chart, to record the thoughts and feelings for each character.

4. Students reread the section on people's eating habits. What do these eating habits tell about them?

5. Questions to consider: As this chapter opens, where is Annie going and who meets her? Describe the people and house where Annie and Sini stay. (Jewish? Activities? Values?) Describe Sini. What seems to be very important to her? Where did Rachel go when Mother died? Relate "The grass is always greener on the other side" to Annie and her wants. How does Annie live different situations vicariously? Where were Annie and Sini on December 31, 1942? What do Annie and Sini dream of doing when they are FREE?

ASSESSMENT

Student's metacognitive questions:

Teacher assessment of students:

FOLLOW-UP

Content: Students are to write a letter to Uncle Bram in the United States as if they were Annie, and tell him what has happened to Annie's family and ask him questions about his new life in the United States.

Process: Read Chapter 5.

Notes:

LESSON PLAN FOR LESSON: 6

TITLE: Families

OBJECTIVES

Content: Students will examine different family values.

Process: Students will compare and contrast family values in the story.

Products: Paragraph on where you would hide out

MATERIALS AND RESOURCES: "The Upstairs Room," Chapter 5

TIME ESTIMATED: 1 period

INTRODUCTION OF LESSON (PROMPTS)

Objectives stated?   √   yes   no

If no, how is interest to be raised?

Students recall prior knowledge? Discuss what occurred in Chapter 5.

Students make self-reference?

Points essential to set forth?

ACTIVITIES/SEQUENCE

1. Students compare and contrast the Oostervelds with the previous family—the Hanninks.

2. Students discuss the words or phrases that distinguish Opoe in her speech. They are asked to give support for their answers.

3. Students are to write a paragraph about where they would hide out and give several reasons why this is a good place to hide.

4. Teacher reads several of the paragraphs aloud. Students discuss their viability.

5. Questions to consider: As this chapter opens, where are Annie and Sini? Give the names of the 3 Oosterveld family members and characterize them. Give an example of ethnic dialogue. (Ja, Ja—Johan) What did the Oostervelds do at night? What did Sini ask for that the family only had one of? Where did they get "real" news? Explain. What did Johan build for the girls?

ASSESSMENT

Student's metacognitive questions:

Teacher assessment of students: Letter to Uncle Bram

FOLLOW-UP

Content:

Process: Read Chapter 6.

Notes:

LESSON PLAN FOR LESSON: 7

TITLE: Characters

OBJECTIVES

Content: Students will compare the lives of the girls before the war and at the time of the story and compare the lives of the Oostervelds before the war and during the time they kept the girls.

Process: Draw conclusions, make inferences using Taba chart

Products: Retrieval chart, list of activities

MATERIALS AND RESOURCES: "The Upstairs Room," Chapter 6

TIME ESTIMATED: 1 period

INTRODUCTION OF LESSON (PROMPTS)

Objectives stated?   √   yes   no

If no, how is interest to be raised?

Students recall prior knowledge? Students recall their reading in Chapter 6.

Students make self-reference?

Points essential to set forth?

ACTIVITIES/SEQUENCE

1. Students add facts to their chart of characters. After chart is complete, each group will share their information and support their conclusions with details from the book.

2. Students discuss how the Oostervelds' lives had to change with Annie and Sini now in their home. What did they do for Opoe's birthday? Were the girls included? How was life for the girls now different from life before the war? How did they have to adapt in order to live with the Oostervelds?

3. Students make a list of activities they would do to pass the time while they were in hiding.

4. Questions to consider: Give reasons why Sini made Annie do a page of math every day. Where does Dientje go to borrow books? What occasion gave Annie and Sini the opportunity to go downstairs in the daytime? What is important to Sini that Annie doesn't understand?

ASSESSMENT

Student's metacognitive questions:

Teacher assessment of students:

FOLLOW-UP

Content:

Process: Read Chapter 7.

Notes:

LESSON PLAN FOR LESSON: 8

TITLE: Time of Conflict

OBJECTIVES

Content: Students will understand the different kinds of conflict and how to classify conflicts into the three kinds.

Process: Students will interpret details.

Products: Chart on conflict scenes

MATERIALS AND RESOURCES: "The Upstairs Room," Chapter 7

TIME ESTIMATED: 1 period

INTRODUCTION OF LESSON (PROMPTS)

Objectives stated?   √   yes   no

If no, how is interest to be raised?

Students recall prior knowledge? Students review reading Chapter 7.

Students make self-reference?

Points essential to set forth?

ACTIVITIES/SEQUENCE

1. Students will work in small groups to identify scenes in the first six chapters that demonstrate conflict. The students will classify conflict into three categories—conflict against nature, conflict against another person, and conflict with one's self.

2. Students discuss the concept of "inner conflict" and whether inner conflict develops into outer conflict.

3. Questions to consider: What conflicting feelings do you think Annie felt toward her dead mother? Do you think you would have been affected the same way as Annie was when she learned the truth about concentration camps? Why or why not? How is Annie's attitude changing about concentration camps? about other people's feelings? (Opoe's cap?) (flippant) Who was conducting a surprise search? Why? Sini is going to the stable with Johan to help him with the cows. How does Annie feel and why? How did Annie feel about lessons? Why do you think she had to have them? What does that tell you about the De Leeuw family's values? What does Sini notice about Annie (healthwise)? What role is Sini now taking in Annie's life? Dientje makes arrangements for Annie to go somewhere. Explain. Was it successful? How old was Annie going to be? What did Annie get for her birthday? Explain whether she liked each present and why. Who or what told Annie about the murder camps?

ASSESSMENT

Student's metacognitive questions:

Teacher assessment of students:

FOLLOW-UP

Content: Students write an entry in a diary from Sini's point of view. They are to describe one of her major problems and her feelings about resolving it.

Process: Students will enter in their logs an example of each of the three kinds of conflict that they have experienced. Students will cut an article from a magazine or newspaper that describes a military conflict somewhere in the world. How can small conflicts result in major conflicts? Read Chapter 8.

Notes:

LESSON PLAN FOR LESSON: 9

TITLE: Turning Points

OBJECTIVES

Content: Students will identify a turning point in the story.

Process:

Products:

MATERIALS AND RESOURCES: "The Upstairs Room," Chapter 8

TIME ESTIMATED: 1 period

INTRODUCTION OF LESSON (PROMPTS)

Objectives stated?   √   yes   no

If no, how is interest to be raised?

Students recall prior knowledge? Students recall homework reading.

Students make self-reference?

Points essential to set forth?

ACTIVITIES/SEQUENCE

1. Students discuss newspaper articles that describe a military conflict somewhere in the world today. They are asked if they can think of other conflicts that might come from these present conflicts.

2. Students discuss what a turning point is. They are to find the turning point in this chapter and reflect upon it.

3. This chapter ends at New Year's, "What is this a sign of?" (HOPE)

4. Questions to consider: How does this chapter open? Explain. What was Sini interested in? How does Annie use her imagination? Where had the English landed? Find it on the map. Who was coming for a visit? How does everyone feel? What does she bring? By the end of Chapter 8, how long had the girls been with the Oostervelds? What year was ending? When does the war end?

ASSESSMENT

Student's metacognitive questions: Students are to think of another book they have read recently. What was the turning point in it? Students should be prepared to discuss it and support their conclusion. Also see question 2 above (reflect).

Teacher assessment of students: Diary entry

FOLLOW-UP

Content:

Process: Read Chapter 9.

Notes:

LESSON PLAN FOR LESSON: 10

TITLE: Motivation

OBJECTIVES

Content: Students will be able to identify the factors motivating each main character (Annie, Sini, Father, Rachel) to keep going.

Process:

Products:

MATERIALS AND RESOURCES: "The Upstairs Room," Chapter 9

TIME ESTIMATED: 1 period

INTRODUCTION OF LESSON (PROMPTS)

Objectives stated? _____√_____ yes _____ no

If no, how is interest to be raised?

Students recall prior knowledge? Students recall homework reading.

Students make self-reference?

Points essential to set forth?

ACTIVITIES/SEQUENCE

1. Students will answer the following question in a class discussion: By the time in this chapter, how has the war progressed?

2. Students locate on the map the position of the Russian troops, the American troops, and the British troops. They locate Normandy.

3. Students discuss what each character was looking forward to after the war. They are asked to explain the effect this had on the characters in this difficult time.

4. Questions to consider: Who came to see the girls at the beginning of this chapter? Who else wanted to come for a visit? When would she come? What did Annie's father write about and why? What role did Rachel take now with her younger sisters? What did Johan want Sini to teach him? Why? Where do the girls want to go? Why? What happens?

ASSESSMENT

Student's metacognitive questions:

Teacher assessment of students:

FOLLOW-UP

Content:

Process: Read Chapter 10.

Notes:

LESSON PLAN FOR LESSON: 11

TITLE: Prediction

OBJECTIVES

Content: Students will be able to relate situations in which courage was expressed.

Process: Students will be able to make predictions based on various incidents in this chapter.

Products:

MATERIALS AND RESOURCES: "The Upstairs Room," Chapter 10

TIME ESTIMATED: 1 period

INTRODUCTION OF LESSON (PROMPTS)

Objectives stated? _____√_____ yes _____ no

If no, how is interest to be raised?

Students recall prior knowledge? Students recall reading.

Students make self-reference?

Points essential to set forth?

ACTIVITIES/SEQUENCE

1. Teacher reads aloud events that begin in Chapter 10. S/he stops at the end of an event and asks students to predict. Teacher asks, "How do you think the story will end?" Teacher lists several predictions on the board. The class works through them. The students predict what will happen in each case.

2. Teacher asks, "If you were in Annie's place, how would you have felt when the soldiers were searching the house? If you were Opoe or Dientje, how would you have felt? Discuss the kind of courage each of these had."

3. Teacher reads aloud the section where Annie comes face to face with the soldier. Students make predictions as to what will happen.

4. Students list other kinds of courage required of people in difficult situations during World War II.

5. Questions to consider: What scares Sini and Annie at the beginning of the chapter? Whom did the German soldiers find? How did they know about them? What does Johan offer to do? What bad news does Johan bring about the Germans? What will happen with Sini and Annie? Why did the girls have to stay in bed? How did it make them feel? What did Annie do that was so dangerous? How did Johan get her out of the predicament? At the end of the chapter, what change occurred?

ASSESSMENT

Student's metacognitive questions:

Teacher assessment of students:

FOLLOW-UP

Content: Each student will write a paragraph about a time s/he demonstrated courage.

Process: Read Chapter 11.

Notes:

LESSON PLAN FOR LESSON: 12

TITLE: Courage

OBJECTIVES

Content: Students will be able to identify Annie's mood swings and infer what caused them.

Process:

Products: Drawing of Annie's mood swings, homework assignment on courage

MATERIALS AND RESOURCES: "The Upstairs Room," Chapter 11

TIME ESTIMATED: 1 period

INTRODUCTION OF LESSON (PROMPTS)

Objectives stated?　　　　　√　　　yes　　　　　　　　　　　no

If no, how is interest to be raised?

Students recall prior knowledge?　Students recall homework reading.

Students make self-reference?

Points essential to set forth?

ACTIVITIES/SEQUENCE

1. Students read their paragraphs about their personal courage.

2. Students will continue the discussion on courage of people during World War II after discussing the paragraphs they wrote. Student groups list ways their courage might have been tested if they had lived during World War II. They will decide as a group the difficulty of these challenges.

3. In groups, the students draw the different scenes of Annie's mood swings.

4. Questions to consider: Who wants the girls to leave and why? Who came to get the girls? Which of the sisters gets claustrophobic and HAS to get out? What is the solution? What does Annie do that shows she is depressed? Trace Annie's feelings in this chapter. Discuss the possible causes of these periods of depression.

ASSESSMENT

Student's metacognitive questions:

Teacher assessment of students: Paper on courage

FOLLOW-UP

Content:

Process: Read Chapter 12.

Notes:

LESSON PLAN FOR LESSON: 13

TITLE: Reflection

OBJECTIVES

Content: Students will dramatize the different feelings of the characters now that the war has ended.

Process:

Products: Group answers to questions, create street scene

MATERIALS AND RESOURCES: "The Upstairs Room," Chapter 12

TIME ESTIMATED: 1 period

INTRODUCTION OF LESSON (PROMPTS)

Objectives stated? _____√_____ yes _____ no

If no, how is interest to be raised?

Students recall prior knowledge? Students recall Chapter 12.

Students make self-reference?

Points essential to set forth?

ACTIVITIES/SEQUENCE

1. In small groups, students can discuss why Johan says he wished the war wasn't over.

2. Still in groups, students will discuss the following questions and write their answers: Is Annie depressed or happy as the chapter opens? Explain. What does Opoe put on to greet the Canadians? What did Johan want from the Canadians? How does Johan feel when he is telling the different townspeople about Annie and Sini? What opinion do Johan, Dientje, and Opoe have about themselves now that the girls will go back to Winterswijk? Who came to take the girls home? Did they want to go? Why or why not? What was Sini's excuse for not going? Where did Annie eventually go? What did Opoe give her? Why was Annie crying when she showed her daughters the upstairs room and the hiding place?

3. The class will dramatize the street scene when the Canadians come through the town. They are instructed to make sure all groups, townspeople and Canadians, are included so that the entire class has parts.

ASSESSMENT

Student's metacognitive questions:

Teacher assessment of students: Observation

FOLLOW-UP

Content:

Process:

Notes:

LESSON PLAN FOR LESSON: 14

TITLE: Post writing

OBJECTIVES

Content: Students will identify the theme and purpose of the author.

Process: Students will write an autobiographical story (family story). Students will draw the turning point.

Products: Stories (end of second day), drawings of turning point

MATERIALS AND RESOURCES:

TIME ESTIMATED: 2 periods

INTRODUCTION OF LESSON (PROMPTS)

Objectives stated? _____√_____ yes _____ no

If no, how is interest to be raised?

Students recall prior knowledge?

Students make self-reference? See activities.

Points essential to set forth?

ACTIVITIES/SEQUENCE

1. Students discuss the theme of the story. Were any lessons learned? Does the book have historical value? Each group will draw their idea of the turning point in the story.

2. Students divide into groups of 4 or 5. Each group chooses one of the following tasks: Write a short paper on how your life would change if a discrimination situation came up in the United States. Where would you go? What would you and your family do? Compare and contrast "The Upstairs Room" and "The Diary of Anne Frank." Do a time line with specific historical events from the story. If there were a museum for the Oosterveld house, what objects would you put in the museum? Explain what each signifies. Make similes about each character; for example, Johan thought he was as dumb as an ox.

ASSESSMENT

Student's metacognitive questions:

Teacher assessment of students: Sketches both written and drawn

FOLLOW-UP

Content:

Process: Each student is to make a time line of his or her life. Each student will write a short autobiographical story about him or herself. It is to include setting, plot, theme, and one conflict. Students are to limit what is included—not too much.

Notes:

LESSON PLAN FOR LESSON: 15

TITLE: The Author—Johanna Reiss

OBJECTIVES

Content: Students will discuss why the author wrote the book, why she cried when she revisited the place.

Process: Students will make inferences and draw conclusions.

Products:

MATERIALS AND RESOURCES:

TIME ESTIMATED: 1 period

INTRODUCTION OF LESSON (PROMPTS)

Objectives stated?   √   yes   no

If no, how is interest to be raised?

Students recall prior knowledge?

Students make self-reference?

Points essential to set forth?

ACTIVITIES/SEQUENCE

1. Students will describe Johanna Reiss's return to the upstairs room with her children. Teacher will raise the following questions: Why do you think she cried? Why did she write this book? Do you feel the writing of the book is an act of courage? Why or why not? Why do you think young people should learn about the treatment of people during World War II?

ASSESSMENT

Student's metacognitive questions:

Teacher assessment of students: Students' autobiographical sketches and time lines

FOLLOW-UP

Content: Test tomorrow

Process:

Notes:

LESSON PLAN FOR LESSON: 16

TITLE: Test

OBJECTIVES

Content: Students will demonstrate knowledge and understanding of the book "The Upstairs Room" by Johanna Reiss.

Process:

Products: Test paper

MATERIALS AND RESOURCES: Test

TIME ESTIMATED: 1 period

INTRODUCTION OF LESSON (PROMPTS)

Objectives stated?   √   yes   no

If no, how is interest to be raised?

Students recall prior knowledge? On test

Students make self-reference?

Points essential to set forth?

ACTIVITIES/SEQUENCE

1. Students will complete test.

ASSESSMENT

Student's metacognitive questions:

Teacher assessment of students: See test.

FOLLOW-UP

Content: Could have videos, speakers, survivors of the holocaust—museum on holocaust opened in Washington, DC, in spring 1993.

Process:

Notes: Test included on pp. 174–76

Test on *The Upstairs Room*

Name_____

Date_____

Multiple Choice

Put the letter of the answer that BEST fits the question.

_____1. What is the genre of this story?
- A. Historical fiction
- B. Science fiction
- C. Contemporary history
- D. Autobiography

_____2. From who's point of view is the story told?
- A. First person
- B. Third person
- C. Neither of the above

_____3. As the story opens (and throughout) what was the theme on the radio?
- A. Events leading up to World War I
- B. Events leading up to World War II
- C. A cooking course for Opoe who loved to cook

_____4. In what line of business was Annie's father?
- A. Cattle
- B. Pigs
- C. Merchant
- D. He was retired.

_____5. What do you remember most about the mother?
- A. Always complaining
- B. Always learning to cook
- C. Wanting to go to America
- D. Always had headaches

_____6. Which event came first?
- A. Annie lives with the Hanninks.
- B. Annie lives with the Oostervelds.
- C. Annie lives in Winterswijk.
- D. World War II begins.

_____7. Why do you think Annie's mother wanted to stay?
    A. She did not want to leave her friends.
    B. She did not want to leave her job.
    C. Her children would learn a new language.
    D. She really wanted to divorce her husband.

_____8. How would you describe Sini?
    A. Conceited
    B. Greedy
    C. Vain
    D. Dishonest

_____9. What did the Hanninks have that the Oostervelds did not have?
    A. Books
    B. Relatives
    C. Friends
    D. Cattle

_____10. Sini said that Annie was sick. What was wrong with her?
    A. Kidney infection
    B. Weak muscles
    C. Headaches
    D. Bad cold

Quotes

Decide who said the following and put the letter identifying the person (A, B, C, D, or E) by the appropriate number.

    A. Annie's mother   B. Annie's father
    C. Johan   D. Marie   E. Opoe

_____11. "A high school teacher coming here? God-o-god-o-god, what's next?"

_____12. "You've always been good to me, and I like the girls very much, but you see it's my boyfriend. He wants me to leave you."

_____13. "But, Ies, I never kept you from going."

_____14. "I don't want to wait any longer. I'm nervous about staying in town. We're moving!"

_____15. "Na, woman, I couldn't sit up here all day and I don't fit in the hiding place."

Conflicts

Select the letter (A, B, or C) to tell which type of conflict each selection is.

    A. Man vs. nature or society

    B. Man vs. man

    C. Man vs. self

_____16. Mother and Father were arguing over whether or not to go to America.

_____17. Sini wants to go outside.

_____18. The Gentiles (or non-Jewish citizens) dared to help the Jews hide.

_____19. Sini thought, "I think I do look better with a tan…yes I do."

_____20. Johan must kill the snitch who told on those who helped the Jews hide.

All Quiet on the Western Front

The plan for a secondary language arts unit based on the book *All Quiet on the Western Front* is presented below.

UNIT PLAN

TOPIC: "All Quiet on the Western Front"

SUBJECT

Grade level or group: Secondary

Primary: Literature

Estimated time: 15 periods

Others: History

EDUCATIONAL OUTCOMES OF UNIT

Content: Students will be able to identify and characterize persons and events in the novel.

Process: Students will be able to compare and contrast, make decisions, and engage in levels of questioning (à la Bloom).

Products: Cognitive map, commercial for book, short essay, double-entry journals (product of reading)

RATIONALE: The approach is to introduce the concepts, place students in cooperative groups, allow practice and transfer of knowledge of processes.

ASSESSMENT PLAN

Purpose: Assess objectives above

How?		Observation		Checklist	√	Informal Questions		Product
	√	Written assignment		Demonstration	√	Test		Other

Test?	√	Multiple choice	√	Completion	√	Short essay		Long essay
	√	Combination						

SPECIAL NEEDS FOR UNIT (IF ANY)

Materials: Copies of novel

Time:

Resource persons:

Space:

LESSON TOPICS/TITLES

1. Introduce "All Quiet on the Western Front." Hand out vocabulary list; examine words in double-entry journals. Add words from double-entry journal to those given by teacher. Write definitions for these words.

2. Concept mapping on effects of war—examine novel's symbols that reflect the effects of war.

3. Groups are assigned major characters to study. Introduce Bloom's taxonomy and questioning techniques.

4. Each student will pick a major character and compose a question at each level of the taxonomy about that character. Teacher will introduce the Taba Retrieval Chart on characteristics which reflect the effects of war as illustrated on the concept map.

[Continued on next page.]

NOTE: This unit developed by Judith Askins and Kathryn Kearse, secondary teachers.

5. Teacher will demonstrate Taba Retrieval Chart using a character. Students will do the same with their charts.

6. Introduce compare/contrast concept using life at home and life on the front. Free response paper—students compare and contrast two characters of their choice.

7. Students who picked the same characters will work in small groups to compare and contrast their characters using different strategies. Ideas will be written in compare/contrast paper.

8. Students work in pairs to edit. Teacher conferences with students.

9. Students prepare final draft. Requirements will be given for creating a commercial to sell the book. Students pick groups.

10. Small-group discussion on important places, things, and quotes in the novel. Students will use their Bloom questions.

11. Test. Complete plans for presentations.

12. Discuss and list characteristics of a good friend, using a cognitive map technique. Discuss the concept of friendship as found in the novel. Give findings to class.

13. Write short personal essay reflecting on which character would make the best or worst friend.

14. Work in small groups on commercials.

15. Commercials are presented and discussed; videotape commercials.

Activities: In lesson plans

Chapter Twelve

Mathematics

Mathematics teachers have said that it is difficult to develop math units that incorporate higher order thinking because there is so much emphasis on operations and their practice. The National Council of the Teachers of Mathematics (NCTM) issued the new standards for mathematics in 1988. As the standards have filtered down to the classrooms, the need for units which intentionally direct students to higher order thinking strategies as applied to mathematics has become more apparent. In the higher order thinking books and manuals, less attention has been directed at mathematics than some other subject areas. We have, therefore, chosen mathematics as the third subject area in which to demonstrate both the unit outline and the lessons.

UNIT PLAN

TOPIC: Nonroutine Problems/Strategies

Grade level or group: 4th grade

Estimated time: 13 periods

SUBJECT

Primary: Math

Others:

EDUCATIONAL OUTCOMES OF UNIT

Content: Students will be able to solve everyday problems which require them to demonstrate some kind of organizational skill or strategy.

Process: Students will engage in problem solving and demonstrate its steps.

Products: Students will create and write their own problem and its solution for each strategy.

RATIONALE: Students are given mechanical-type problems to solve in school with little emphasis placed on solving problems as they apply to everyday-life situations. The use of nonroutine problems can help students make the transfer from book knowledge to the real world. Students need to learn several different strategies for solving problems.

ASSESSMENT PLAN

Purpose: Assess objectives above

How?							
√	Observation		Checklist	√	Informal Questions	√	Product
√	Written assignment		Demonstration		Test		Other

Test?							
	Multiple choice		Completion		Short essay		Long essay
	Combination						

SPECIAL NEEDS FOR UNIT (IF ANY)

Materials: Problems with multiple answers or multistep problems

Time:

Resource persons:

Space:

[Continued on next page.]

LESSON TOPICS/TITLES

1. Introduction to nonroutine problems

2. Party plan

3. Seating problem

4. Managing the party

5. Greek festival

6. Camping trip

7. Setting up displays

8. Scheduling your time

9. Materials for classroom

10. Design a survey

11. Shared problems

12. Presentations

13. Final report

Activities: In lesson plans

Bibliography: Math texts and problem books

LESSON PLAN FOR LESSON: 1

TITLE: Introduction to Nonroutine Problems

OBJECTIVES

Content: Students will be able to work in groups on a nonroutine problem. They will work through one with teacher scaffolding. They will work through a problem on their own.

Process:

Products: Students will write their solutions to class problems.

MATERIALS AND RESOURCES: Math notebook, problems, fact sheet on fish, overhead

TIME ESTIMATED: 1 period

INTRODUCTION OF LESSON (PROMPTS)

Objectives stated? _____√_____ yes _____ no

If no, how is interest to be raised?

Students recall prior knowledge?

Students make self-reference?

Points essential to set forth? There is no formula or rule for nonroutine problems. You have to go through steps in problem solving, but how you carry out the steps will vary with each problem. Organizing the problem is the secret of good problem solving.

ACTIVITIES/SEQUENCE

1. Teacher talks to students about developing a plan for solving problems. The students' plans need to be flexible because nonroutine problems are not as defined or specific as many they have been doing in math. There may be more than one acceptable answer.

2. Introduce the problem. Read or pass out copies of the principal's note (provided on p. 182).

3. Students identify what the problem is. Teacher explains that when the problem is clarified and you have looked at what you know and what you need to know, the result is called problem representation. Teacher writes on the board: Identify the problem. Students receive flier with information on problem and chart on fish that are available. Teacher cautions students to be sure they have represented the problem with everything that is relevant and that they know what the end results need to be. Teacher writes on board: Problem Representation.

4. Students work in small groups to come up with a plan, then brainstorm ideas on the board. Teacher asks each group to select a plan to try first. Teacher explains to them that it is all right to have different plans. Students are told they can modify their plans if necessary. Teacher writes on board under "Problem Representation" the following steps: clarify, collect data, generate solutions, select a solution to try.

5. Students are told to work on their plan and try to solve the problem. Teacher writes on board: Operation of solution set.

6. Teacher writes on board: Evaluation—check your work. Students are asked to check to see that their calculations and solutions fit any stipulations which have been set up. Teacher asks, "Did you get the most for your $25, stay within the size constraint of the fish and the aquarium, and consider all of the special needs of the fish selected? Could you have devise a chart or organizer to help you manage the information?"

[Continued on next page.]

7. Teacher reviews the steps with students several times. Teacher checks to see if students can remember the steps. The teacher then asks students if the steps fit what the students did. S/he asks students to volunteer their answers and has them write their solution in their math notebook.

8. Students will write a letter to the principal with the information s/he requested—how many of each kind of fish, reason for choices, summary of spending, and reason the fish will not be too crowded.

ASSESSMENT

Student's metacognitive questions: See activities 6 and 7 above.

Teacher assessment of students: Oral questioning and monitoring

FOLLOW-UP

Content: Students will know steps in problem solving.

Process: Students will try to work the zoo problem for homework (see below).

Notes: Principal's note (below), fish infomation sheet (p. 183), fish descriptions (p. 184), zoo problem (below)

Principal's Note

The principal's note to the students is as follows:

Your class will be getting a 30-gallon aquarium. The class will have $25.00 to spend on fish. You will plan which fish to buy. Use the "Choosing Fish for Your Aquarium" brochure to help you choose the fish. The brochure tells you things you must know about the size of the fish, how much they cost, and their special needs.

Choose as many different kinds of fish as you can. Then write a letter to me explaining which fish you chose. In your letter

1.　tell me how many of each kind of fish to buy;

2.　give your reasons for choosing those fish; and

3.　show that you are not over spending and that the fish will not be too crowded in the aquarium.

(NOTE: This problem was developed by the New Standards Project.)

Zoo Problem

You are to be manager of a local zoo that is being built. You have been told that you have $20,000 to spend on fencing. The fence costs $1 per running foot. You are trying to get the most space enclosed, but you know that certain animals do not get along. The animals that you know you will have in your zoo are elephants, lions, tigers, monkeys, giraffes, hippos, bears, and antelope. The aviary and reptile complexes are separate. How might you arrange the animals and how would you allocate the fencing?

(NOTE: This problem was developed from an idea proposed by sixth grader Michael McGovern.)

Choosing Fish for Your Aquarium

Planning Ahead

Use the information in this brochure to help you choose fish that will be happy and healthy in your aquarium. To choose your fish, you must know about the size of the fish, their cost, and their special needs.

Size of Fish

To be healthy, fish need enough room to swim and move around. A good rule is to have one inch of fish for each gallon of water in your aquarium. This means that in a ten-gallon aquarium, the lengths of all your fish added together can be ten inches at the most.

Cost of the Fish

Some fish cost as little as one dollar; others cost much more. The prices of each kind of fish are listed in the chart on the next page.

Special Needs

Use the chart on the next page to learn about the special needs of each kind of fish. Some fish need to live together in schools—a group of four or more of the same kind of fish—while others live in pairs or alone. A few kinds of fish have other special needs, which are listed in the chart.

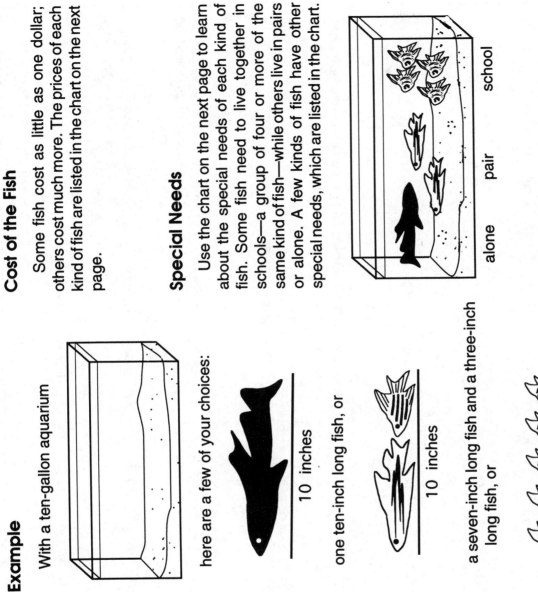

Example

With a ten-gallon aquarium

here are a few of your choices:

|___10 inches___|
one ten-inch long fish, or

|___10 inches___|
a seven-inch long fish and a three-inch long fish, or

|___10 inches___|
five fish if each is only two-inches long.

alone   pair   school

CHART FOR FRESHWATER FISH

Picture	Name	Cost	Length in Inches	Color	Special Needs, Facts
	Zebra Danio	$1.00	1.5 inches	blue with gold lines	Lives in schools; gets along with other kinds of fish
	Marbled Hatchetfish	$1.00	2 inches	yellow	Lives in schools; can leap 3–5 yards
	Guppy	2 for $3.00	2 inches	red, blue, and green	Lives in schools
	Red-tailed Black Shark	$5.00	4.5 inches	black with red tail	Fights with other sharks, but gets along with other kinds of fish
	Cardinal Tetra	$5.00	1.5 inches	red and green	Lives in schools
	Blind Cave Fish	$2.00	3 inches	silvery rose	Lives in schools; uses its sense of smell and vibration to find food
	Ramirez' Dwarf Cichlid	$5.00	2 inches	rainbow	Lives in pairs; rarely lives longer than 2.5 years; gets along with other fish
	Velvet Cichlid	$5.00	12.5 inches	olive with stripes	Can be trained to take food from the hand and can be petted; must be kept only with other cichlids

LESSON PLAN FOR LESSON: 2

TITLE: Party Plan

OBJECTIVES

Content: Students will be able to solve nonroutine problems.

Process: Students will practice the steps in problem solving.

Products: Problems students created for homework, entries in math notebook

MATERIALS AND RESOURCES: Problems, restaurant menu (see p. 187)

TIME ESTIMATED: 1 period

INTRODUCTION OF LESSON (PROMPTS)

Objectives stated?   √   yes   _____   no

If no, how is interest to be raised?

Students recall prior knowledge? Students recall steps in problem solving.

Students make self-reference? Students share their solution to the zoo problem.

Points essential to set forth? Problem-solving steps are the same, but strategies may be different

ACTIVITIES/SEQUENCE

1. Students review the steps in problem solving. Several students present their solution to the zoo problem to the class. Class discusses each by going through the steps.

2. Teacher introduces the problem to students as follows: Today we are going to look at a real-life situation and see if we can solve the problem. Your classroom is having a party for 25 students and 25 parents. It will be catered by Capri's Italian Restaurant. You have $150 to spend on the food for 50 people. How can you get the most food that you like for your money? Use the menu from the restaurant to make your selections.

3. Teacher asks students to set up Problem Representation. Questions teacher might ask are, What is being asked? What information is known? What information is unknown or missing? Is there a way to figure out what you need to know? (Example: How many servings of pizza can you get from a 10 inch pizza? How many servings of cake can you cut from a two-layered 9-inch cake that has been iced?)

4. Students work in small groups to generate several solutions for solving the problem. Teacher may suggest organizer of some kind to assist. Student will enter solutions under "Problem Representation" and select one to try.

5. Groups carry out their solution set (operation). Students will do the mathematical work and any subproblems that arise. They will prepare a paper from their group to hand in.

6. Students will evaluate their solution to see if the plan will feed 50 people and still be within the $150 limit.

7. Students will report their solutions to the class. Class will see that there are multiple solutions to the problem.

[Continued on next page.]

NOTE: Sixth grade student Carter Willis suggested this problem.

ASSESSMENT

Student's metacognitive questions: See activity 6 above.

Teacher assessment of students: Teacher will monitor groups to keep them on task and offer assistance. S/he will raise feasibility questions if appropriate.

FOLLOW-UP

Content: Students will construct similar problem. On a separate sheet of paper, the students will write their solutions. These will be discussed in class tomorrow.

Process: See content above.

Notes: Keep problems students generate for future use.

Great Italian Restaurant

Appetizers

Fried Mushrooms	3.50
Minestrone Soup	3.50
Fettucini Alfredo	4.50

Drinks

Soft Drinks	1.05
Milk	.75
Tea	.85
Coffee	.75

Entrees

Spaghetti	8.99

• Includes garlic bread, salad, fruit, and drink

Ravioli	5.99

• Includes garlic bread and salad

Linguini	plain	6.99
	meal	10.99

• Meal includes salad, garlic bread, and seafood

Children's Menu

Hamburger	2.50
Hot Dog	2.50
Spaghetti	2.50

• All Children's Menu items include french fries or salad, garlic bread or roll, and drink.

Desserts

Cheesecake	2.99
Chocolate Cake	2.99
Apple Pie	3.99
Grilled Cheese	2.99

Pizza
—Our Speciality

Toppings	Individual	Small	Medium	Large
pepperoni	4.00	6.00	8.00	10.00
hamburger	4.00	6.00	8.00	10.00
sausage	4.00	6.00	8.00	10.00
onions	3.20	4.00	6.00	8.00
bell pepper	3.20	4.00	6.00	8.00
ham	4.00	6.00	8.00	10.00
extra cheese	4.00	4.00	6.00	8.00

	2 toppings	3 toppings	Supreme
Individual	4.50	5.00	6.00
Small	5.00	7.00	8.00
Medium	8.00	9.00	10.00
Large	11.00	12.00	12.00

LESSON PLAN FOR LESSON: 3

TITLE: Seating Problem

OBJECTIVES

Content: Students will solve nonroutine problems.

Process: Students will practice the steps in problem solving.

Products: Students will produce similar problems and their solution.

MATERIALS AND RESOURCES: Problems, overhead

TIME ESTIMATED: 1 period

INTRODUCTION OF LESSON (PROMPTS)

Objectives stated?　　　　　√　　　　yes　　　　　　　　　　　　no

If no, how is interest to be raised?

Students recall prior knowledge? Students recall steps in problem solving.

Students make self-reference? Students share problems they have created.

Points essential to set forth? Setting up the problem is crucial.

ACTIVITIES/SEQUENCE

1. Students review last night's activity—2 or 3 students tell about the problems they wrote. Class will work through each one as a group, or let the student explain his or her problem (be the teacher). Students will be able to create file-folder activities with their problems after they have been checked.

2. Teacher introduces the seating problem to students as follows: You have 6 rectangular tables which can seat 3 people on each side and one at each end. How can you arrange the tables to seat the most people? How can you arrange the tables to seat the least number of people?

3. Each student will work on the problem independently and present his or her solution to the class. Teacher suggests that they may find it helpful to sketch or draw their ideas.

4. Students will write the steps they went through in their thinking in order to come up with their answers (Problem Representation: identify, clarify, collect data, generate solutions, select one to try, operate with solution set, evaluate the outcome).

ASSESSMENT

Student's metacognitive questions: See activity 4 above.

Teacher assessment of students: Monitor problems presented. Teacher will review students' writing of the steps they went through in their own thinking processes.

FOLLOW-UP

Content: Students will construct similar problem. They will solve the problem on a separate sheet of paper and bring both to class.

Process: Same as content above.

Notes:

LESSON PLAN FOR LESSON: 4

TITLE: Managing the Party

OBJECTIVES

Content: Students will sequence the activities necessary to manage the party, obtain food, seat participants, serve, etc.

Process: Students will practice the steps in problem solving.

Products: Each students' plan

MATERIALS AND RESOURCES:

TIME ESTIMATED: 1 period

INTRODUCTION OF LESSON (PROMPTS)

Objectives stated?   √   yes   no

If no, how is interest to be raised?

Students recall prior knowledge? Students will review what they did on the two previous days.

Students make self-reference? Students will pretend that they are a party manager.

Points essential to set forth? There are many ways to plan, but follow the general steps in problem solving; use an organizer if you like.

ACTIVITIES/SEQUENCE

1. Class reviews last night's follow-up activity. Several students share their problems and let the others solve them. All students turn in their problems and solutions.

2. Students review two previous lessons: food and seating.

3. Teacher introduces the problem: The class decided to select a party chairperson who will oversee the whole affair. You have been selected as the chairperson. Write out a sequence of tasks that must be carried out in order for the food to be obtained, the participants seated, the food served, etc. Remember the restrictions and your solutions for the food and the seating.

4. Each student writes out his or her plan. Teacher reminds students to go through the steps in problem solving and suggests that they use an organizer.

5. Students share steps and justify their order.

6. Students are asked if solving this problem was like any other problems they solved? Explain.

ASSESSMENT

Student's metacognitive questions: See activity 5 above.

Teacher assessment of students: Teacher reviews plans.

FOLLOW-UP

Content:

Process:

Notes:

LESSON PLAN FOR LESSON: 5

TITLE: Greek Festival

OBJECTIVES

Content: Students will calculate multiple arrangements of students and guests who will receive 36 pieces of baklava.

Process: Students will practice the steps in problem solving.

Products: Multiple solution sets

MATERIALS AND RESOURCES: Problem

TIME ESTIMATED: 1 period

INTRODUCTION OF LESSON (PROMPTS)

Objectives stated? _____√_____ yes _____ no

If no, how is interest to be raised?

Students recall prior knowledge? Students review problem-solving steps.

Students make self-reference?

Points essential to set forth? More than one answer is possible.

ACTIVITIES/SEQUENCE

1. Teacher introduces the problem: Your classroom is having a Greek festival. The teacher said she has figured that 36 pieces of baklava will be exactly enough to give one piece to each student and each guest. Two-thirds (2/3) of the class are girls. How many girls are there? How many boys? How many guests are coming? There are more than one set of numbers you can find that will meet the conditions in the problem. List as many as you can.

2. Students review the steps in problem solving. Students consider, How does the model help with this problem? Or does it?

3. Students work in small groups to solve this problem.

4. Groups report their solutions to the class and explain how they got their answers. Students discuss different strategies used by different groups and whether one is better than another for this type of problem. Why?

ASSESSMENT

Student's metacognitive questions: See activity 4 above.

Teacher assessment of students: Teacher listens to explanations and justifications.

FOLLOW-UP

Content: For homework, each student is to construct a problem similar to the one done in class today. On a separate sheet, the students will place the solution. Both are to be brought to class to share and turn in.

Process:

Notes:

TITLE: Camping Trip

OBJECTIVES

Content: Students will develop a plan for feeding students who go on a camping trip for the weekend.

Process: Students will make all calculations necessary.

Products: Each student will produce a plan on the form provided.

MATERIALS AND RESOURCES: Grocery ads from newspapers

TIME ESTIMATED: 1 period

INTRODUCTION OF LESSON (PROMPTS)

Objectives stated?   √   yes   no

If no, how is interest to be raised?

Students recall prior knowledge? Students share their problems.

Students make self-reference?

Points essential to set forth?

ACTIVITIES/SEQUENCE

1. Students will share the problems they constructed for homework. One or two will be worked in class by the group.

2. Teacher introduces the problem: Fifteen girls are going on a weekend camping trip to Lake Arrowhead. Each girl pays a total of $10 for the trip. The transportation costs $2 per person and admittance to the camp is $3 per person. You are on the food committee and need to plan the meals. Using the grocery ad from the local newspaper, plan the meals and snacks for the following meals: Friday, supper and snack; Saturday, breakfast, lunch, supper, snack; Sunday: breakfast, lunch. Remember that the following things will be furnished by the camp: wood, campfire sites, ice, coolers, and fishing pond.

3. Students review steps in problem solving. They are to consider how the steps fit with this problem.

4. Students are given the form to plan their food needs.

5. Students will work in small groups to solve the problem.

6. Groups will report their plan to the class and justify it.

ASSESSMENT

Student's metacognitive questions:

Teacher assessment of students: Students will turn in plans.

FOLLOW-UP

Content: Students will construct and work through a problem like the one they worked in class. They will place their answer on a separate sheet of paper. They are to turn in problem and answer.

Process:

Notes: Form included on p. 192

CAMPING TRIP PLANNING SHEET				
DAY	**MEAL**	**ITEM**	**QUANTITY**	**COST**
Friday	supper			
	snack			
Saturday	breakfast			
	lunch			
	supper			
	snack			
Sunday	breakfast			
	lunch			

LESSON PLAN FOR LESSON: 7

TITLE: Setting Up Display

OBJECTIVES

Content:

Process: Students will use logical reasoning to arrange display of video games.

Products: Order of arrangement

MATERIALS AND RESOURCES: Problem, drawing of display case (see p. 194)

TIME ESTIMATED: 1 period

INTRODUCTION OF LESSON (PROMPTS)

Objectives stated? _____√_____ yes _____ no

If no, how is interest to be raised?

Students recall prior knowledge? Students present homework problems.

Students make self-reference?

Points essential to set forth?

ACTIVITIES/SEQUENCE

1. Several students present the problems they constructed for homework. Class generates solutions.

2. Teacher introduces the problem: There are 7 video game cartridges arranged in a case. They are Rad Racer, Bad Dudes, Contra, Ninja Gaiden, Super Brain, Battle Toads, and Robot Police; they are not necessarily in that order. Contra is first. Ninja Gaiden is between Battle Toads and Super Brain. Super Brain is on top of Robot Police. Battle Toads is second. Bad Dudes is on the bottom of Rad Racer. Using the display case drawing, arrange the games in the correct order.

3. Teacher asks students, "Can we use our problem-solving plan to work this problem? Why or why not?" Students should realize that this is a different kind of problem which requires arranging rather than computing.

4. Students work individually to solve this problem. Because it is a deductive logic problem, there is only one correct answer. The teacher should ask students to think about what was different in the way they solved this problem compared to the problems they solved previously.

ASSESSMENT

Student's metacognitive questions: See activities 3 and 4 above.

Teacher assessment of students:

FOLLOW-UP

Content: For homework, students are asked to design a similar problem and its solution.

Process:

Notes:

NOTE: This problem was developed by sixth grader Jon Krueger.

GAME CARTRIDGE DISPLAY CASE

LESSON PLAN FOR LESSON: 8

TITLE: Scheduling Your Time

OBJECTIVES

Content: Students will learn about time-management scheduling.

Process: Students will be able to plan a personal schedule for a week.

Products: Each student will produce his or her own time schedule.

MATERIALS AND RESOURCES: Blank form with hours and days (see p. 197)

TIME ESTIMATED: 1 period with follow-up activity

INTRODUCTION OF LESSON (PROMPTS)

Objectives stated?   √   yes   _____   no

If no, how is interest to be raised?

Students recall prior knowledge? During lesson, students will recall their activities at various times of the day.

Students make self-reference? Students will do this during entire lesson.

Points essential to set forth? Once students set down the nonnegotiables, they will see that they have more time at their command than they thought they had.

ACTIVITIES/SEQUENCE

1. Students will present 1 or 2 of their homework problems for the class to try. Teacher will collect problems.

2. Teacher introduces the problem: "Many times I hear you say that you don't have time to do your homework or work on a project or study for a test. In small groups, discuss why you think this is so." Students discuss in small groups various activities they engage in and why they don't have time. Students share some of these with the class—Scouts, band, sleep, school, chores, ball practice, piano lessons, etc.

3. Teacher says to students, "Today we are going to set up a time table that will help you better manage your time." Hand out the time-schedule forms. Teacher asks students to fill in specific things that they have to do or are responsible for each day. They should fill in their normal sleeping schedule, time spent eating, the hours they are at school, time spent riding the bus, time for chores, time for teams, extracurricula activities, church commitments, and all preallocated obligations. They are not to fill in time for TV and other recreational activities at this time.

4. Teacher tells students, "Now that you've put in the schedule what we call nonnegotiables, let's look at what time you have left. Is there any time left? How much? Are you surprised at how many hours there are?"

5. "You have not yet put in any homework or TV or telephone conversations. Now think about your favorite TV shows. Put them in. Now find an hour for homework each Sunday–Thursday. Put it in. Now is there anything you really like to do every day or on certain special days of the week? Add that. Do you still have some time? How would you like to spend the rest of the time?" Students respond with activities they have not yet added.

[Continued on next page.]

---

6. "Let's talk about how you are spending your time. Where do you spend most of each day? Are you using your time well? Do you see something you might do, some rearrangement or combination that might make the use of your time more efficient?" Students discuss these questions in groups, then each presents one idea they came up with.

7. "How did the schedule form help you to organize your thinking? Is there a better way to plan your activities?" Students discuss any ideas. "Did you use the steps in problem solving to carry out this solution? Did they work? How were they used and what was different?" Students discuss.

ASSESSMENT

Student's metacognitive questions: See activities 6 and 7.

Teacher assessment of students:

FOLLOW-UP

Content: Students are asked to try to live with their schedule for a week. Find out what doesn't work, adjust and rearrange if necessary. Students are told to bring their schedules in one week from tomorrow. Plan to discuss adjustments at that time.

Process:

Notes:

NAME:	Monday	Tuesday	Wednesday	Thursday	Friday	Saturday	Sunday
6:00							
6:30							
7:00							
7:30							
8:00							
8:30							
9:00							
9:30							
10:00							
10:30							
11:00							
11:30							
12:00							
12:30							
1:00							
1:30							
2:00							
2:30							
3:00							
3:30							
4:00							
4:30							
5:00							
5:30							
6:00							
6:30							
7:00							
7:30							
8:00							
8:30							
9:00							
9:30							

LESSON PLAN FOR LESSON: 9

TITLE: Materials for Classroom

OBJECTIVES

Content: Students will make decision about what to buy with limited resources.

Process: Students will engage in decision making.

Products: Purchase-order list and amounts of items

MATERIALS AND RESOURCES: Supply chart (see p. 199)

TIME ESTIMATED: 1 period

INTRODUCTION OF LESSON (PROMPTS)

Objectives stated?   √   yes   _____ no

If no, how is interest to be raised?

Students recall prior knowledge?

Students make self-reference?

Points essential to set forth? Choices are made for different reasons.

ACTIVITIES/SEQUENCE

1. Teacher presents the problem: You are asked by the principal to be in charge of a committee which is to spend $100 for your classroom. Using the items and prices from the supply chart, make a list of as few items as possible that total $100 or less. Make a list of as many items as possible that total $100 or less. Order no more than one of any item on the supply chart.

2. Students will be given a copy of the supply chart. They will work individually to come up with their answers. Then they will share with a neighbor.

3. Class will discuss choices. Each student will be asked to tell why s/he chose each item.

4. Teacher asks, "How did you organize your information in order to make a decision? Which was harder, least number or largest number? Why?"

ASSESSMENT

Student's metacognitive questions: See activity 4 above.

Teacher assessment of students: Teacher will collect lists.

FOLLOW-UP

Content: Design a similar problem; place solutions on a separate sheet. Both will be turned in as homework.

Process:

Notes:

NOTE: This problem was developed by sixth grader Brian Sieradzki.

SUPPLY CHART			
BELL $5.00	RADIO $20.00	STORAGE BOXES $10.00	TAPE PLAYER $25.00
FLASHLIGHT $5.00	BOX OF YARN $5.00	BATTLEWAGON GAME $10.00	HAND PUPPET $10.00
GEO-SAFARI $99.99	BOX OF GLUE STICKS $5.00	T.V. $100.01	BOX OF POSTER PAPER $15.00
SUPER NEWS PROGRAM $99.99	CRAYONS $1.00	V.C.R. $56.00	SCISSORS $1.50

LESSON PLAN FOR LESSON: 10

TITLE: Design a Survey

OBJECTIVES

Content: Students will be able to plan a research study.

Process: Students will engage in metacognitive activities of planning.

Products: Survey form, survey plan

MATERIALS AND RESOURCES:

TIME ESTIMATED: 1 period plus research time

INTRODUCTION OF LESSON (PROMPTS)

Objectives stated?   √   yes   no

If no, how is interest to be raised?

Students recall prior knowledge? Students review problem-solving procedures.

Students make self-reference?

Points essential to set forth? Planning is the key to good research.

ACTIVITIES/SEQUENCE

1. Students will present homework problems to class. Class will solve one or two.

2. Teacher will introduce problem: You are to plan a research study which you will then carry out during the next few days. Compose a question that can be asked of students in your grade level or school. The question must be set up so that the results may be tabulated and reported in numerical form. (See example under notes.)

3. Students will meet as a class and later in 4 groups to do the following: find a topic (total class); identify to whom the survey will be given (total class); develop several items to include in the survey (4 groups); select the questions or items to be used (total class); design the survey form (1 group); and plan the sequence of events to carry out the study.

4. Students prepare form for reproduction (same small group who designed the form).

ASSESSMENT

Student's metacognitive questions: How can we design this so we can get answers that we can analyze? What do we need to think about?

Teacher assessment of students: Monitor and observe process.

FOLLOW-UP

Content: Get survey reproduced.

Process:

Notes:

Sample Survey

Of the following meals served in the school cafeteria, which is your favorite? Check only one.

____pizza   ____tacos   ____fried chicken
____hamburger   ____hot dog   ____fish

LESSON PLAN FOR LESSON: 11

TITLE: Shared Problems

OBJECTIVES

Content: Students will be able to list steps in problem solving. Students will be able to tell how strategies change depending on the type of problem.

Process: Students will be able to solve nonroutine problems.

Products: Group problem solutions

MATERIALS AND RESOURCES: Previous problems and student's homework problems (with solutions)

TIME ESTIMATED: 1 period

INTRODUCTION OF LESSON (PROMPTS)

Objectives stated? _____√_____ yes _____ no

If no, how is interest to be raised?

Students recall prior knowledge? Students review process steps.

Students make self-reference?

Points essential to set forth?

ACTIVITIES/SEQUENCE

1. Teacher will review different examples of nonroutine problems which the students have solved over the past two weeks. Students will write down the problem-solving steps, then discuss how the strategies were different for various problems.

2. Students will get into 4 groups. Each group will be given a different problem. Students in each group will solve their problem and plan how they will present it to the class the next day. They are asked to focus on what strategies they used and why. The teacher will have selected these problems from the ones constructed by the students for their homework assignments.

ASSESSMENT

Student's metacognitive questions: See activity 2 above.

Teacher assessment of students: Teacher will observe group work to assess how each individual is contributing to the group's task.

FOLLOW-UP

Content: If any group has not finished their preparations for their presentations tomorrow, they will be responsible for doing that as homework.

Process: Distribute survey to target sample.

Notes:

LESSON PLAN FOR LESSON: 12

TITLE: Presentations

OBJECTIVES

Content: Students will be able to explain their metacognitive processes in solving the problem their group had.

Process: Students in groups will make class presentations of their problem-solving endeavor.

Products: Presentations

MATERIALS AND RESOURCES:

TIME ESTIMATED: 1 period

INTRODUCTION OF LESSON (PROMPTS)

Objectives stated? _____√_____ yes _____ no

If no, how is interest to be raised?

Students recall prior knowledge? The whole lesson is on this.

Students make self-reference? The lesson involves metacognition.

Points essential to set forth?

ACTIVITIES/SEQUENCE

1. Each group will present its problem, its solution, and how they arrived at the solution.

2. At the end of the four presentations (if time permits), the teacher will once again review the problem-solving steps and the various strategies that they used.

ASSESSMENT

Student's metacognitive questions: See activities 1 and 2 above.

Teacher assessment of students: Teacher will evaluate presentations using checklist (see p. 114).

FOLLOW-UP

Content:

Process: Collect surveys.

Notes:

LESSON PLAN FOR LESSON: 13

TITLE: Final Report

OBJECTIVES

Content:

Process: Students will be able to tabulate a survey and produce a report of the results.

Products: Report on survey.

MATERIALS AND RESOURCES: Completed survey forms

TIME ESTIMATED: 1 period

INTRODUCTION OF LESSON (PROMPTS)

Objectives stated?   _____ √   yes   _____ no

If no, how is interest to be raised?

Students recall prior knowledge?

Students make self-reference?

Points essential to set forth?

ACTIVITIES/SEQUENCE

1. Students will decide how to tabulate data.

2. Students will carry out tabulations. (Whether this needs to be done in groups will depend on how many items there are to tabulate, the number of students surveyed, and the topics covered.)

3. Students will plan how to report the data. (Teacher may want to show them how to convert count to percents). They will need a graph or table as well as a narrative report.

4. Students will discuss what they can infer or generalize from the data. They will need to be able to justify their findings using the data they have collected. This will be part of the narrative.

5. Students will decide what to do with the report. They may want to send the report to the principal, to the classes of students who participated, to parents, to teachers, and/or to other staff members of the school (for example, if the survey concerned health issues, the school nurse should receive the report).

ASSESSMENT

Student's metacognitive questions: Almost all activities above require students to ask themselves how they should proceed, plan, infer.

Teacher assessment of students: Student reports

FOLLOW-UP

Content:

Process: Report will be sent to appropriate persons.

Notes:

Metrics

The middle school unit for mathematics shown below deals with metrics as a system of measurement. It includes conversion activities and information about the metric system.

UNIT PLAN		

TOPIC: Metric System of Measurement

Grade level or group: 6th grade

Estimated time: 11 periods

SUBJECT

Primary: Math

Others:

EDUCATIONAL OUTCOMES OF UNIT

Content: Students will convert within the metric system and solve real-life metric measurement problems.

Process: Students will use the process of comparing and contrasting ideas, using teacher-directed structured questioning strategies, a Taba Rterieval Chart, and cognitive mapping to understand the metric system and its uses.

Products: Math journals, Taba Retrieval Chart, cognitive map

RATIONALE: Since most of the world uses the metric system, students need to understand the system and how it works.

ASSESSMENT PLAN

Purpose:

How?	_____ Observation	_____ Checklist	_____ Informal Questions	√ Product
	_____ Written assignment	_____ Demonstration	√ Test	_____ Other

Test?	_____ Multiple choice	√ Completion	_____ Short essay	_____ Long essay
	_____ Combination			

SPECIAL NEEDS FOR UNIT (IF ANY)

Materials: Any textbook with metric measures, transparencies   **Time:**

Resource persons: **Space:**

LESSON TOPICS/TITLES

1. Teacher will give an introduction to the metric system. S/he will include how it differs from the U.S. system and why the United States has not converted to the metric system. Students start their math journals.

2. Students will learn the metric system prefixes using a mnemonic device. Develop cognitive map about uses and measures. Use story "Millie Meter" to motivate. Use "King Henry Died Monday Drinking Cold Milk" for mnemonic. Make conversions in metric using distance. (2 periods).

3. Conversions with mass in metrics. Develop Retrieval Chart on mass, distance, and capacity as they relate to various units of metric system. Worksheet.

[Continued on next page.]

NOTE: This unit developed by Cynthia Heaney, teacher.

4. Conversions with capacity in metrics. Plan a trip to Myrtle Beach, SC, using metrics. Analyze and calculate.

5. Estimation of common objects using metrics. Measure and compare with estimate.

6. Measure common items using metric measures (continuation).

7. Students will practice metric conversions for mass, capacity, and length from customary measures. Write persuasive entry in journal as to why classmates should use one of the two systems—metric or customary (English).

8. Students will solve real-life problems using metrics. They will use estimation to determine reasonableness of their answers. Skill drill.

9. Students will construct word problems of metric conversions. Students will evaluate for reasonableness.

10. Test. Journals checked.

Activities: In lesson plans

Nonroutine Problem Solving— Secondary

The secondary unit for mathematics addresses nonroutine problem solving. The topic could be presented in tech math, general math, vocational math, and any math subject where the concept of authentic problems and the development of problem-solving skills are taught.

UNIT PLAN

TOPIC: Nonroutine Problem Solving

Grade level or group: Secondary

Estimated time: 10 periods

SUBJECT

Primary: Math

Others:

EDUCATIONAL OUTCOMES OF UNIT

Content: Students will be able to solve nonroutine problems.

Process: Students will learn a repertoire of strategies for solving nonroutine problems and will be able to select (decision making) appropriate ones to solve given problems.

Products:

RATIONALE: Students need to have a variety of problem-solving skills in mathematics and be able to apply the skills appropriately for a variety of nonroutine types of problems.

ASSESSMENT PLAN

Purpose: Assess objectives above

How?	____ Observation	____ Checklist	____ Informal Questions	____ Product
	____ Written assignment	√ Demonstration	√ Test	____ Other

Test?	____ Multiple choice	√ Completion	____ Short essay	____ Long essay
	____ Combination			

SPECIAL NEEDS FOR UNIT (IF ANY)

Materials: A math text would be helpful, but not essential—need sets of word problems which use real-life situations. Problems must include ones which call for each of the solution strategies.

Time:

Resource persons:

Space:

[Continued on next page.]

NOTE: This unit adapted from project developed by Judy Merritt, teacher.

LESSON TOPICS/TITLES

1. Solve problems using the guess-and-check strategy

2. Solve problems using the strategy of solving simpler related problems

3. Solve problems by drawing a diagram

4. Solve problems using the strategy of working backwards

5. Knowing which strategy to use—decision making

6. Solve problems using the strategy of writing an equation

7. Solve problems using formulas

8. Solve problems using the strategy of logic

9. Reinforce the ability to make proper decisions about which strategy to use

10. Test

Activities: In lesson plans

Bibliography: Math texts and various other sources

Chapter Thirteen

Other Subject Areas

Space prohibits giving complete units and lessons in all subject areas; space even prohibits giving unit plans in all areas. A few subject areas have been selected to serve as examples, but it is important to realize that unit development can and should occur in every subject area or course. It is just as important in a hands-on vocational educational subject as it is in Advanced Placement English. Most of the examples we have chosen have come from K–12 classes. The procedure for developing and planning is as applicable to college, tech centers, vocational centers, and adult education programs as it is to the K–12 grades and subjects.

We have included in this chapter unit plans in science, foreign language, guidance, and media.

Science

UNIT PLAN	
TOPIC: 6 and 8 Legged Critters	SUBJECT
Grade level or group: Grades K–1	Primary: Science
Estimated time: 10 hours	Others:

EDUCATIONAL OUTCOMES OF UNIT

Content: Students will have a general understanding of insects and spiders

Process: Students will develop listening skills, sequence, compare/contrast, draw conclusions, and estimate.

Products: Insect show, bug jar, ant farm, food projects, retrieval chart

RATIONALE: Students should learn early about the wonders of nature. They are curious about bugs and enjoy learning about them.

ASSESSMENT PLAN

Purpose: To measure objectives informally

How?	√ Observation		Checklist	√ Informal Questions		√ Product
	Written assignment		Demonstration	Test		Other
Test?	Multiple choice		Completion	Short essay		Long essay
	Combination	(NOTE: Observation will serve as test due to the grade level.)				

[Continued on next page.]

NOTE: This unit developed by Barbara Hilton, teacher.

SPECIAL NEEDS FOR UNIT (IF ANY)

Materials: See list below   Time:

Resource persons: Space: Outdoors—insect show

LESSON TOPICS/TITLES

1. Introduce unit. Discuss assumptions about insects. Discuss insect body parts.

2. Caterpillars—life cycle

3. Butterflies—compare and contrast with caterpillars

4. Lady bugs, beetles (2 days)

5. Honeybees—sequencing

6. Ants, colonies

7. Grasshoppers

8. Spiders

9. Insects and spiders

10. Insect show

Activities: In lesson plans

List of materials:

quart glass jar for each child

insects

cheesecloth

rubber band

plastic insects

songs

finger plays

stories

sequence cards

paper plates

magazines

chart paper

clothespins

colored tissue paper

construction paper

ladybug hand puppet

cotton balls

fish bowl

sand and loose soil

sugar

20 ants

bread crumbs

masking tape

Snacks:

bread

Chinese noodles

raisins

bananas

candy (for eyes)

licorice (for feelers)

carrot sticks

cream cheese

peanut butter

UNIT PLAN	
TOPIC: Space Travel	SUBJECT
Grade level or group: Grade 6	Primary: Science
Estimated time: 15 periods	Others: Math

EDUCATIONAL OUTCOMES OF UNIT

Content: Students will learn how advancements in technology have enabled astronauts to travel in space.

Process: Students will collect data, make inferences, make predictions.

Products: Time line, rockets, space shuttle, costumes, essays, launch

RATIONALE: Students need to experience some of the aspects of space travel. They need to understand the many arrangements and technical activities that accompany a space launch. They also need to comprehend what it might be like to travel in space.

ASSESSMENT PLAN

Purpose:

How?	√ Observation	√ Checklist	√ Informal Questions	√ Product
	√ Written assignment	√ Demonstration	Test	Other

Test?	Multiple choice	Completion	Short essay	Long essay
	Combination			

SPECIAL NEEDS FOR UNIT (IF ANY)

Materials: Model of space shuttle (toy), shuttle kit to make plastic model one-half size, materials to make small rockets to launch, material for costumes, materials for mission control mock-up

Time:

Resource persons:

Space: To assemble module

LESSON TOPICS/TITLES

1. Introduce unit—famous people in space, astronauts from your state

2. Important space facts from 1961–1969, make time lines

3. How rockets work

4. Rocket experiments—shoot rockets in school yard, record data.

5. Assess the importance of rockets to the space program—small groups, report to class.

6. Space shuttle—parts and reusable parts

7. Living on the shuttle—examine food, clothing, sleep, exercise, personal hygiene.

8. Value of space shuttle to the space program

9. Brainstorm about occupations of those on the ground and in space. Each will pick which part they wish to play.

10. Toys in space—video and experiments (NASA)

[Continued on next page.]

11. Set up space shuttle; organize ground crew; make costumes; learn parts. (3 days)

12. Talk about problems astronauts face today. Write short essay for homework. Practice for space launch.

13. Space launch—discuss how it went afterward.

Activities: In lesson plans

BIBLIOGRAPHY

Baker, Wendy. 1986. *Americans in Space*. New York: Crescent Books.

Blumberg, Rhoda. 1980. *The First Travel Guide to the Moon: What to Pack, How to Go, and What to See When You Get There*. New York: Four Winds Press.

Dwiggins, Don. 1971. *Into the Unknown: The Story of Space Shuttles and Space Stations*. San Carlos, CA: Golden Gate Junior Books.

Eggen, Paul, and Main, June. 1990. *Developing Critical Thinking through Science, Book Two*. Pacific Grove, CA: Critical Thinking Press & Software.

Elementary School Aerospace Activities: A Resource for Teachers. Washington, DC: US Government Printing Office, Superintendent of Documents, 20402.

Gallant, Roy A. 1971. *Man's Reach for the Stars*. Garden City, NY: Doubleday.

Halpin, Myra. Space activities, suits, games, tapes, kits, slides, scripts, toys, etc. 605 Hammond St., Durham, NC 27704.

Kamerman, Sylvia E., ed. 1981. *Space and Science: Fiction Plays for Young People.* Boston: Plays, Inc.

Johnson Space Center, National Aeronautics and Space Administration, Houston, TX 77058

National Aeronautics Education Council, 806 15th St., N. W., Washington, DC 20005.

O'Connor, Karen. 1983. *Sally Ride and the New Astronauts.* New York: Franklin Watts, Inc.

United States National Aeronautics and Space Administration publications. Many are available free to teachers of all grade levels. NASA, Community and Education Services Branch, Public Affairs Division, 400 Maryland Ave., S. W., Room F6051, Washington, DC 20546

UNIT PLAN

TOPIC: Periodic Table

Grade level or group: Secondary

Estimated time: 9 periods

SUBJECT

Primary: Chemistry

Others:

EDUCATIONAL OUTCOMES OF UNIT

Content: Students will be able to use information about halogens and about the third row of the periodic table to apply to given situations.

Process: Students will be able to observe, record, analyze, and conclude about nonroutine experiments involving halogens and elements on the third row of the periodic table. They will be able to make predictions and evaluate outcomes.

Products: Experiment write-ups

RATIONALE: Chemistry students need to learn about the elements in the periodic table. However, its complexity and specificity makes the task a difficult one. The purpose of this type of presentation is that the students will discover the properties and behavior of various elements in specific groups through experimentation and analysis.

ASSESSMENT PLAN

Purpose: Measure knowledge of halogens and the third row of the periodic table

How?	√	Observation		Checklist	√	Informal Questions		Product
	√	Written assignment	√	Demonstration	√	Test		Other

Test?		Multiple choice		Completion		Short essay		Long essay
	√	Combination						

SPECIAL NEEDS FOR UNIT (IF ANY)

Materials: Lab equipment—test tubes, treated paper, apparatuses, burners, etc.—element samples, periodic table, chemistry text

Time:

Resource persons:

Space: Lab

LESSON TOPICS/TITLES

1. Halogens—electron configurations, prediction of size due to position on periodic table, role of oxidation

2. Students will perform the electrolysis of aqueous potassium iodide, observe, and draw conclusions.

3. Students will generalize to other halogens what they learned from their experiments and discussions. They will compare and analyze data and draw conclusions.

4. Small groups review findings and extensions.

5. Third row of periodic table will be introduced. Students will be asked to take what they know about properties of elements already studied and make predictions about the behavior of the elements in the third row. Teacher demonstration. Students will ask questions while the demonstration is taking place. They will be challenged to make predictions concerning other elements in the row.

[Continued on next page.]

6. Acid-base reactions—Students will perform lab experiments, observe, and record data. They will observe the reaction of an amphoteric substance and form a concept about this.

7. Students will discuss their experiments, make predictions about other elements in row, and discuss new concept: amphoteric.

8. Small group review of materials on two topics, halogens and the elements in the third row of the periodic table. Then total class will discuss any questions or concepts.

9. Test—Students will be asked to apply, analyze, and evaluate. They will be asked to design an experiment to find specific information.

Activities: In lesson plans

BIBLIOGRAPHY

Collette, A. T., and Chiapetta, E. L. 1984. *Science Instruction in the Middle and Secondary Schools.* St. Louis, MO: The Times Mirror/Mosby College Publ.

Malm, L. E. 1963. *Chemistry: An Experimental Science Laboratory Manual.* San Francisco, CA: W. H. Freeman, 80–81, 84–85.

McClellan, A. L. 1963. *Chemistry: An Experimental Science Teachers Guide.* San Francisco, CA: W. H. Freeman, 635–80.

Pimentel, G. C. 1963. *Chemistry: An Experimental Science.* San Francisco, CA: W. H. Freeman, 352–76.

Foreign Language

UNIT PLAN

TOPIC: Spanish and Spanish Culture

Grade level or group: Grades 7–8

Estimated time: 13 periods

SUBJECT

Primary: Spanish

Others: Social Studies, Art, Music

EDUCATIONAL OUTCOMES OF UNIT

Content: Students will increase their knowledge of Spain and their appreciation of Spanish culture. Students will be able to use SER and ESTAR appropriately.

Process: Students will use verbs in sentences, written and oral, and will be able to discuss the content in Spanish with the teacher and other students. Students will be able to reason abstractly.

Products: Food, drawings

RATIONALE: Students need to appreciate the Spanish culture while improving their Spanish skills and vocabulary.

ASSESSMENT PLAN

Purpose: To assess objectives above

How?		Observation		Checklist	√	Informal Questions	√	Product
	√	Written assignment	√	Demonstration	√	Test	√	Other

Test?		Multiple choice	√	Completion	√	Short essay		Long essay
		Combination						

SPECIAL NEEDS FOR UNIT (IF ANY)

Materials: Overhead transparencies, maps, slides, pictures, food

Time:

Resource persons: Use peer tutors

Space: Food preparation

LESSON TOPICS/TITLES

1. Students engage in activities to differentiate SER and ESTAR. They infer reasons to use each and respond orally and in written form in Spanish.

2. Students study vocabulary to be used with ESTAR to describe temporary conditions. Teacher acts out expression and students play charades.

3. Students use SER and ESTAR with maps and pictures (places in a Spanish town), geographic points, mountains, World's Fair, people and their occupations. Discuss in Spanish. Take notes. Expand vocabulary.

4. Students study families. They use SER and ESTAR to describe their family and friends. Draw family member(s) or friend(s).

5. Cataluna. Towns, location, Badalona. Students will learn song. Increase vocabulary about towns.

[Continued on next page.]

NOTE: This unit developed by Margaret Roberts, teacher.

6. Spanish time line. Discuss in Spanish the time line. Slide presentation. Olympics. Pen Pal.

7. Separation of Cataluna from Spain. Discuss and debate both sides. Learn about language, history. Listen to tape in Catalan and Spanish (elementary level). Overhead transparencies on language differences.

8. Foods from different areas of Spain. What comes from different groups who settled there. Use maps.

9. Prepare food "pa amb tomquet" (bread and ham). Eat it. Learn how to use "bota."

10. Art from famous Catalan artists—Antoni Gaudi, architect; Salvador Dali, surrealism; Joan Miró, surrealism—and music by Casals. Produce similar art work. (3 periods)

11. Open-book questions. Questions and responses all in Spanish.

Activities: In lesson plans

BIBLIOGRAPHY

All Barcelona. 1975. Barcelona, Spain: Escudo de Oro, S. A.

All Montserrat. 1974. Barcelona, Spain: Escudo de Oro, S. A.

Barnard, C. N. 1991. Barcelona. *National Geographic Traveler* 8 (6) (Nov/Dec): 96.

Bon Appetite 1992. 37 (5).

Cross, E., and Cross, W. 1985. *Spain.* Chicago: Children's Press.

Gaudi. 1991. Barcelona, Spain: Escudo de Oro, S. A.

Leon, V. 1984. *Seventy Spanish Culture Activities.* Portland, ME: J. Weston Walch.

Llovet, J. 1982. *Barcelona.* Barcelona, Spain: Peralt Montagut-Ediciones.

Morris, J. 1988. *Spain.* Englewood Cliffs, NJ: Prentice Hall.

Peffer, R. 1984. "Catalonia: Spain's Country within a Country." *National Geographic* 95 (Jan).

Time-Life, eds. 1986. *Spain.* Amsterdam, Holland: Time-Life Books.

Serrat, Joan Manuel. 1978. *Que Bonita es Badalona* on audio tape. Ariola Eurodisc, S. A.

Valette, J. P., and Valette, R. M. 1984. *Spanish for Mastery I.* Lexington, MA: D. C. Heath.

Woods, G. 1987. *Spain, A Shining New Democracy.* Minneapolis, MN: Dillon Press.

Guidance

UNIT PLAN

TOPIC: Learn How to Stick Up for Yourself

Grade level or group: Grade 6

Estimated time: 10 periods

SUBJECT

Primary: Guidance

Others: Reading, Health

EDUCATIONAL OUTCOMES OF UNIT

Content: Students will know ways of developing their personal power.

Process: Students will be able to implement techniques which empower them to be assertive and feel good about themselves.

Products: Matrix, activities, "happiness list," situation matrix, "I did it list"

RATIONALE: The assumption is made that personal power and self-esteem have strategies or skills which students can learn. Each student needs to know what these are and how to go about enhancing their feelings about themselves.

ASSESSMENT PLAN

Purpose:

How?   √ Observation   ____ Checklist   √ Informal Questions   ____ Product

       √ Written assignment   ____ Demonstration   ____ Test   ____ Other

Test? ____ Multiple choice   ____ Completion   ____ Short essay   ____ Long essay

       ____ Combination

SPECIAL NEEDS FOR UNIT (IF ANY)

Materials: Time:

Resource persons: Space:

LESSON TOPICS/TITLES

1. What does it mean to stick up for yourself?

2. You are responsible for your behavior and feelings.

3. Making choices

4. Naming your feelings

5. Claiming your feelings

6. Naming and claiming your dreams

7. Naming and claiming your needs

[Continued on next page.]

NOTE: This unit developed by Penelope Fulton, teacher.

8. Getting and using power

9. Learning to like yourself

10. Sticking up for yourself from now on

Activities: In lesson plans

BIBLIOGRAPHY

Addenholdt-Elliott, M. 1987. *Perfectionism: What's Bad about Being Too Good?* Minneapolis, MN: Free Spirit Publ.

Dinkmeyer, D., and Losoncy, L. 1987. *The Encouragement Book*. Englewood Cliffs, NJ: Prentice Hall.

Good, P. 1987. *In Pursuit of Happiness*. New View.

Kaufman, G., and Raphael, L. 1990. *Stick up for Yourself! Every Kid's Guide to Personal Power and Positive Self-esteem*. Minneapolis, MN: Free Spirit.

Schmitz, C., and Galbraith, J. 1985. *Managing the Social and Emotional Needs of the Gifted*. Minneapolis, MN: Free Spirit.

Wind by the Sea. Needham Heights, MA: Silver, Burdette & Ginn.

Media

UNIT PLAN

TOPIC: Media and Research

SUBJECT

Grade level or group: Secondary

Primary: Research

Estimated time: 8 periods

Others:

EDUCATIONAL OUTCOMES OF UNIT

Content: Students will be able to locate various types of material in the media center/library.

Process: Students will be able to direct themselves in finding various kinds of material in the library—reference sources for research topics, personal information, and recreational materials. They will use analysis to plan their search.

Products:

RATIONALE: All students need to be able to direct themselves in finding materials in a media center/library. They need to learn a procedure for locating various kinds of information.

ASSESSMENT PLAN

Purpose:

How?	√ Observation	___ Checklist	___ Informal Questions	___ Product
	___ Written assignment	___ Demonstration	___ Test	___ Other
Test?	___ Multiple choice	___ Completion	___ Short essay	___ Long essay
	___ Combination			

SPECIAL NEEDS FOR UNIT (IF ANY)

Materials: Reader's Guide to Periodical Literature, computer, software, Short Story Index, Granger's Index to Poetry

Time:

Resource persons:

Space: Media Center or Library

LESSON TOPICS/TITLES

1. How to find a needle in a haystack—students will construct a logical search of the Reader's Guide.

2. Searching the future today—using simple on-line search of an electronic bibliographic database.

3. Fitting pieces of a puzzle with biographies—locate biographical information on any person.

4. Taking the short cut to the Short Story—locating short stories.

5. The short story—locate and integrate information on short story writers and their writing styles.

6. Pinpointing the poem—locate a poem from a collection.

7. Teaching strategies for an integrated search—operate a computer terminal for an Occupational Information Service.

8. Teenagers in their world—putting it into practice. Assessment—given information on books, poems, stories, authors, students will locate them.

Activities: In lesson plans

Chapter Fourteen

Helping Students Do Research

Students in the 21st Century will need research skills. The need to obtain current information is already a critical skill for students at institutions of higher learning. Strides in making information accessible have been mind boggling. In media centers, a student can use a computer terminal to access in seconds the references s/he needs. Annotated references tell the student at a glance if the content will be useful. An entire set of encyclopedia can be on a disc in the media center or library. Interlibrary loans can be done with on-line access. Microfilm/fiche store locally other needed data.

How do you get students into the research mode? Piaget believed that if you told children the answers to their questions, you robbed them of the joy of finding out for themselves. Kindergartners can look for answers to questions in material that you arrange for them to examine. Primary grade students can gather information from their homes and communities.

Upper grade students can learn what resources are available. Most classrooms have resources in the room—atlases, encyclopedia, dictionaries, textbooks. Start early on taking classes to the media center/library and showing them how to find things there. These are all good beginnings.

Students need to learn that there are systematic, effective ways to obtain and describe information. You could display graphic organizers from data in newspapers, magazines, textbooks, and reference sources. Most study-skills programs include a section on finding information. Not only is it important to find the data, but students need to know effective ways to record the data for future use and later referral.

Access to computers in school will make changes in how students record, reference, and write their reports. In spite of all these changes, the processes of collecting data, organizing, and synthesizing them into some coherent whole still need to be taught using whatever tools are available.

Although the processes described below are particularly designed for middle and secondary students (1987), they can be modified for elementary students.

Selecting the Question

Students experience surprising difficulty in choosing topics to research. They seem to have no topic or a dozen topics. You will need to assist them in selecting or generating a topic.

Two major areas of constraint must be addressed in selecting a topic for research: personal limitations and environmental limitations. Personal constraints refer primarily to commitment. How much time, effort, money, is s/he willing to spend? The extremes in this—no effort to need for perfection—are probably both disadvantageous.

Most teachers strive to inculcate good work habits in students, work habits which include doing the best you can at whatever task you are attempting. There are some students, however, who believe that their work needs to be perfect. Since perfection is not usually attained, these students may translate their performance as a failure. This leads to low self-concept and undue pressure by the student on him or herself. In these few cases, you would be doing such students a favor by helping them to conceptualize "close enough."

The much more frequent situation is one where the student has ideas that far exceed his or her commitment. This is where the meta-cognitive operations of planning come to bear. Before you allow a student to embark on a research project of any complexity, the student needs to analyze what the project will entail. In doing this, the student should be aware of the environmental constraints which may prevent or limit the project's successful outcome.

The research project worksheet presented on p. 223 may be helpful.

In considering what topic to choose, students may ask themselves some of these questions:

- What am I curious about but have not had time to learn about? (curiosity)

- Is there some theory or idea I would like to prove or disprove? (theory)

- Is there some technique or method of research I would like to try? Do I already have some data I could treat in some way? (methodology)

- What am I interested in that I would like to know more about? (exploration)

- Is there a topic or idea that is a "hot issue" or difficult to research that I might get some recognition for researching? (prestige)

- Is there a current issue or topic that I should consider? (immediate issue/ topic)

The answers to these questions can be entered in the matrix on p. 223.

Research Design

Once the topics have been evaluated and one selected, the student can use the problem-solving worksheet (Chapter 5, p. 60) to plan the steps in his or her research. One of the first questions to be answered is about the research design; will it be qualitative or quantitative, and will it be descriptive or experimental? The question or topic drives the design; the design drives the research process.

Qualitative Design

Qualitative design is a systematic study of an individual and/or group within their natural surroundings. This design is used in case studies, ethnographic research, anthropological studies, and various ecological studies. Some of these require the researcher to take extensive field notes, keep logs, and spend considerable time sifting through material collected. The report will require a synthesis of findings.

Because of its complexity, qualitative research should probably be encouraged only in students who are serious about their study and have the developmental level of cognition necessary to engage in inducing patterns and concepts from large amounts of data. They will need to use a neutral vocabulary and report in a logical and unbiased language. The case study is probably the least complicated of qualitative investigations because it limits its topic to one individual.

Advise students of the ethics of research and the privacy concerns brought about when one studies someone else. You may want to set up an ethics panel in the class to approve student topics which involve intervening in the lives of other individuals or collecting private information on them. The American Psychological Association has published criteria and these are summarized in most psychology textbooks. The major questions are as follows: "Will what is being proposed in any

RESEARCH PROJECT WORKSHEET

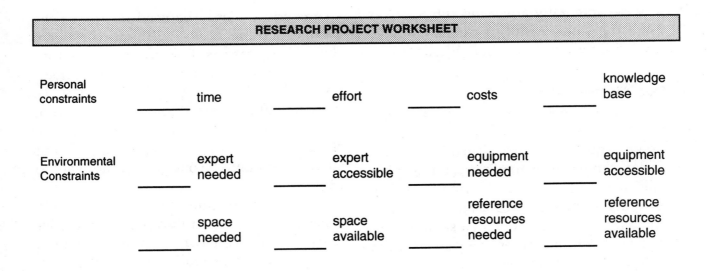

Personal constraints _____ time _____ effort _____ costs _____ knowledge base

Environmental Constraints _____ expert needed _____ expert accessible _____ equipment needed _____ equipment accessible

_____ space needed _____ space available _____ reference resources needed _____ reference resources available

Source/ Topics	Constraints						
	maturity level	information level	social acceptance	time, money, equipment	adult assistance	intended audience	ethics
curiosity							
theory							
methodology							
exploration							
prestige							
immediate issue/topic							

way detrimentally affect the subjects?" and "Will the study result in public display of private information on individuals without their consent?"

Quantitative Design

Quantitative designs are used to show relationships and to describe phenomena. Surveys and questionnaires fall in this category of designs. Interviews, mailings, and telephone calls are used to collect information on attitudes about and understandings of some topic. The effort is made to obtain a sample that is representative of a larger group so that generalizations can be inferred from the responses. Such reports usually have frequency numbers, percents, and analyses by subgroups. The wording of a survey's statements or questions and its format contribute to the accuracy obtained. The percentage of responses received is also important. There are several excellent publications available on sociometric instruments, such as questionnaires and surveys. If students are going to be engaging in this type of research, you will want your media center or your class resources to include one or more of these references.

Predictive quantitative studies collect data on one or more measures which have established predictive value for some element, usually one for which direct data is difficult to obtain or measure. For instance, there are studies that show that when students "enjoy" reading, they check out more books. If one of your students wanted to measure the number of checkouts for a certain group prior to some program and after the program, s/he could infer whether the program enhanced students enjoyment of reading. Such a measure is called an *unobtrusive measure* since the subjects of the study are not aware that the data are being collected and, in and of itself, the process is not any kind of treatment or intervention.

Teachers and other professionals might look at the at-risk research. There are characteristics of middle and high school students who drop out or fail, characteristics that can be observed in primary grades. A survey of these characteristics could be used to predict the number of students who will be at-risk later in their school careers. Because this would involve information about achievement, attendance, discipline referrals, intersocial skills, parental status, family incomes, etc., this is not likely to be a suitable topic for secondary students but might be appropriate for adult students. It might be one you would want to explore!

The *passive* quantitative method is used to collect data in order to investigate the relationships between two or more variables. These correlational studies do not establish cause-effect relationships; rather, if the correlation coefficients are significant, they show that a relationship exists between the variables. Only a controlled study such as those in experimental research can establish cause-effect.

Experimental Studies

Experimental studies are those where the researcher sets up or obtains a control group(s) to be used with the experimental group (the one to be treated) so that when common measures are compared on the two (or more), any differences in the results can be attributed to the treatment. In education and all social sciences, these studies are quasi-experimental because it is impossible to control all the variables as a physicist might do. Human elements always enter into educational research.

Quasi-experimental studies must be carefully planned before they are begun. If you are doing a naturalistic study where you are observing behavior at various times and under various conditions, you are not "treating" anyone; you are observing them in their habitat. On the other hand, in experimental studies, everything possible is held constant in the experimental and control groups except the one variable of interest. If there are differences in outcomes between the groups and all else is the same, the researcher can conclude that the introduced variation produced the difference in the groups. Most student research studies will not be this rigorous because there are constraints that cannot be overcome—time, space, equipment, cost.

Resources

When the students have listed what they know and what data they need to gather (on the problem solving worksheet), they need to list the resources they have available and what other kinds they need. At this point, you will be able to assist them in expanding their resource list. Your media specialist might also be able to help. Media specialists sometimes can provide a list of available basic resources before the students try to select their topics.

Preparing Results

All quantitative methods will require some mathematical computation and usually some kind of graphic display—graph, matrix, table, illustration, diagram or spatial array—along with the narrative report. Students' mathematical capabilities will dictate to some extent what kind of study they will do and what kind of help they will need to process the data.

Surveys and questionnaires require the least sophisticated types of calculations since they usually report frequencies and percents. The passive and predictive quantitative studies are usually treated with correlational statistics. Many current calculators can perform correlations if the data is entered in pairs. Computer programs will carry out more complex interrelationships. Regression coefficients are also used in some of these reports. In addition, most reports include measures of central tendency (averages). These are mean, median, and mode. If measures of variation are needed, then variance and standard deviations can be computed as well. These, too, can be performed on some calculators and most computer statistical programs.

The most complex statistics will be part of the experimental designs. Descriptive data for almost any study include means and standard deviations for the total group and subgroups and correlation coefficients. With experimental designs, the questions center around whether there are significant differences between and among groups after some kind of treatment has occurred. There also are tests calculated to reveal the significance of differences between groups or between the same group over time (repeated measures). These will be beyond the training of most of your students. If you are using a mentor system for the students who are doing research and the mentors want to serve as resources to assist with the data analysis, these types of studies will be more feasible.

Types of Data

Students need to know that the kind of data they collect will limit the kind of analyses they can calculate. The four basic kinds of data are nominal, ordinal, interval, and ratio.

Nominal data simply designate that individuals or things belong or do not belong to some group. Frequency tables show how many people are Republicans, how many are Democrats, and what percent of the total each represents. Studies in the daily newspapers reflect this kind of descriptive data: What percent of the work force is female? How many homes are below the poverty level on income? What percent of the nuclear weapons are controlled by the United States or Russia? What percent of your tax dollars is spent for each of the categories of county or federal expenditures? Nominal data are important and interesting, but after you have counted and expressed them in percent or some other ratio, no further analysis can be made.

Ordinal data are ranked data. They are ordered so that one is higher than another, but the distance between any two is not necessarily the same as the distance between any other two. If you line up the students in your class by height and write down their rank in relation to the other students, you will know their rank, but not how tall they are or if the difference in height between student 5 and student 6 is one-half inch or two inches or whether the difference between student 6 and student 7 in the row is one inch or six inches.

Ordinal measures are useful in obtaining

medians. For instance, if you were interested in income levels in your town, you would determine the wages of all the income-receiving individuals who lived in the city limits. If you averaged these for a mean, the results would be misleading because Mr. Jones is a multimillionaire and his income will inordinately influence the "average" income. If you arrange all the incomes in order of amount, you can obtain the income of the person in the middle (the median)—half the town earns less and half earns more. This would be more representative of the earnings of the town. Percentile ranks may also be obtained for any point on the range. You can determine that 75% of the townspeople make less than a certain amount, etc.

Interval data refer to measures on a continuum of numbers in which the distance between each quantity and the next is the same amount. You grade a set of papers and the maximum number of points a student can earn is 100. Each student receives a number which represents how much of the 100 points s/he has earned. The supposition is that the distance between 69 and 70 is the same as between 98 and 99. The properties of interval data allow researchers to carry out many tests and analyses. It is the type of data most often reported in experimental studies.

The last category, *ratio*, assumes that there is a defined point where a scale begins and ends. Such sets of numbers would have absolute zeroes. This category is used in physics and mathematics, but it is not appropriate in education. Can you say without any doubt that the students know nothing?

Conclusion

In summary, the student needs to select a topic after considering the personal and environmental constraints it presents. Then the student needs to design the type of study to be done. The topic will influence this choice. Once the design has been selected, the ways of collecting the data necessary for carrying out the design need to be planned. When the data are collected and analyzed, the student will prepare a report of the collection and analyses and the conclusions of his or her study. The report may be both oral and written, and it may have products and constructions. It is usually important for students to have an opportunity to present to others what they have done.

Chapter Fifteen

Curriculum and Instruction

Four levels of curriculum and instruction will be discussed in this chapter: classroom, grade, school, and district.

Classroom

There is no teaching mandate that is going to effect instruction if the teacher does not philosophically agree with the concept. The key is the teacher—any change in education will fail unless the teachers support it. HOT is no different, and since it is an instructional component, the teacher is even more vital to its success.

What are the steps in bringing about a change in curriculum and instruction within the classroom?

1. The teacher believes all children can learn.
2. The teacher believes all children can engage in higher order thinking.
3. The teacher decides to integrate higher order thinking into the content s/he teaches.
4. The teacher plans units and lessons to teach for, of, and about thinking.
5. The teacher implements the plans.
6. The teacher evaluates the effectiveness of the instruction.
7. The teacher revises/modifies his or her plans for the future.

As you can see, the attitude of the teacher toward change is a major factor in infusing HOT into the content areas. When teachers are already feeling pressured to do more and more in less and less time, it is no wonder that they may throw up their hands when someone suggests just one more thing. The reason to implement a new program, then, must be compelling. This is why this book opened with a rationale for teaching higher order thinking.

If you are a teacher and have read this far, you have no doubt agreed with the need to continue and/or augment the teaching of HOT in your classroom. There are many teachers who are willing to teach HOT but do not feel able to initiate the changes it will take—some because they cannot generate the energy, others because they do not know how to begin. It doesn't take as much effort as you might think. You can infuse HOT without changing the subject matter but merely by changing the processes the students use in studying the subject and by developing some process objectives to go with the content objectives you already have. If you do not know how to begin, you can take the ideas from the sample lessons and incorporate them into your own lessons. Part II of this book contains many examples which may be useful. Also, check with other teachers who may be developing lessons you can observe.

Those of you who feel comfortable developing HOT lessons can invite other teachers to observe. The test of any staff development program is, "Did I get anything I can use in my classroom tomorrow?" The ease of implementing HOT processes is sure to make the answer "Yes" and your staff development a success.

The 4th step above deals with the teacher planning for, of, and about thinking. (See Chapter 7 for illustrations and more detail.)

Teaching for Thinking

In teaching *for* thinking, you have the students do something to the content in order to reach some content objective. It you look at the thinking skills and strategies taxonomy presented earlier in the book (p. 106), you can decide which of the processes you want the students to use to reach your content objectives. Instead of asking them to regurgitate information from the text or a lecture, you ask them to summarize, outline, make inferences, or whatever seems most appropriate. You do not teach them the process although you may have to clarify what it is.

All lessons can be broken down into three parts—planning, implementing, and evaluating. Planning is the most important because components not built in during planning are not likely to happen. Teaching for thinking can be incorporated in the planning with little change. Consider whether the activity you have selected would be better done individually or in a group. Plan how you will group if that is your choice. During implementation, the only difference may be the amount of time it takes to complete the tasks. Thinking takes a lot longer than copying.

If you decide to use group tasks instead of individual assignments, this will need to be structured for the students. Whenever you use groups, you should ask the groups to reflect upon how it went and how they could have been more effective. This builds group social skills and cooperation. During planning, you construct whatever evaluation instrument you plan to use to see if the students met the objectives. Evaluation, then, is simply the execution of that plan. In teaching for thinking, you do not have a higher order thinking process objective nor do you teach a HOT skill. Your evaluation will only assess your content objectives.

Teaching of Thinking

Teaching *of* thinking in the lesson requires some additional planning. Not only do you have content objectives, you have process objectives—in this case, a higher order thinking skill or strategy. You are going to teach it directly to the students as well as teaching them some content.

If you write your content objectives first, a higher order thinking skill or strategy may suggest itself from the content. Select only one to teach in this lesson. Present the content material and the accompanying activities, and at the place where the higher order thinking process is needed, stop the progression of the content and teach the process as illustrated in Chapter 7.

For review, the steps included defining, illustrating, giving examples of the skill, modelling, working through the skill with the students, and practice. If you want to evaluate how well they mastered the skill, you could give them new material on which they would use the skill. It would be too soon to "grade" them on the process. Since processes take practice and feedback, several practice sessions would be needed before a process could be expected to be carried out effectively and efficiently.

Teaching about Thinking

Teaching *about* thinking deals with the metacognitive aspects of thinking. In the planning stage, you may want to plan a time when the students reflect upon their thinking. Early in the lesson, you may want to have them engage in planning what they will do, how they will do it, and what they predict will happen. At the end of some part of the lesson, you may want to build in questions such as the following: How did we arrive at our answer? How did the group function? What did we do best? What do we need to work on? How can I keep track of how well I'm doing? Is there a better way to organize this material? Is there a better way to solve this problem?

For further suggestions on how you might integrate higher order thinking into your classroom, you may want to read sections under special content areas in Part II of this book. Remember to be alert to possibilities for transfer of processes to different content areas or of content to different processes. You can borrow from more than one and put them together in a different way. That is the hallmark of strategies; they can be adjusted and recombined depending on the situation. In another time and place with a different set of circumstances and content, another arrangement of skills and strategies might be indicated. One's ability to make these adaptations to ever-changing conditions is what makes humans so unique.

Grade

Until you have tried some of the skills in your lessons, you probably should not try to influence other teachers who teach the same students and/or the same grade to try what you are doing. If all of the teachers at your grade level have received some training in teaching higher order thinking, then discussions could be very valuable in saving each of you instructional time and planning time. Suppose one of you plans to teach organizing in social science class. Teachers teaching these same students other content could develop ways to practice organizing in their subject after you have taught the strategy. If you are in a self-contained classroom, you can share your successes with the other teachers in grade-level meetings. They will not want your students to be able to do something theirs cannot do.

Teacher agreement on what skills or strategies to work on at your grade level would be an important step in the orderly presentation of higher order thinking to the students at your level of instruction. If the other teachers at that grade level in your school do not want to work together on teaching a skill or strategy, it is probably better to let the idea lie. This does not mean that you should not go ahead with your teaching and try to make it as interesting and exciting as you can. Word will get around. Meanwhile, you can informally share in the lounge some of the things you are doing.

Teachers will steal ideas in a minute! Be willing to share with anyone who asks. The grade level chairperson can place the topic on the agenda of your monthly or weekly meetings; each person can share what s/he has tried and how it worked. Communication is vital to nurturing and spreading opportunities to learn in different ways. The national and local impetus to integrate the curriculum

may make the task of transfer easier to accomplish. If writing, spelling, science, mathematics, and social studies are integrated into a unit on ecology, the use of HOT skills and strategies can also be suggested by the teacher(s) in the various activities/subjects. Ideas on curriculum integration can be found in the October 1991, issue of *Educational Leadership*.

School

School-level planning for curriculum and instruction which incorporates higher order thinking is usually a product of teacher's meetings. While it would be best if such an offering came at the request of teachers following a needs assessment instrument or faculty discussion, the school may offer staff development for integrating higher order thinking in the content areas because it is part of the adopted curriculum.

Many schools first utilize a motivational speaker who can present an inspirational session on infusing higher order thinking. That can be a good beginning. Without follow-up, little is likely to come from such a one-day stand. Teachers need some nitty-gritty know-how, help, and support over a prolonged period of time. If the teachers are the ones who want this and are doing the staff-development planning, they will build these follow-ups into their plans.

Subsequent sessions for teachers in a school should address which higher order thinking skills and strategies should be taught *directly* at which grade levels. You cannot teach all skills and strategies at every grade level, nor would you want to. Since all upper strategies presume competence in the skills and strategies below them, the teachers might want to develop a rather loose scope and sequence for where the skills will be taught and where the strategies will be addressed and practiced for mastery. In order to do this, the group will need to select a taxonomy or set of skills. For instance, the group might use the taxonomy presented in this book or use Bloom's taxonomy or *Tactics for Thinking's* set of skills or one of the other commercially available programs. (See taxonomies in Chapter 3 and programs in Chapter 16.)

The teachers are the best equipped to answer questions concerning developmental appropriateness. They may want to consider a spiral curriculum where a skill is introduced early, then recycled, expanded, and elaborated at a higher grade, much as curricula treat American history (Beyer 1988).

District

District implementation of thinking skills programs may offer resources a school could not afford but may tap the greatest resistance on the part of teachers. New demands from central offices are not well received by most teachers unless the rationale and resources are made clear. Grass-root movements starting at the teacher level will have greater acceptance. If the teachers at one or more schools have developed procedures for implementing higher order thinking in their curriculum, the district may be able to build on that.

If a district curriculum committee, with representatives from each school, could initiate the development of a program and invite teacher suggestions and requests for assistance, the success ratio would probably go up. Such a committee could also develop a scope and sequence of activities in higher order thinking.

The important goal is to improve students' ability to think at higher levels of complexity and efficiency. There is no guarantee that they will all be good problem solvers, only that they will be *better* problem solvers. A district committee could also respond to requests for support in the schools' and teachers' efforts in planning staff development and in obtaining resources to assist teachers.

Typically, a district will select a particular approach to higher order thinking, obtain materials, and offer training. There are many programs on the market. Most require staff development; almost all have materials. A district may choose to write its own higher order thinking program. Some districts having the skilled staff to develop such programs have elected to do this. For each one of those, there are 99 who will select one of the commercial programs or do nothing at all. Many of the commercial programs, particularly those which require a pull-out or separate class time for HOT, have a scope and sequence developed.

Selecting a commercial program does not end the problem of implementation in schools, grade, and classroom because some arrangements must be made to deliver the staff development, and funds must be found to purchase the materials. In the chapter on commercially available programs (Chapter 16), some criteria for selecting a program will be suggested.

Most teachers are teaching *for* thinking; however, most schools do not have any systematic or schoolwide plan for selecting and sequencing a set of skills and strategies. Some states have mandated teachers to engage students in higher order thinking. Legislators argued that the schools would not get around to doing it unless they passed legislation and funded the efforts at the state level. It is doubtful that you can mandate thinking. Putting higher order thinking skills and strategies in the curriculum guides for districts and states will not assure implementation. It might lead to behaviors by teachers of "all right students, now we are going to think. There are five steps to thinking. Today we will take up the first one...." If only it were that easy!

District personnel who may be assigned to implement a program in higher order thinking would do well to review the steps in curriculum books on how to bring about change. One such book is *Taking Charge of Change* (Hord, Rutherford, Huling-Austin & Hall, ASCD, 1987). The reform movements are not going to let this lie dormant. The International Assessment of Education results have been too embarrassing for the United States. Some state departments of education have initiated statewide efforts on higher order thinking. One of the earliest was the state of Maryland, which began its program in 1984, funding projects in the school districts to develop higher order thinking (McTighe & Cutlip 1986). Delaware put out its assessment and plans in 1988. In 1989 South Carolina's legislature mandated the developing of higher order thinking in the schools. Other states have approached the need in different ways.

The most essential ingredient to improving student achievement is improving the quality of curriculum and instruction. Appropriate assessment is, of course, important also. To improve curriculum and instruction, educators will need to embed higher order thinking in all curricula. In the 1988 ASCD Yearbook (Brandt, ed.), this concept was addressed at the curriculum level in ten different content areas and included general observations and recommendations.

The plan to develop national tests may give impetus to these changes. The emphasis will, hopefully, be on how well students achieve the published objectives and not on how well students compare with one another. The National Assessment of Educational Progress has approached student achievement in subject areas by reporting what students at certain ages know and do not know, rather than how one group of students ranks compared to another. This type of information could be a basis for changing instruction and curriculum. It could also guide students and parents as to what students need to achieve next.

Chapter Sixteen

Programs Available from Outside Sources

When mandates are handed down to districts and/or schools, the first question that usually comes from the recipient of the mandate is, Is there a program already out there that will do the job? Although there are some people who insist on doing everything themselves even if someone else has already done it, most educators do not want to reinvent the wheel. On the other hand, some administrators buy everything that comes along, looking for a "quick fix" without consideration of whether there is any evidence that the program in question works. Unfortunately, in education there are no quick fixes. Tight budgets have reduced some of these purchases, but millions of dollars are spent each year on programs that sound good but have not been adequately evaluated.

Resnick (1987) laments the lack of adequate research on the effectiveness of many of the higher order thinking (HOT) programs. These programs have proliferated in the past ten years, and many of them have little research data showing whether or not they are effective in improving students' ability to think. Part of the problem is that there is lack of agreement on what constitutes higher order thinking and how to measure it. (This was discussed in more detail in Chapter 8.)

Since some HOT programs are very expensive and require one to three years of teacher training by certified trainers, a district does not want to make a poor choice. Consumable materials for each child can make the cost of such programs prohibitive.

Over 550 programs have been reviewed by the authors. Some are not included below because they lacked research evidence of effectiveness, did not have a complete staff-development program easily available, were not comprehensive enough for general use,

lacked sufficient information, or some other specific reason. The authors have received training in more than ten of the better known programs and have either visited sites where others were implemented or have interacted with the materials.

Many programs are for only a few grade levels, others are subject specific, and training in others is difficult to arrange or inordinately expensive. Each program selected for review will be presented with the same format. Omitted information was unavailable at the time of writing. If the developer is someone other than the contact person, it will be noted in the description.

Costs of these programs are variable depending on

- staff-development requirements—the number of staff-development days required, their location (out of town or on site), the number of trainees attending

- the option to train local teachers as trainers—the availability of teachers to train, length of training, accommodations

- materials required—the types of manuals needed (student/teacher), the necessity to purchase student materials (may make many programs' cost prohibitive), whether student materials are consumable, whether computers are required for implementation

- class set-up required—whether separate physical facilities, class sections, and/or new teachers are needed

- the availability of trainers

The first set of programs are separate from the regular curriculum of a school. All of these assume that the skills and strategies learned in the program will transfer to the content areas and to life, yet few have explicit experiences to teach transfer. A few, by nature of the content used in the examples, have a better chance of achieving some transfer.

The second set do not stand alone, although they may not be clearly integrated into content curricula.

Should the reader wish to explore further the programs available, the following sources will prove helpful:

- *Resources for Teaching Thinking* (Research for Better Schools 1990), an overview of 520 programs;

- *Educational Programs That Work* (National Diffusion Network 1991), overview of 180 programs;

- *Developing Minds: A Resource Book for Teaching Thinking*, (Costa, ASCD, 1985), overview of 54 programs (revised edition 1990); and

- *Developing a Thinking Skills Program*, (Beyer 1988), overview of 20 programs.

On page 235 is a list of questions which may be helpful when exploring commercially available HOTS programs.

Remember, programs do not teach higher order thinking to students; teachers do. Whatever program is being considered, it must be usable by the teachers.

Program Evaluation

The inclusion of a program in the following pages does not constitute approval by the authors. The information is listed for your consideration in making decisions for your district or school. As noted above, the first group (beginning p. 237) offers a separate course and are not integrated into the content areas. The second group (beginning p. 246) are integrated into the content areas. Both sets are arranged in alphabetical order by program title.

Other Programs

The above programs only scratch the surface of those on the market. There are others which will be mentioned here that are also useful for particular needs.

Two programs which have summer institutes each year to train teachers in creative problem solving are the Center for Creative Learning (PO Box 619, Honeoye, NY 14471) and the Creative Education Foundation (1050 Union Rd., Buffalo, NY 14224). Each of these also publishes materials which may be used to work with students in the creative problem-solving processes.

There are programs in future problem solving which are extensions of the creative problem-solving models. Whimbey and Whimbey (1975) developed some of the first materials to be used with junior high/middle school students. The student books were devoted to analyzing reading and reasoning. These were used in language arts classes. Although these are still being used and have been found to be effective for their stated objectives, many schools and districts are needing to augment or choose more comprehensive programs. Whimbey and Lockhead (1982) have a book of problems teachers can use to stimulate and coach students in using matrices and spatial arrays to solve certain types of problems. These have been used with gifted students for some time.

Several other National Diffusion Network (NDN) approved programs, in addition to those listed separately above, are Comprehensive School Mathematics Program (CSMP), K–6; Reading Education Accountability Design: Secondary (READS), 5–12; and Critical Analysis and Thinking Skills (CATS), 7–12.

Zaner-Bloser publishes a series of teacher and pupil edition units entitled *Breakthroughs: Strategies for Thinking*. These are on science topics and ecology and are for grades K–8.

Midwest Publications has been a major source of published materials in critical thinking. The name of the publisher has been changed to Critical Thinking Press and Software to reflect the extensive list the company has of thinking materials. Dr. Merle Karnes' books on *Primary Thinking Skills*; the *Building Thinking Skills* K–12 series by Hill and Edwards and Howard and Sandra Black; and the *Critical Thinking* series by Anita Harnadek are

Questions for Evaluating HOTS Programs

- Do the program objectives match the district/school objectives for its HOT outcomes?
- Does the program cover the grade levels needed locally?
- If the program does not cover grade levels needed, is there another program which would cover the other grades?
- Is the program limited to a particular content area?
- If so, are those limitations consistent with the district's outcomes?
- Is the program a separate or integrated program?
- If separate, does it include a curriculum to teach for transfer?
- Is the program comprehensive in skills and strategies taught?
- If not, does the district have a plan to supplement the program?
- Does the program teach skills and develop strategies directly in contrast to teaching for thinking where students engage in HOT activities but are not taught the procedures?
- Does the program have a well-developed staff development component?
- Does the staff development component include training trainers?
- Are there provisions for peer coaching?
- How long does the staff development take? Over what time span? Trainer training? Over what time span?
- Is the training available on site or would district personnel have to go elsewhere to receive training?
- How long does it take to implement the program completely? Is this realistic with the district's plans and needs?
- Is there a maintenance program?
- How much does the training cost? If away, room and board and transportation need to be included. If local, substitute pay may need to be budgeted. If summer, would stipend be necessary per teacher? per trainer? per pupil?
- How much do the materials cost per teacher? per trainer? per student?
- Are the materials consumable? reproducible?
- How much does the maintenance program, if any, cost?
- How soon could the district begin?
- Does the program mesh well with current special programs in the district?
- Are the texts and support materials consistent philosophically and instructionally with the district's policies and philosophy and consistent with the goals of the program itself?
- Is there any provision for parent involvement/parent education presented by the program? For example, various terms may not have the same meaning as we would use them everyday.
- What research and evaluation are available to support the validity and reliability of the program? Were they carried out by the author(s) of the program? Were the instruments developed by the author(s) of the program? What evidence do you have of the reliablitiy of the results? How else might you check on this program?

some of the series available. There are also applications to science, math, and history, as well as mind benders, games, etc.

The Junior Great Books program is used in many schools to develop students' abilities to read interpretively and to think independently. The program may be used from second grade through high school. For more information, contact the Great Books Foundation, 40 E. Huron St., Chicago, IL 60611.

The Institute for Creative Education (ICE) developed an approach to developing creative thinking and published a book of activities which can be used in specific areas, some at each grade level/subject (Educational Improvement Center-South, Box 209, Delsea Dr., Sewell, NJ 08080).

Two programs that deserve mention because of their historical importance are Project Intelligence and Productive Thinking. Each of these was developed when there were not many programs in progress and the research on problem solving was much less. Productive Thinking Program (Covington, Crutchfield, Davies & Olton 1974) is a self-instructional program composed of fifteen books of materials for fifth and sixth graders. Evaluations were promising for the types of problems the students worked in the books.

Project Intelligence was begun in 1979 as a joint project between David Perkins of Harvard University; Bolt, Beranek & Newman, Inc.; and the Venezuelan Ministry of Education to improve the intellectual skills of students. Six-lesson series (100 lessons) addressed foundations of reasoning, understanding language, verbal reasoning, problem solving, decision making, and inventive thinking. It was for seventh grade students. The evaluation results showed significant gains for the experimental groups over the control groups (1983). The commercial program Odyssey is a follow-up of the materials developed in this program.

Connections is another program authored by Perkins and others (not based on the Venezuela program); it is being published by Addison Wesley.

Odyssey of the Mind (originally called Olympics of the Mind) is a program of competition between teams of three grade ranges, K–5, 6–8, and 9–12. The problems each year are developed by the national organization. Memberships are purchased by schools. This entitles teams from the school to participate in the annual competition. All work and solutions are student produced; adult coaches may be teachers, parents, and/or community resource people. Most states and some foreign schools have a competition to determine which teams may compete in the World Finals. The problems include structural problems, ones based on performing arts, vehicular problems, and situational problems (in which a dilemma is presented and students must design solutions). In addition, each team must engage in spontaneous brainstorming-type activities which are also part of their total score. For more information, contact OM Association, Box 27, Glassboro, NJ 08028.

Strategic Reasoning (Glade) has sets of pencil-and-paper lessons to develop thinking in six areas: identification, description, classification, structure analysis, operation analysis, and seeing analogies.

Ennis (1987) has contributed to the understanding of critical and creative thinking with his essays, presentations, articles, and, cited here, his taxonomy of critical thinking, dispositions, and abilities. He emphasizes that individuals are disposed to think in certain ways and these dispositions need to be developed.

Marzano and Arredondo (1986) introduce the *Tactics for Thinking* program of skills as a basement level to be built on with other programs, either commercial or locally developed. After the introduction of *Tactics*, Marzano collaborated with Brandt, Hughes, Jones, Presseisen, Rankin, and Suhor (1988) to develop a framework for a thinking-skills curriculum. This was published by ASCD as *Dimensions of Thinking: A Framework for Curriculum and Instruction*. Since this publication, Marzano, Pickering, and Brandt (1990) have analyzed a number of programs on the market to determine which dimensions each stresses strongly, moderately, or relatively little. The programs analyzed include some of the HOT programs above and other curricula not listed. This article is recommended to those who are trying to integrate current programs and staff development with higher order thinking programs or materials. *Dimensions of Learning* (1992) is a recent book which builds on these previous efforts, field testing, and workshops.

In view of the large number of teachers who have been trained in programs based on Madeline Hunter's staff development, the se-lection of an approach to HOT which builds on PET, ITIP, UCLA model, mastery, or other alternative titles for the Hunter model would seem logical. This is not difficult to do if the developers review Hunter's full model with its flexibility and allowance of both deductive and inductive instruction to take place. One example of this approach can be found in Weber's (1990) article on "Linking ITIP and the Writing Process" in *Educational Leadership's* special issue on connections (February 1990, vol. 47:5).

Set I: Separate Programs

PROGRAM:	Building Thinking Skills		
GRADES: K–12	SUBJECT SPECIFIC? No		SEPARATE PROGRAM? Yes

DESCRIPTION

Building Thinking Skills is a series of five books of activities designed to develop thinking skills. Each book has reproducible pages and there is a teacher's manual for each. Books for younger children have activities which use hands-on blocks and materials. All types of skills from similarities and differences to analogies to patterning to classifying to sequencing to deductive reasoning are included in the series. There are two books at the 7-12 levels, one on figural and one on verbal skills. Teacher's manuals provide instructional directions, dialogue, and solutions. Research in several school districts in Florida and California report significant results with the use of this series.

TRAINING

LENGTH: ---	LOCATION: ---	NUMBER OF TRAINEES: ---
TRAINER TRAINING: No	LENGTH: ---	CYCLE OF TRAINING: No

MATERIALS NEEDED

TRAINER MANUAL: No	TEACHER'S MANUAL: Yes	STUDENT MATERIALS: Yes (required—reproducible on a classroom basis)

DEVELOPED BY:	Primary book and manual are by Dr. Warren Hill and Dr. Ronald Edwards; the other four books and manuals are by Dr. Howard Black and Sandra Parks Black.
CONTACT PERSON:	Critical Thinking Press & Software (formerly Midwest Publications) P.O. Box 448 Pacific Grove, CA 93950 800-458-4849

PROGRAM:	CORT (Cognitive Research Trust)		
GRADES: 3–adult	SUBJECT SPECIFIC? No		SEPARATE PROGRAM? Yes

DESCRIPTION

Six sets of lessons to be spread over three years with 35 minutes in one lesson per week. The purpose is to develop specific thinking skills to improve performance in all subject areas. The program has been revised with a second edition published by SRA. It is concerned with higher order thinking, comprehension, and communication skills. There are structured group discussion. The six sets are entitled Breadth, Organization, Interaction, Creativity, Information and Feeling, and Action. No prescribed staff development seems to be required.

TRAINING

LENGTH:	1 day seminars can be arranged	LOCATION: ---	NUMBER OF TRAINEES: ---
TRAINER TRAINING: No		LENGTH: ---	CYCLE OF TRAINING: ---

MATERIALS NEEDED

TRAINER MANUAL: No	TEACHER'S MANUAL: Yes	STUDENT MATERIALS: Yes (required)

DEVELOPED BY:	Dr. Edward de Bono
CONTACT PERSON:	Science Research Associates, Inc. 155 N. Wacker Drive Chicago, IL 60606

PROGRAM:	Higher Order Thinking Skills (HOTS)		
GRADES: 4–6	SUBJECT SPECIFIC? No		SEPARATE PROGRAM? Yes

DESCRIPTION

HOTS is designed to develop higher order thinking skills in students who are achieving poorly academically, specifically for Chapter I students. It is a pull-out program which requires computers, special teacher training, and 35 minutes a day, 4 days a week for two years. The lessons include work with metacognition, inferencing, decontextualization, and information synthesis. Since Chapter I students are identified because of deficiencies in reading or math, the lessons relate to these subjects, but are not designed to replace their instruction. The teacher assists students in developing their verbal abilities through the use of Socratic dialogue. No management system, no grades.

TRAINING

LENGTH: 5 days	LOCATION: your school	NUMBER OF TRAINEES: ---
TRAINER TRAINING: No	LENGTH: ---	CYCLE OF TRAINING: ---

MATERIALS NEEDED

TRAINER MANUAL: No	TEACHER'S MANUAL: Yes	STUDENT MATERIALS: Yes (required)

CONTACT PERSON:	Dr. Stanley Pogrow University of Arizona College of Education Tucson, AZ 85721 NDN (National Diffusion Network) approved

PROGRAM:	IDEAL		
GRADES:	Secondary, College	SUBJECT SPECIFIC? No	SEPARATE PROGRAM? Yes

DESCRIPTION

The acronym IDEAL stands for Identify the problem, Define it and represent it with precision, Explore possible strategies, Act on these strategies, and Look at the effects (Bransford & Stein 1984). The program has been carefully researched with college students and with the use of computers. Video tapes of portions of films have been used to develop the problem-solving strategies. The tasks are separate from the curriculum. High-interest material has been used for the exercises.

TRAINING

LENGTH:	---	LOCATION:	---	NUMBER OF TRAINEES:	---
TRAINER TRAINING:	---	LENGTH:	---	CYCLE OF TRAINING:	---

MATERIALS NEEDED

TRAINER MANUAL:	---	TEACHER'S MANUAL:	---	STUDENT MATERIALS:	Yes (required); also computer required

CONTACT PERSON: Dr. John Bransford
Learning Technology Center
Peabody College, Vanderbilt University
Nashville, TN 37235

PROGRAM:	Instrumental Enrichment		
GRADES: 4–8	SUBJECT SPECIFIC? No		SEPARATE PROGRAM? Yes

DESCRIPTION

The program contains fifteen sets of lessons which are introduced at a separate time from content. Each works on developing a particular skill. The first group of sets deals with spatial analysis tasks, the second group with orientation in space and several other topics, the third group involves categorization, relations, and representations. The program recommends that the student spend from 20 minutes to 1 hour, four days a week. At this pace, the program will be completed in two to three years. The student materials are consumable. Teachers are expected to offer students opportunities to "bridge" to the subject curricula. Students are asked to think about (mediate) their thinking. Lessons are interesting, perhaps more so for the spatially inclined.

TRAINING

LENGTH:	5 days the first year	LOCATION:	your school	NUMBER OF TRAINEES:	25
TRAINER TRAINING:	No	LENGTH:	NA	CYCLE OF TRAINING:	Yes, 2–3 years

MATERIALS NEEDED

TRAINER MANUAL:	No	TEACHER'S MANUAL:	Yes	STUDENT MATERIALS:	Yes (required)

DEVELOPED BY:	Dr. Reuven Feuerstein
CONTACT PERSON:	Dr. Frances Link Curriculum Development Associates, Inc. 1211 Connecticut Avenue NW, Suite 414 Washington, DC 20036

PROGRAM:	Intelligence Applied		
GRADES: Secondary, College	**SUBJECT SPECIFIC?** No	**SEPARATE PROGRAM?** Yes	

DESCRIPTION

The program is designed to train students to use their intellectual abilities and is divided into five parts: background, components of human intelligence, facets of human intelligence, functions of human intelligence, and personality/motivation. Designed for one semester or year. It is a separate curriculum designed to develop students' understanding of intelliegence and how to use theirs.

TRAINING

LENGTH: ---	LOCATION: ---	NUMBER OF TRAINEES: ---
TRAINER TRAINING: ---	LENGTH: ---	CYCLE OF TRAINING: ---

MATERIALS NEEDED

TRAINER MANUAL: ---	TEACHER'S MANUAL: Yes	STUDENT MATERIALS: Yes (required)

DEVELOPED BY:	Dr. Robert Sternberg Department of Psychology Yale University New Haven, CT 06520-7447
CONTACT PERSON:	Harcourt Brace Jovanovich College Division 7555 Caldwell Avenue Niles, IL 60648 800-237-2665

PROGRAM:	Odyssey		
GRADES:	4–9	SUBJECT SPECIFIC?　No	SEPARATE PROGRAM?　Yes

DESCRIPTION

Six teacher's manuals and student books cover the topics of foundations of reasoning, understanding language, verbal reasoning, problem solving, decision making, and inventive thinking (in that order). Three to five lessons per week, 45 minutes. Developed from Project Intelligence by David Perkins and Bolt, Berarek,& Newman Inc. for project in Venezuela.

TRAINING

LENGTH:	---	LOCATION:　--	NUMBER OF TRAINEES:　---
TRAINER TRAINING:	---	LENGTH:　---	CYCLE OF TRAINING:　---

MATERIALS NEEDED

TRAINER MANUAL:	---	TEACHER'S MANUAL:　Yes	STUDENT MATERIALS:　Yes (required)

DEVELOPED BY:	Dr. David Perkins and Bolt, Berarek,& Newman Inc. from Project Intelligence for a project in Venezuela

CONTACT PERSON:	Mastery Education Corp. 85 Main Street Watertown, MA 02172

PROGRAM:	Philosophy for Children		
GRADES:	5–10	SUBJECT SPECIFIC? Usually language/ literature	SEPARATE PROGRAM? Yes

DESCRIPTION

The program is designed to develop the natural philosophical interests and skills in children through discussion of issues important to them and presented through stories which are read and discussed by them. The role of teacher as an inquirer/facilitator requires extended training varying from 2 1/2 hours per week for a year to two weeks of intensive training at a summer camp. Because stories developed by the program must be used, it is considered a separate program even though some schools may have replaced part of their language arts block with these activities and texts.

TRAINING

LENGTH:	14 days	LOCATION:	New Jersey	NUMBER OF TRAINEES:	---
TRAINER TRAINING:	No	LENGTH:	---	CYCLE OF TRAINING:	Yes, 1–2 years

MATERIALS NEEDED

TRAINER MANUAL:	No	TEACHER'S MANUAL:	Yes	STUDENT MATERIALS:	Yes (required)

DEVELOPED BY:	Dr. Matthew Lipman
CONTACT PERSON:	The Institute for the Advancement of Philosophy for Children (IAPC) Montclair State College Montclair, NJ

PROGRAM:	Structure of Intellect (SOI)		
GRADES: 4–up	SUBJECT SPECIFIC? Some		SEPARATE PROGRAM? Yes

DESCRIPTION

The SOI Systems developed instructional materials to be used on an individual basis for students whose scores are deficient in certain areas of the Structure of Intellect-Learning Abilities profile. In addition to these sets of materials which can be used almost independently by students, the SOI Systems has published materials. "How to Reason: A Handbook for Critical Thinking" (Meeker) is recommended to be used with students from grade 4 and up. The SOI-LA is based on Guilford's Theory of Intellect, one of the factor theories of intelligence. The instrument has scores for both divergent and convergent thinking. Two 1/2-hour lessons a week.

TRAINING

LENGTH: 2 days	LOCATION: ---	NUMBER OF TRAINEES: ---
TRAINER TRAINING: ---	LENGTH: ---	CYCLE OF TRAINING: ---

MATERIALS NEEDED

TRAINER MANUAL: ---	TEACHER'S MANUAL: Yes	STUDENT MATERIALS: Yes (required)

CONTACT PERSON:	Dr. Mary Meeker M & M Systems 45755 Good Pasture Road Vida, OR 97488

Set II: Intergrated Programs

PROGRAM:	Dimensions of Learning		
GRADES: K–12	SUBJECT SPECIFIC? No		SEPARATE PROGRAM? No

DESCRIPTION

The Dimensions of Learning is an integrative instructional framework. It offers instruction in how to integrate higher order thinking skills and strategies into the classroom. It deals with acquiring and integrating knowledge (declarative and procedural), enabling skills, extending knowledge, and dispositions of effective learning. The completed program has recently been published.

TRAINING

LENGTH: 3–5 days	LOCATION: Washington, DC & Denver	NUMBER OF TRAINEES: ---
TRAINER TRAINING: Yes	LENGTH: 3–5 days	CYCLE OF TRAINING: ---

MATERIALS NEEDED

TRAINER MANUAL: Yes (video tapes also)	TEACHER'S MANUAL: Yes	STUDENT MATERIALS: ---

CONTACT PERSON: Dr. Robert Marzano, Director of Research
Mid-Continent Regional Educational Laboratory
12500 E. Iliff Avenue, Suite 201
Aurora, CO
—Materials are being published by ASCD, 1250 N. Pitt Street, Alexandria, VA 22314

PROGRAM:	Infusion of the Teaching of Thinking		
GRADES: K–12	SUBJECT SPECIFIC? No		SEPARATE PROGRAM? No

DESCRIPTION

The Infusion of the Teaching of Critical and Creative Thinking into standard subject-area instruction is probably best used from upper elementary. The recommended practices, however, are suitable for all grade levels. The infusion procedures are taught in staff development two-day lesson-design sessions at different locations around the country. There are texts that have been developed by the trainers but they are not required for the training. Handouts furnished by the trainers are used. One book for elementary and one for secondary are available for teachers and trainers (who have two additional days of training) to implement staff development in districts/schools. On-site support and demonstrations are available by the consultants.

TRAINING

LENGTH: 2 days	LOCATION: varies	NUMBER OF TRAINEES: up to 70
TRAINER TRAINING: Yes	LENGTH: 2 days	CYCLE OF TRAINING: No

MATERIALS NEEDED

TRAINER MANUAL: Yes	TEACHER'S MANUAL: Yes	STUDENT MATERIALS: No

CONTACT PERSON:	Dr. Robert Swartz and Sandra Parks, Co-Directors The National Center for Teaching Thinking P.O. Box 334 Newton Center, MA 02159

PROGRAM:	Patterns		
GRADES:	K–12	SUBJECT SPECIFIC?　No	SEPARATE PROGRAM?　No

DESCRIPTION

A staff development program for teachers to incorporate various creative and critical aspects of thinking in their classrooms. Explicit lessons and modeling with practice and feedback and transfer are integrated in the training design. Extensive use of cooperative learning techniques for classroom organization are presented.

TRAINING

LENGTH:	5 days	LOCATION:	your school	NUMBER OF TRAINEES:	60
TRAINER TRAINING:	Yes	LENGTH:	3 days	CYCLE OF TRAINING:	Yes (for trainers only)

MATERIALS NEEDED

TRAINER MANUAL:	Yes	TEACHER'S MANUAL:	Yes	STUDENT MATERIALS:	No

CONTACT PERSON:	Jim Bellanca, Executive Director Illinois Renewal Institute, Inc. 200 E. Wood Street, Suite 250 Palatine, IL 60067 National Diffusion Network (NDN) approved

PROGRAM:	Project IMPACT		
GRADES: 5–12	SUBJECT SPECIFIC? No		SEPARATE PROGRAM? No

DESCRIPTION

Staff development program designed to train teachers to teach critical thinking skills in their classrooms. A hierarchy of skills which lead to critical thinking and its applications are presented. Enabling skills such as perceiving, conceiving, and seriating; processes under analyzing, questioning, and inferring; and operations of logical reasoning and evaluation are presented to teachers within context of classroom content.

TRAINING

LENGTH: 3 days	LOCATION: your school or CA	NUMBER OF TRAINEES: 30
TRAINER TRAINING: Yes	LENGTH: 2 days	CYCLE OF TRAINING: No

MATERIALS NEEDED

TRAINER MANUAL: Yes	TEACHER'S MANUAL: Yes	STUDENT MATERIALS: No

CONTACT PERSON:
Dr. Lee Winocur
Center for Teaching Thinking
21400 Magnolia Street
Huntington Beach, CA 92648

National Diffusion Network (NDN) approved

PROGRAM:	Strategies for Teaching Thinking across the Curriculum		
GRADES: 7–12	**SUBJECT SPECIFIC?** No		**SEPARATE PROGRAM?** No

DESCRIPTION

Program trains teachers to teach students to perform six major skills: classification, concept formation, representing related concepts, identifying patterns and relationships, formulating and testing hypotheses, and constructing meaning. Teachers work with hands-on activities and redesign lesson plans to integrate skills in their subject areas.

TRAINING

LENGTH: 4 days	LOCATION: your school or Atlanta	NUMBER OF TRAINEES: ---
TRAINER TRAINING: Yes	LENGTH: 3 days	CYCLE OF TRAINING: No

MATERIALS NEEDED

TRAINER MANUAL: Yes	TEACHER'S MANUAL: Yes	STUDENT MATERIALS: No

CONTACT PERSON:	Director of School Services Educational Testing Services Mail Stop 88–D, Rosedale Road Princeton, NJ 08541

PROGRAM:	Tactics for Thinking		
GRADES:　K–12	SUBJECT SPECIFIC?　No		SEPARATE PROGRAM?　No

DESCRIPTION

Tactics is a set of 22 thinking skills and the instructions for how to present each to students. There are three types of skills: learning to learn, content thinking skills, and reasoning skills. The program has been used widely because it is not a separate program and teachers can be taught how to present the skills within their classes. Developed by the Mid-continent Regional Educational Laboratory, authors Marzano and Arredondo, the materials have been published by ASCD. Marzano calls it a beginning. There is no curriculum or scope and sequence. The skills can be used at any grade level by adapting to the developmental level of the students. The availablility of video tapes of Marzano teaching each skill facilitates staff development and the training of trainers.

TRAINING

LENGTH:　3 days	LOCATION:　---	NUMBER OF TRAINEES:　---
TRAINER TRAINING:　Yes	LENGTH:　---	CYCLE OF TRAINING:　---

MATERIALS NEEDED

TRAINER MANUAL:　Yes (video tapes also)	TEACHER'S MANUAL:　Yes	STUDENT MATERIALS:　No

CONTACT PERSON:	Dr. Robert Marzano, Director of Research Mid-Continent Regional Educational Laboratory 12500 E. Iliff Avenue, Suite 201 Aurora, CO —Materials are being published by ASCD, 1250 N. Pitt Street, Alexandria, VA 22314

PROGRAM:	Talents Unlimited		
GRADES: 1–6	SUBJECT SPECIFIC? No		SEPARATE PROGRAM? No

DESCRIPTION

Program promotes the development of talents which all students have. Teacher provides systematic instruction in each of the six areas in the regular subject areas. Includes productive thinking, decision making, planning, and communication skills. Teachers develop lessons using models in manual.

TRAINING

LENGTH: ---	LOCATION: ---	NUMBER OF TRAINEES: ---
TRAINER TRAINING: ---	LENGTH: ---	CYCLE OF TRAINING: ---

MATERIALS NEEDED

TRAINER MANUAL: No	TEACHER'S MANUAL: Yes	STUDENT MATERIALS: No

CONTACT PERSON:	Mobile County Public Schools Talents Unlimited 1107 Arlington Street Mobile, AL 36605

Chapter Seventeen

Technology and Higher Order Thinking

Computer literacy is one of the outcomes education has added to its list of competencies during the 1980s. No student should lack the ability to use computers. Some curricula are more ambitious than others about the extent of this usage. Software has proliferated; unfortunately, some of it is not educationally sound. As users become more computer literate, they are asking hard questions about what various packages can do. This is particularly true in the instructional design/curriculum domain. The advertising blurb states that the software will develop problem-solving abilities in students in grade x; how do you decide whether it can? Later in the chapter a checklist will be offered to assist you in making some judgments, but first, a general discussion of what technology can and cannot do and some of the problems with using various kinds of technology.

Computers have added dimensions to instructional design. As instructional technology burgeons, computers have become only one part of the picture, albeit an important part. They have made remedial instruction interesting through games and simulations. Computers offer individualized instruction adapted to a student's particular needs for repetition and practice. Hypermedia provides different students with the opportunity to explore knowledge using the most appropriate media and knowledge organization. At the same time that one student works on the development of one skill, another student can select or have selected for him or her a set of tutorial exercises on another skill. At one time, these programs were loaded on each individual computer each time the computers were turned on. Now, the computers can be hooked together and parts of the complete instructional system can be accessed as needed for individuals or groups of students.

Another advance in computers is user friendliness. Although learning to use a computer takes time, whether the user is the student or the teacher, computer manufacturers have made tremendous advances in making the process palatable. The personal computer market demanded this added assistance. Unless the customer could learn to access the computer's offerings, s/he was not going to buy it. The mouse is one of the most notable efforts in making computers user friendly, and touch-sensitive screens are slowly gaining in popularity. Selection from a menu is easily accomplished by novices with either of these devices. The improved graphics have increased the potential use of computers in instruction as well as in desktop publishing.

In ten years, schools have gone from no computers to at least some. Most schools have computers in labs or classrooms. Cost has limited the number of computers in schools; however, computer companies, in cooperation with various businesses and industries, have made it possible for schools with few financial resources to obtain computers. Such programs continue. It appears that access to computers is no longer the problem it was; the question now is, How will teachers use the computers? How you use computers depends on what software you have available or can purchase and whether you have the expertise to develop tailor-made instruction.

NOTE: Special assistance on this chapter was provided by University of South Carolina professors, Drs. Joan Gallini and Margaret Gredler and doctoral student Neal Helman. The authors are grateful for their help.

Because software is expensive, you need to make good use of the funds you have. One option is to join a network. One such consortium is MECC. By being a member, the district has use of all the software the network has purchased. This has been a boon to small schools and those districts with few resources. If you are not aware of whether your district has such a catalogue of programs available or not, ask your principal or the person in the district office who serves as the computer-resource person.

If you have a list of programs available to you, you may still need assistance in selecting appropriate ones. Previewing those which have descriptions that sound appropriate is the best way to select what you will use. It is time consuming, however, to sit and work through a program just to find out that it will not do what you need it to. You need to limit your choices before you preview. If the annotation or description is properly done, it should tell you what objective the program will address and for what audience it is recommended.

As in all aspects of instructional design and planning, the objectives should drive the instruction. Activities that are fun and similar to video games are fine for "sponge" activities, but you need to be sure that they address the objective you have for your students if you are using them for instruction, not amusement. One book you may find helpful is Gredler's *Designing Games and Simulations* (1992).

Multimedia Learning Environments

Exciting advances have been taking place in technology which will affect educational use of videodiscs, hypermedia, and computers. Interactive programs which use a videodisc to present a knowledge base or situation and computers which allows students to interact with the videodisc are going to change the face of computer-assisted instruction. The potential for using all or part of such a knowledge base is tremendous.

Hypermedia combines text with video, audio, and computer graphics so that students can explore the connections or associations between the components of a knowledge base. The definition of computer-assisted instruction (CAI) is changing. Schools can now have a complete encyclopedia with sound and graphics available through a computer menu.

As the technology progresses and videodisc production costs decrease, the capability of videoing events or staged lessons/example and then tying these videos to teacher-developed activities opens a whole new realm of educational opportunities. Such interactions can permit multiple solutions to problems and multiple access to data collections according to the needs or interests of individual students. The spread of such opportunities will be delayed by the capabilities of the educational staff and the funds to purchase equipment and materials. The personnel in the technology lab in the College of Education at the University of South Carolina have been repurposing videodiscs in order to use them for such multimedia simulations. For example, computer-accessible shopping scenes on videodiscs give physically/developmentally handicapped populations opportunities to solve problems and develop strategies—even though they are limited by their mobility or the need for and cost of supervision.

Jasper, a multimedia-learning-environment program (Peabody College, Vanderbilt University) is an example of a program being developed from "scratch" for math/science problems. It uses real-life situations and has students solve problems that arise. Other programs deal with environmental issues, cultures, and situations around the world.

IBM and CNN have a multimedia program about hurricanes, called HUGO. Students try to solve problems about how to keep a boat afloat during a storm, learn in a game format what it takes to create a hurricane, and recount the history of hurricanes (Hurricane Hugo in particular). ABC has a new interactive division which has produced materials pertaining to the 1989 California earthquake. One company which distributes some of these programs is Video Discovers (1700 Westlake Avenue N, Suite 600, Seattle, WA 98109).

Interactive multimedia programs allow students to engage in processes not normally tapped in most CAI programs. Simulations developed this way permit more flexibility, real-life references, and variety. They also provide students with emotional multisensory connections to the subject matter. Such procedures would facilitate the learning-to-learn skill, also called deep processing, where the person tries to visualize, feel with senses, call up emotions, and associate linguistic input with a person, place, or event. Memory is strongly encoded with such self-referencing practices.

Laboratory equipment and supplies for science can be expensive, and certain activities may be dangerous when the students do not follow prescribed rules and directions. There are computer simulation programs which will let the students choose what chemicals to combine in an experiment, then tell the students if they have just "bombed" the school or turned loose a poisonous gas or obtained the desired solution.

In distance education, where students in remote areas receive instruction through telecommunications, this type of simulation can allow students to "carry out" experiments without the dangers of unsupervised labs. Animal activists have protested the dissecting of various animals in high school biology labs. Simulation may be the next best thing. This is not to say that such simulation is as good as or better than the "real thing," but it can be substituted and achieve some or all of the objectives of a particular lesson. In addition, companies such as IBM and Broderbund, among others, produce sensors (i.e., light, touch, temperature) that can be connected to a computer to create a micro computer-based laboratory instrument. With the software accompanying the sensors, students can focus on organizing and applying the data while the computer manages the data gathering, recording, calculating, and display.

One program that has been developed in physical science uses a videodisc of the Tacoma bridge collapse. The science unit developed to go with it deals with stress, tension, force, waves, etc. Although there is a program developed for this (John Wiley & Co.), a person familiar with an authoring language such as LinkWay could develop other instruction using the same knowledge base.

Most of the programs developed like this are for college students. One of the most interesting ones is "The Would-Be Gentleman" which takes a 17th-century French family through two generations with the goal of manipulating numerous variables to improve the family's status/prestige. The college students who analyzed the program found it challenging and interesting; the major drawback is that it requires a great deal of knowledge about 17th-century France: economics, history, politics, institutions, and other cultural information. For a student of French history, the game encourages some shrewd judgments; without this knowledge, it becomes more of a guessing game.

Computerized Communication Contexts*

Another exciting development is the use of computers to link large numbers of teachers and students across the world. Besides letting teachers share resources, such as papers, lesson plans, picture files, or computer programs, computers connected through telephone lines allow students to participate in large-scale projects with others from near and far. The Associated Student News Network, coordinated by a teacher in Alaska, is one example.

As part of the Associated Student News Network, students from around the world digest local news and electronically send ar-

* NOTE: Special thanks to Neal Helman for his assistance with this section.

ticles that interest them (and that they think will interest the rest of the subscribers) to the central "publishing office" in Alaska; the articles are combined into a global gazette that is then distributed electronically to all subscribers. Such an activity can help students develop writing skills, foreign language skills, skills needed to select, digest, and summarize, and skill at shifting their viewpoint. Recognizing point of view can be very difficult for students, but it is required in choosing news that will be of interest to students in other countries.

Using computers to link students with local, regional, national, or even international experts can offer students the opportunity to develop communication, cooperative, and inquiry skills, as well as skills tied more closely to subject content. One example of such large-scale cooperative learning involved several thousand students across the country in a project sponsored by the National Geographic Foundation.

Several hundred classes were given individual responsibility for gathering local data about acid rain by taking water and soil samples, conducting the appropriate lab tests, and recording and reporting the results. By the end of the project, a national map of environmental damage from acid rain had been created. In the process, students discussed the project and related issues with professional scientists. Students raised questions about the causes of the problem and the length of time it will take to solve it; the scientists also helped, from a distance, with conducting and interpreting the lab tests.

In addition to the interpersonal communication occurring through linked computers, on-line data bases provide a great resource for both teacher and student. They are becoming more prevalent worldwide, enabling students to gather information more easily than in the past. A primary advantage to on-line data bases is that they make available information inaccessible locally or even regionally. These data bases store anything from government documents to scientific research reports to articles from popular magazines. On-line data bases are somewhat similar to multimedia data bases (e.g. Grolier's Electronic Encyclopedia on compact disc), except that the on-line versions include neither graphics nor sound—and you can only access them through telecommunications. They are accessible by many people simultaneously, and individual schools or teachers need not maintain the data base (done by purchasing updates or adding the information themselves).

The hardware and software that allow you to link computers through telephone lines has been around for nearly three decades. As this sort of technology is used more and more in government, business, and the scientific community, hardware manufacturers and software authors realize the need for simpler systems. This has pushed the technology forward so that it is much less of a burden on the novice than it once was. This trend of simplifying computerized communication will, of course, continue as more people become involved in its use. These simpler systems will make more and more sense in the educational environment as the technology becomes somewhat less noticeable, letting you focus on communication and skill development. This is analogous to the way telephones proliferated and became, essentially, an invisible technology. An important benefit of these types of links is that the brand of computer you use does not always affect your ability to take advantage of this communicative medium. Telecommunications technology makes good sense as a way to increase the instructional value of the computer hardware available to you.

Computer Software

Most computer software developed to offer students activities in problem solving, decision making and other higher order thinking activities has been faulted because it accepts only one right answer, it is not challenging enough, and/or the user is limited to trial and error performances rather than reasoning logically.

Authentic problem solving should permit more than one choice as acceptable if a rationale can be put forward. Many of you may have worked with software, such as Oregon Trail, where no matter how good you are at predicting, you will be the victim of random error. This is not to say that such software packages are not useful; an analysis of the processes involved will determine whether they are useful for your students, given your instructional objectives.

Pogrow (1990) recommends using the software, but adapting it to your classroom using a Socratic approach. He states that we have been using the programs in ways which do not enhance learning. His program, HOTS, designed for Chapter I students, takes many of the software packages on the market and uses them in other ways. He uses them primarily to stimulate interest. Then the teacher builds on these games, adventure stories, and simulations to teach principles and concepts in reading and mathematics.

There is danger in using software that tells students that there is only one right answer and that no matter what one does or how well one reasons, s/he is at the mercy of the world (trial and error solution setup). That is not a message teachers want to impart to students who are trying to develop their ability to regulate their own learning, monitor their own thinking, and act planfully and reflectively.

If you have the responsibility of selecting software, some things that you may want to consider are presented on page 258. You can circle and notate answers as you investigate a piece of software. Many of the ideas for elements in this checklist can be found in the Courseware Evaluation Instrument in Gallini and Gredler (1989, pp. 263–68).

Technological courseware is expensive; it takes time and planning on the part of the teacher to obtain it, and much of it can be used advantageously only in limited settings with specific equipment. No matter how interesting and challenging courseware may be, it is only useful if it contributes to your instructional objectives. None of it is designed to replace the teacher; in fact, it makes the teacher even more significant in the teaching-learning setting. You need not be afraid to use it, but remember it will not replace good teaching and quality interactions between students and teachers, students and students, and students and materials, situations, and events.

COURSEWARE EVALUATION

Name:	Produced by:
Subject:	Level:
Hardware needed:	Purpose:

Description:

Features:

Instructional objective(s):

Previewed:	Yes	No	Recommended:	Yes	No	By whom?

Available from: Cost:

Limitations of use:

CURRICULUM / INSTRUCTION COMPONENTS

Pretest:	Objectives:	Expertise level:
Vocabulary level:	Free of bias:	Graphics quality:

Directions:	Adequate	Needs assistance	Available on screen
Formatting:	Nondistracting	Easy to follow	Allows corrections by student

Pacing:	Controlled by student	Controlled by program

Program response:	Immediate feedback	Positive response to correct answer	No punishment for errors	Offers adequate practice of process	Presents examples of concepts	Permits more than one correct answer	Requires justification of student response
Simulation:	Realistic	Abstract	Transfer explicit	Permits student hypotheses	Permits student analysis	Permits experimentation	Permits multiple routes to solutions

Student organization:	Single student	Pair	Group

Teacher's manual:	Yes	No	Overall quality of manual:

RATING

Format:	Excellent	Good	Fair	Poor
Features:	Excellent	Good	Fair	Poor
Instruction:	Excellent	Good	Fair	Poor
Ease of Obtaining:	Easy	Some difficulty	Difficult	
Cost:	High	Moderate	Relatively inexpensive	
Overall:	Excellent	Good	Fair	Poor
Objective match:	Excellent	Good	Fair	Poor
Will use:	Yes	No	When needed:	

AFTER USE

Overall :	Excellent	Good	Fair	Poor
Use again?	Yes	No	Why?	

Chapter Eighteen

Parents and Teachers Working Together

Teacher/parent conferencing has become an important part of standard operating procedures in schools, and since parents frequently ask what they can do to help their children, this chapter is included in the hopes that it may give teachers a quick reference to use when needed. Research on intervention programs in schools inevitably reports that those programs which were successful had parental involvement. Thus, if you can help parents to support and maintain the healthy development of their children (physically, cognitively, and affectively), you will help the children, enhance your task as teacher, and contribute to society in general.

The major tasks parents can accomplish are as follows:

- encourage independence and reasoned risk-taking;
- express confidence in the child's abilities;
- have high expectations for child's performance;
- model behaviors that are constructive, i.e., reflective thinking, persistence in tasks, trying to do one's best, valuing educational pursuits;
- spend quality time, and more of it, with your children;
- offer experiences that are distinctive and varied;
- never do for a child what s/he can do for him or herself;
- ask the child questions for which s/he can find answers;
- structure some order to your and his or her life;
- monitor child's progress—academic, social, health, and
- ask for child's opinions, and thoughts on family decisions.

Each of the above will be briefly elaborated upon in the following paragraphs. They are not placed in any order of importance—all of them are important. Developing a child's confidence in his or her abilities and the willingness to try are critical to developing self-reliance and to developing self-regulation in a learner. All of these contribute in some way to these ends.

If a child is going to develop into a mature adult, s/he must learn to make good decisions and solve problems. These cannot be learned by someone telling the child about them, they must be experienced by the child. Since these processes are procedural knowledge, they need practice and feedback. Parents have many opportunities to allow children to develop by letting children make choices, endure the consequences of their choices, and learn how to be better decision makers/problem solvers.

Encourage Independence

Encouraging independence includes many actions on the part of parents. The parents need to set limits on the child's behavior, but allow for choices within the limits. A child will not necessarily make good choices by having the whole world to choose from. Parents have the responsibility of setting the limits, giving hints or cues when needed, and allowing a child to make a poor choice. If the parents do not want the child to wear woolens in July, then woolens are not among the choices the child can make. This is far-fetched, of course, but the idea of laying out several outfits for school and allowing the child to choose from them exemplifies the idea of limits and choices within limits.

As the child gets older, the limits are expanded as are the choices. This also sets the stage for the child's understanding of the fact that there will always be limits on one's behavior. When parents no longer set them, government or nature will.

Breaking laws has a set of consequences—government fines or imprisonment. Nature's consequences may be faster. If a child defies the law of gravity by jumping off the garage, the consequences will be immediate and probably painful. If someone abuses his or her body with alcohol, drugs, poor nutrition, etc., the consequences will eventually catch up with him or her.

A child needs many small opportunities, such as the choice of clothing named above, to experience the consequences of choices, whether happy or sad. The only way to learn to make good choices is by having many experiences where engaging in careful planning/reflecting have resulted in the child making reasoned choices and receiving feedback/consequences of those choices.

Independence from parents does not mean that the parent has lost the child. Some parents fear that if they do not keep their child dependent upon them, the child will not love them. Growing in independence can be painful for both the parent and the child, but it is so important. One definition of adolescence is from the onset of puberty until the person is self-governing. By these standards, there are many adolescents who are in their thirties and forties. Self-governing suggests that the person makes his or her own decisions; it does not mean that the person does not seek advice and counsel from friends, parents, and professional associates.

If a child is self-reliant, it implies that s/he has confidence in his or her ability to carry on without having to rely on constant support. Everyone needs support, but some need it so constantly and emotionally that they cannot proceed without it.

Express Confidence in Child's Ability

Because children do not perform at the standards one sets for adults, it is easy for parents to fall into the habit of finding fault with a child's performance. They may defend their behavior by saying, "Well, how is he ever going to learn if I don't tell him what's wrong?" It only takes a little searching of one's own history to remember how difficult it was to learn some tasks, how discouraging it was when the behavior was inadequate, and how helpful it was to receive encouragement about what one was doing right, not criticism about what one was doing wrong.

Criticism is translated by many as the criticizer saying that the person is not all right. The fact that the criticism had to do with the behavior rather than the person becomes blurred. The end result is discouragement on the part of the person who is trying to learn some new and/or difficult task. Persistence and effort need to be nurtured and encouraged. If a child's effort is recognized and progress is noted, the child is more likely to persist. Berating tears down confidence.

Once the behavior is established, motivation has become intrinsic, and interest has been created, then behavior can be refined with constructive criticism. This is assuming that the person wants to refine his or her behavior and that the person who offers the constructive criticism is the appropriate one to do so. Unless a person can tell someone how to improve his or her performance, the criticizer does not have the right to be critical. If the parent expresses confidence in the child's ability, then the child is more likely to try again; the child is more likely to understand one has to make "errors" to get better; the child is more likely to engage in "risk-taking" behavior.

Some parents may not understand why it is beneficial to encourage risk taking. If the only tasks one will try are those which are "sure bets," a person will stagnate. S/he will not try anything new or different. How would such a person fare in our world of technology? If people won't try new products and ideas or new ways of doing things, what will happen? They will lose out. There is no doubt about it. All children need to be able to try something new, something they do not know how to do. By the same token, they need to be willing to learn new information and delve into new fields of knowledge.

Taking risks in themselves is not necessarily advisable; taking reasoned risks is advisable. One does not step out in front of a truck in order to prove himself to be a risk taker. One needs to weigh the predicted consequences to see if the odds are in the risk taker's favor. Jumping off cliffs won't do much for one's self-confidence and is not a decision one would make after reasoned reflection; however, never going in the water or learning to drive a car won't help one's self-confidence either. Inertia may keep one safe, but life will be passing him or her by.

Research on characteristics associated with self-reliance, independence, and risk taking in children found that not only is it important to express confidence in the child, but the parents need to exhibit self-confidence and high self-esteem in themselves (Santrock 1992). This is another example of the value of modeling, which is discussed below.

Hold High Expectations for Child's Performance

This may sound contradictory to the admonition above about criticism when someone is attempting to learn a new task; it is not. Parents may expect a child to perform to a high level of competence, yet be realistic in expectations of how long it will take for the child to reach the expected performance.

First-born children are often saddled with educating their parents to the fact that they are not perfect and they are not adults. Later born children may have more tolerant parents. The high achievement of firstborns suggests that those parental beliefs may not be all bad. The literature is full of the accomplishments of firstborn children. What the literature does not say is that there are more firstborns in mental institutions and suffering from psychoneurotic disorders. Some children can take the pressure from parents and rise above it; however, humans come in infinite varieties, and not all can handle the stress and pressure of overly ambitious parents.

Expectations must be based on the child's age, development, health, personality disposition, and other factors. A high expectation for one child might be an impossible expectation for another. Parents must exercise care in setting their expectations for each child on an individual basis, and of course, parents should not compare their offspring with one another or with other children. The use of comparison should be reserved for evaluating current performance against past performance of the same child. As the child matures, expectations change.

Along with high expectations is the belief that the child can do the task. Parental confidence and support cannot be minimized. There are individuals who have risen above adversity to reach great heights, but they are few. Most humans need a little help and support; no one is in a better position to offer that to a child than his or her parents.

Model Desired Behaviors

The old saying of "Do as I say, not as I do" has never been very successful in guiding behavior. Children enjoy mimicking their parents. Early on, children believe that anything their parents do is right. Therefore, the parent needs to model the behaviors s/he values and wants to see the children exhibit.

A parent lamented that she could not get her child to eat salads. During the conversation, she commented that she didn't like salads although she knew they were good for her. She also admitted that she seldom served them at home and that her child rarely had seen her eat a salad. It is not hard to figure out that some of the child's resistance to salad might be found in the parent's modeling behavior. How much more important it is for parents to model behaviors demonstrating values and interpersonal relations than to talk about them!

Some of the desired behaviors to be modeled are persistence (particularly in the presence of adversity), trying to do one's best (even on simple tasks), reflective thinking, fairness and honesty in dealing with others, patience, tolerance, concern, caring, etc. Listing characteristics that a parent admires in others would be a good beginning for choosing behaviors to model for their children. No one said parenting was easy!

Value Educational Pursuits

When the term *educational pursuits* is used, it is chosen because educational activities are not limited to school classrooms. Parents are particularly responsible for the experiences the children have outside of the school walls. Several areas of concern might be included in this section: television, trips, books/libraries, computers/software, magazines, special events (historical, cultural, community), parental support of school and its activities, appreciation of the contribution of oral history and local events, and parents' leisure time activities. Some of these will be elaborated upon.

Television is a mixed blessing. Never have we had history, past and present, at our fingertips as we have now. Never have we had such entertaining ways to learn. Never have we had so much responsibility for monitoring our children's TV watching. There are wonderful educational programs on the television every hour of every day; there are also programs that depict amoral behavior, crime, violence, and degenerate social relations in the name of entertainment. Many times, they are entertaining and mature audiences may select to view them, but that does not mean that parents should allow young children to watch such fare.

In addition to what the child watches is the decision of how long the child watches TV. Some children now have TV's in their bedrooms. It becomes increasingly difficult to monitor their watching unless you have a switch to cut the power off after certain hours or for a specific time slot. Under the section below on structuring your child's day are some suggestions about how you might do this and still allow the child some say-so in his or her TV watching.

Family trips are another area of parental influence. Some families arrange trips for their children that may be educational, others take trips to visit relatives in neighboring communities, still others take no trips at all. In a rural school one of the authors visited, over half the students had never been seventeen miles to the county seat and only two had been outside the county. The parents are hardworking, low-socioeconomic individuals who are not likely to ask the school what they can do to help their children. They are doing well if they can even make a PTA meeting.

Schools try to arrange trips for students each year: community service offices (police, fire, aid), courts, historical sites, museums, legislative sessions, industry, and many other locations or events. This in no way should hamper a parent from arranging such an experience for his or her child. If a family lives in a town with a dairy farm, a pulp/paper mill, a meat processing/packing plant, or any of 1000s of industrial or business pursuits, the parents might arrange a trip to the site. If travel out of state is proposed, such as a visit to a distant relative, selecting to visit a historical site on the way transmits to the child that you value educational experiences.

In the section on modeling above, the pursuit of leisure activities by the parent was listed as one way of influencing children. In valuing educational pursuits, the parent can choose to read during leisure time; the parent can also make regular trips to the library and start the child early in checking out books to "read." Taking the child to the local library and getting him or her involved in summer reading programs are both ways to let children know you value education and learning.

Subscriptions to magazines can also reflect a love for learning. Magazines such as *National Geographic, Smithsonian, Challenge, Time, Newsweek, US News & World Report, Life*, nature magazines, and many others have as their mission to inform. Subscribing to and reading them (by parents) can raise a child's interest in learning more about nature, culture, history, and current events. Publications such a *G/C/T (Gifted, Creative, Talented)* offer many good activities for children. The magazine is published to give parents and teachers of gifted children ideas about things their children could do. Many of the activities are also appropriate for children who are not classified as gifted.

In addition to demonstrating to children that you are interested in the world, a parent can also indicate an interest in what is new and important. Some parents knock computers just because they don't know anything about them or their operation. Others have computers in their homes and encourage their children to operate them. It is not necessary to have a computer at home in order to value the contribution computers and technology can make to education.

"Field trips" for the family were mentioned above. Other local trips can involve attending historical/cultural/community events. Oral history and the contributions individuals have made can be more fully appreciated through some of the community programs and local events.

One other way to show children that parents value and support education is through active involvement in the school and its activities. Parent/teacher organizations, school improvement councils, special projects and celebrations, and volunteerism are all avenues of school support. Also, parents should have conferences with the teacher about their children's progress and behavior. A parent should not reserve visits to the school or teacher when there are problems, but should monitor children's progress during appropriate visitation times.

Spend Quality Time with Children

Parents are rushed and often feel guilty about the amount of time they spend with their children. Research has shown that the quality of the time is as important as the quantity of the time (Santrock 1992). If a parent is with a child all day but only watches to see that the child does not get hurt or engage in undesirable behavior, and does not interact with the child or communicate with him or her, the quantity is great, but the quality is minimal. Listening to the child, reading to the child, holding the child may be the most important things a parent can do, particularly with young children. Many older children accuse their parents of not listening to what they have to say.

Quality time is the important idea, but this is not to say that one can spend 15 minutes of quality time a day and that they will have met their quota. The research which points to the importance of quality over sheer quantity was not suggesting that the time could be minimal if it was "quality." A parent cannot instill moral, ethical, and social values in children in a few minutes. There has to be enough contact over a prolonged period of time, so that the child can observe parents modeling desired behavior, as well as encouraging and supporting the child's good behaviors. In studies by Baumrind (1966, 1986), children who were self-reliant, independent, sociable, etc. were found to come from homes where parents were controlling (set limits, expectations), nurturing, communicating, and held high maturity demands for their children.

Variety and Distinctiveness of Stimuli

In order to develop children's cognitive abilities, the children need many sensory stimuli—sights, sounds, tastes, smells, touches. Sheer numbers, however, will not help. Two characteristics which have been found to be important in cognitive stimulation are variety and distinctiveness. Not only do children need a wide variety of different experiences, the experiences need to be spaced so that they are distinctive one from the other. A child who lives in a tenement apartment where two adults and six children coexist in two rooms is not lacking stimulation; the noise and confusion must be awful. What s/he lacks is the variety and the distinctiveness of the events in his or her life. There is a sameness about a din of noise. One can become jaded by the sameness. Just as individuals find they have less interference in their learning when they separate similar materials by studying something dissimilar in between, children will get more cognitive stimulation when experiences stand out from what came before and after.

Do Not Do for the Child What S/he Can Do for Him or Herself

Many women say they never learned to cook when they were growing up because their mothers did not want them "messing" in their kitchens. It was easier for the mother to do whatever needed to be done than to clean up the mess after someone else tried to learn to do it. Unfortunately, helping children learn is more exhausting than doing it oneself. If the child never has the opportunity to stumble through the process, however, how will s/he ever learn?

Do not rob a child of the act of discovery. Vygotsky (1978) believed that there is a zone of proximal development in which children cannot successfully do something alone, but can be successful with hints, explanations, and/or assistance from an adult. The school functions in this capacity to make learning more approachable as well as more efficient and effective. Parents should also be aware that they can serve this function with their children. If a parent thinks back to the period of a child's initial language acquisition, the parent will doubtlessly remember a great amount of shaping, helping, reinforcing, supplying, and practicing. The adult offered the scaffolding on which the child could build a language system. Given time and exposure to the native language, a child will acquire it, but with the adult's support, the process is accomplished in a much shorter time.

Ask Questions for Which the Child Can Find or Figure Out the Answers

When a child asks a parent a question, the parent typically answers it. Parents need to think a moment before responding, and if the question is one the child can answer, ask them how they might find the answer. Parents can also be on the lookout for opportunities to ask children why they think something happened, what they think caused something, what something is called, where something came from, etc. Parents should be generous with help if children get stumped but persist in helping children get the answer themselves, rather than telling them the answer.

Structure the Child's Day

Organization is one of the processes we are slow to develop. One way to help children to manage their days is to have predictable parts of it so that they know what will happen at certain times. Setting up the time to get up, eat breakfast, leave for the bus, come home, eat supper, and go to bed, allows other events in the children's lives to be chosen by them.

During the afternoon and evening hours, TV, chores, play, telephoning, reading, hobbies, and homework must be completed. Have the child choose when these will be done. There is a tendency for parents to say, You must do your homework before you can play. Actually, it does not matter which one is done first unless the child has demonstrated that s/he falls asleep over the homework if it is postponed. If there is a special TV program which the child wants to watch, there should be some negotiable way for him or her to juggle times. Allowing the child to manage his or her own time to do what is really important to him or her is developing the metacognitive strategy of planning.

Monitor the Child's Progress

Without standing over the child, a parent needs to monitor the child's activities and progress. If needs are assessed, the parent can intervene. The academic realm, the social realm, and the child's health and physical habits all require monitoring. They are inter-related. Sometimes it is difficult to know where one starts and the other stops. If the child's vision is such that s/he cannot see the board, the academic performance of the child may be affected. If the child feels left out or inad-equate in social situations, it may affect the child's confidence and attitudes, which may in turn affect his or her health or school perfor-mance.

Consult on Family Decisions

When decisions are to be made which af-fect the entire family, parents should get in the habit of asking each child his or her opinion, and ask the child to tell why that is his or her choice. After each is asked and the results polled, the parents will make the decision and give the children the rationale for their choice. These types of behaviors have been found in families where children have high self-esteem, confidence, and independence.

***

Although there are many other sugges-tions that could be made, these probably cover the major areas. All individuals want to main-tain and enhance their self-esteem; they want to feel good about themselves. If children feel confident, supported, and have a track record of successful experiences and coping behav-iors, they will probably be well-adjusted and successful. In turn, they will be disposed to use their abilities, skills, and strategies to adapt to new situations and, hopefully, contribute to society.

Bibliography

Anderson, J. R. 1990. *Cognitive Psychology and Its Implications.* 3rd ed. San Francisco: W. H. Freeman.

Angell, J. R. 1908. "The Doctrine of Formal Discipline in the Light of the Principles of General Psychology." *Educational Review*, 36: 1–14.

Applebee, A. N.; Langer, J. A.; and Mullis, I. V. S. 1991. "Crossroads in American Education: A Summary of Findings from the Nation's Report Card." In *Developing Minds: A Resource Book for Teaching Thinking*, edited by A. L. Costa, 17–18. Alexandria, VA: Association for Supervision and Curriculum Development.

Arredondo, D.E., and Block, J. H. 1990. "Recognizing Connections between Thinking Skills and Mastery Learning." *Educational Leadership* 47 (5): 4–10.

Arter, J. A., and Salmon, J. R. 1987. *Assessing Higher Order Thinking Skills: A Consumer's Guide.* Portland, OR: Northwest Regional Educational Laboratory.

Ausubel, D. 1963. *The Psychology of Meaningful Learning.* New York: Greene & Stratton.

Baker, L., and Brown, A. 1984. "Metacognitive Skills and Reading." In *Handbook of Reading Research*, edited by P. D. Pearson. New York: Longman.

Barell, J. 1991. *Teaching for Thoughtfulness.* New York: Longman.

Baron, J. B., and Sternberg, R. J., eds. 1987. *Teaching Thinking Skills: Theory and Practice.* New York: W. H. Freeman.

Baumrind, D. 1967. "Childcare Practices Anteceding 3 Patterns of Preschool Behavior." *Genetic Psychology Monograph* 4.

———. 1986. *Familial Antecedents of Social Competence in Middle Childhood* (unpublished monograph, Ch. 9). Berkeley, CA: Institute of Human Development, University of California at Berkeley.

Bereiter, C., and Scardamalia, M. 1987. "An Attainable Version of High Literacy: Approaches to Teaching Higher-order Skills in Reading and Writing." *Curriculum Inquiry* 17:1, 9–30.

Beyer, B. K. 1985. "Teaching Critical Thinking: A Direct Approach." *Social Education* 49 (4): 257–303.

———. 1987. *Practical Strategies for the Teaching of Thinking.* Boston: Allyn & Bacon.

———. 1988. *Developing a Thinking Skills Program.* Boston: Allyn & Bacon.

Black, H., and Black, S. 1990. *Organizing Thinking Book 2.* Pacific Grove, CA: Midwest Publications (now Critical Thinking Press & Software).

Bloom, B. S., ed. 1956. *Taxonomy of Educational Objectives, Handbook I: Cognitive Domain.* New York: McKay.

Bloom, B. S. 1976. *Human Characteristics and School Learning.* New York: McGraw-Hill.

Boyer, E. 1983. *High School: A Report on Secondary Education in America*. New York: Harper & Row.

Brandt, R., ed. 1988. *Content of the Curriculum*. Alexandria, VA: Association for Supervision and Curriculum Development.

Brandt. R. 1990. "On Knowledge and Cognitive Skills: A Conversation with David Perkins." *Educational Leadership* 47 (5): 50–53.

Bransford, J. D., and Stein, B. S. 1984. *The IDEAL Problem Solver*. New York: W. H. Freeman.

Bransford, J. D., and Vye, N.J. 1989. "A Perspective on Cognitive Research and Its Implications for Instruction." In *Toward the Thinking Curriculum: Current Cognitive Research*, edited by L. B. Resnick and L. E. Klopfer, 173–205. Alexandria, VA: Association for Supervision and Curriculum Development.

Brooks, J. G. 1990. "Teachers and Students: Constructivists Forging New Connections." *Educational Leadership*, 47 (5): 68–71.

Bruner, J. S. 1968. *Toward a Theory of Instruction*. New York: Norton.

———. 1973. *Beyond the Information Given: Studies in the Psychology of Knowing*. New York: Norton.

Callahan, C. 1989. *Evaluation of Gifted Programs*. Paper presented at the annual meeting of the National Association for Gifted Children. Cincinnati, November 1989.

Campione, J. C., and Brown, A. L. 1978. "Toward a Theory of Intelligence: Contributions from Research with Retarded Children." *Intelligence* 2: 279–304.

Carbo, M. 1990. "Igniting the Literacy Revolution through Reading Styles." *Educational Leadership* 48 (2) (Oct): 26–30.

Case, R. 1978. "A Developmentally-based Theory and Technology of Instruction." *Review of Educational Research* 48: 439–63.

Center for the Teaching of Thinking. *IMPACT*. Huntington Beach, CA: Huntington Union High School District.

Chi, M. T. H.; Feltovich, P. J.; and Glaser, R. 1981. "Categorization and Representation of Physics Problems by Experts and Novices." *Cognitive Science* 5: 121–52.

College Board 1990. *Background on the New SAT–I and SAT–II*. College Board National Forum, October 31, 1990.

Costa, A. L., ed. 1985. *Developing Minds: A Resource Book for Teaching Thinking*. Vol 1 & 2. Alexandria, VA: Association for Supervision and Curriculum Development.

Costa, A. L., and Lowery, L. F. 1989. *Techniques for Teaching Thinking*. Pacific Grove, CA: Midwest Publications (now Critical Thinking Press & Software).

Covington, M. V.; Crutchfield, R. S.; Davies, L.; and Olton, R. M. 1974. *The Productive Thinking Program: A Course in Learning to Think*. Columbus, OH: Merrill.

Curry, J. 1981. Gifted Training Workshop, Wilmington Island, GA.

Derry, S. J., and Murphy, D. A. 1986. "Designing Systems That Train Learning Ability: From Theory to Practice." *Review of Educational Research* 56 (1): 1–39.

Dishon, D., and O'Leary, P. W. 1984. *A Guidebook to Cooperative Learning.* Holmes Beach, FL: Learning Publications, Inc.

Dole, J. A.; Duffy, G. G.; Roehler, L. R.; and Pearson, P. D. 1991. "Moving from the Old to the New: Research on Reading Comprehension Instruction." *Review of Educational Research* 61: 239–64.

Dunn, R.; Beaudry, J. S.; and Klavas, A. 1989. "Survey of Research on Learning Styles." *Educational Leadership* 46 (6) (Mar): 50-58.

Educational Programs That Work. 17th ed. 1991. Longmont, CO: Sopriswest. US Department of Education and National Dissemination Study Group.

Eggen, P. D., and Kauchak, D. P. 1988. *Strategies for Teachers: Teaching Content and Thinking Skills.* 2nd ed. Englewood Cliffs, NJ: Prentice Hall.

Eggen, P. D.; Kauchak, D. P.; and Harder, R. J. 1979. *Strategies for Teachers: Information Processing Models in the Classroom.* Englewood Cliffs, NJ: Prentice Hall.

Ennis, R. H. 1987. "A Taxonomy of Critical Thinking Dispositions and Abilities." In *Teaching Thinking Skills: Theory and Practice,* edited by J. B. Baron and R. J. Sternberg. New York: W. H. Freeman.

Feuerstein, R. 1980. *Instrumental Enrichment: An Intervention Program for Cognitive Modifiability.* Baltimore: University Park Press.

Flavell, J. H. 1978. *Cognitive Monitoring.* Paper presented at the Conference on Children's Oral Communication Skills, University of Wisconsin.

Gagné, E. 1985. *The Cognitive Psychology of School Learning.* Boston: Little, Brown.

Gagné, R. M. 1985. *The Conditions of Learning and Theory of Instruction.* New York: Holt, Rinehart & Winston.

Gagné, R. M.; Briggs, L. J.; and Wager, W. W. 1992. *Principles of Instructional Design.* 4th ed. Fort Worth, TX: Harcourt Brace Jovanovich.

Gagné, R. M., and Driscoll, M. P. 1988. *Essentials of Learning for Instruction.* Englewood Cliffs, NJ: Prentice Hall.

Gallini, J. K., and Gredler, M. E. 1989. *Instructional Design for Computers.* Glenview, IL: Scott, Foresman.

Gardner, H. 1983. *Frames of Mind: The Theory of Multiple Intelligences.* New York: Basic Books.

Gick, M. L., and Holyoak, K. J. 1980. "Analogical Problem Solving." *Cognitive Psychology* 12: 306–55.

———. 1983. "Schema Induction and Analogical Transfer." *Cognitive Psychology* 15: 1–38.

Glover, J. A.; Ronning, R. R.; and Bruning, R. H. 1990. *Cognitive Psychology for Teachers.* New York: Macmillan.

Goodlad, J. 1983. *A Place Called School: Prospects for the Future.* New York: McGraw-Hill.

Goodman, K. S.; Bird, L. B.; and Goodman, Y. M. 1992. *The Whole Language Catalog Supplement on Authentic Assessment.* Santa Rosa, CA: American School Publishers. (Printed by SRA).

Gray, J., and Myers, M. 1978. "The Bay Area Writing Project." *Phi Delta Kappan* 59: 110–13.

Gredler, M. 1992. *Designing Games and Simulations: A Process Analysis*. London: Kogan Page.

Guskey, T. R. 1990. "Integrating Innovations." *Educational Leadership* 47 (5): 11–15.

Halpern, D. F. 1989. *Thought and Knowledge*. 2nd ed. Hillsdale, NJ: Lawrence Erlbaum Associates.

Hansen, J., and Pearson, P. D. 1983. "An Instructional Study: Improving the Inferential Comprehension of Good and Poor Fourth-grade Readers." *Journal of Educational Psychology* 75: 821–29.

Harvard University. 1983. *Project Intelligence: The Development of Procedures to Enhance Thinking Skills*. Final report, submitted to the Minister for the Development of Human Intelligence, Republic of Venezuela, October.

Hayes, J. R. 1989. *The Complete Problem Solver*. 2nd ed. Hillsdale, NJ: Lawrence Erlbaum Associates.

Herman, J. L.; Aschbacher, P. R.; and Winters, L. 1992. *A Practical Guide to Alternative Assessment*. Alexandria, VA: Association for Supervision and Curriculum Development.

Herman, J. L.; Morris, L. L.; and Fitz-Gibbon, C. T. 1987. *Evaluator's Handbook*, UCLA Center for the Study of Evaluation *Program Evaluation Kit*. Newbury Park, CA: SAGE Publications.

Herrmann, B. A. 1988. "Two Approaches for Helping Poor Readers Become Strategic." *The Reading Teacher* 42: 24–28.

Higher Order Thinking Assessment Committee. 1990. *Higher Order Thinking Assessment Committee Report*. Columbia, SC: South Carolina Department of Education, May 22, 1990.

Hord, S. M.; Rutherford, W. L.; Huling-Austin, L.; and Hall, G. E. 1987. *Taking Charge of Change*. Alexandria, VA: Association for Supervision and Curriculum Development.

Hunley, M. L. 1989. Personal interview. University of North Carolina, Charlotte, NC.

Hunter, M. 1983. *Mastery Teaching, Improved Instruction*. El Segundo, CA: TIP Publications.

Hyde, A. A., and Bizar, M. 1989. *Thinking in Context*. New York: Longman.

Hyde, J. S. 1984. "How Large Are Gender Differences in Aggression? A Developmental Metanalysis." *Developmental Psychology* 20: 722–36.

Johnson, D. W.; Johnson, R. T.; and Holubec, E. J. 1991. *Cooperation in the Classroom*. rev ed. Edina, MN: Interaction Book Co.

Jones, B. F.; Palinscar, A. S.; Ogle, D. S.; and Carr, E. G., eds. 1987. *Strategic Teaching and Learning: Cognitive Instruction in the Content Areas*. Alexandria, VA: Association for Supervision and Curriculum Development and Elmhurst, IL: North Central Regional Education Laboratory.

Joyce, B., and Weil, M. 1972. *Models of Teaching*. Englewood Cliffs, NJ: Prentice Hall.

Kallison, J. M., Jr. 1986. "Effects of Lesson Organization on Achievement." *American Educational Research Journal* 23: 337–47.

Kearney, C. P.; Kean, M. H.; Roeber, E. D.; Stevens, B. L.; Baron, J. B.; Fremer, J.; and Daniel, M. 1985. *Assessing Higher Order Thinking Skills* (ERIC/TME Report 90). Washington: American Institutes for Research.

Larkin, J. H.; McDermott, J.; Simon, D. P.; and Simon, H. A. 1980. "Expert and Novice Performance in Solving Physics Problems." *Science* 208: 1335–42.

Linnemeyer, S. A. 1989. *Responsive Evaluation of Programs for the Gifted and Talented*. Paper presented at the annual meeting of the National Association for Gifted Children. Cincinnati, November 1989.

Lipman, M.; Sharp, A. M.; and Oscanyan, F. 1980. *Philosophy in the Classroom*. Philadelphia: Temple University Press.

Luchin, A. S. 1942. "Mechanization in Problem Solving: The Effect of Einstellung." *Psychological Monographs* 54 (6).

Macoby, E. E., and Jacklin, C. N. 1974. *The Psychology of Sex Differences*. Stanford, CA: Stanford University Press.

———. 1980. "Sex Differences in Aggression: A Rejoiner and Reprise." *Child Development* 51: 964–80.

Markham, E. M. 1979. "Realizing That You Don't Understand: Elementary School Children's Awareness of Inconsistencies." *Child Development* 59: 643–55.

Marsh, H. W., and Parker, J. W. 1984. "Determinants of Self-concept: Is It Better to Be a Relatively Large Fish in a Small Pond Even if You Don't Learn How to Swim as Well?" *Journal of Personality and Social Psychology* 47: 213–31.

Marzano, R. J., and Arredondo, D. E. 1986. *Tactics for Thinking*. Alexandria, VA: Association for Supervision and Curriculum Development.

Marzano, R. J.; Pickering, D. J.; and Brandt, R. S. 1990. "Integrating Instructional Programs through Dimensions of Learning." *Educational Leadership* 47 (5): 17–23.

Mayer, R. E. 1983. *Thinking, Problem Solving, Cognition*. New York: W. H. Freeman.

McCarthy, B. 1990. "Using the 4MAT System to Bring Learning Styles to Schools." *Educational Leadership* 48 (2) (Oct): 31–37.

McTighe, J., and Cutlip, G. 1986. "The State's Role in Improving Student Thinking." *Educational Horizons*, Summer, 1986.

McTighe, J., and Ferrara, S. 1988. "Assessing Student Thinking: Work in Progress in Maryland." *Teaching Thinking and Problem Solving* 10 (4): 1–4.

Miyasaka, J. R. 1990. *Evaluating Instructional Programs*. Paper presented to South Carolina Educators for the Practical Use of Research, Columbia, SC, October.

Molnar, A., ed. 1985. *Current Thought on Curriculum*. Alexandria, VA: Association for Supervision and Curriculum Development.

Mussen, P. H.; Conger, J. J.; and Kagan, J. 1979. *Child Development and Personality*. 5th ed. New York: Harper & Row.

National Assessment of Educational Progress. 1981. *Reading, Thinking, and Writing*. Denver: Education Commission of the States.

National Assessment of Educational Progress. 1986. *The Writing Report Card*. Princeton, NJ: Educational Testing Service.

National Commission on Excellence in Education. 1983. *A Nation at Risk: The Imperative for Educational Reform*. Washington, DC: U. S. Department of Education.

National Diffusion Network. 1991. *Educational Programs That Work*. Washington, DC: Office of Education.

National Forum on Assessment. 1991. *The Criteria for Evaluation of Student Assessment System*. Washington, DC: National Forum on Assessment, c/o Council for Basic Education.

New Standards Project. 1992. *Mathematics, Aquarium Problem*. Pittsburgh, PA: Learning Research and Development Center at the University of Pittsburgh and the National Center on Education and the Economy.

Nickerson, R. S.; Perkins, D. N.; and Smith, E. E. 1985. *The Teaching of Thinking*. Hillsdale, NJ: Lawrence Erlbaum Associates.

Norris, S. P., and Ennis, R. H. 1989. *Evaluating Critical Thinking*. Pacific Grove, CA: Midwest Publications (now Critical Thinking Press & Software).

North Carolina Department of Public Instruction, Division of Accountability Services 1992. *Sample Scoring Guide for Released Open-ended Items: Reading, Mathematics, Social Studies*. North Carolina End of Grade Testing. Raleigh, NC: North Carolina Department of Public Instruction.

O'Neil, J. 1992. "National System of Standards, Exams Piloted." *Update* 34 (8): 1, 3–5. Alexandria, VA: Association of Supervision and Curriculum Development. (October).

O'Reilly, K. 1983. *Critical Thinking in American History*. Pacific Grove, CA: Midwest Publications (now Critical Thinking Press & Software).

O'Tuel, F. S., and Bullard, R. 1987, August. *Helping Students Do Research*. Paper presented at the meeting of the South Carolina Consortium for Gifted, Spartanburg, SC.

———. 1988. "Strategy Teaching for Fifth-grade Gifted and Nongifted." *Research Briefs, 1988*. Research and Evaluation Committee, National Association for Gifted Children.

———. 1990. "Use of Strategies in Gifted and Nongifted Students." In R. Swassing, ed., *1990 Research Briefs*. Washington, DC: National Association for Gifted Children.

Olson, D. R. 1976. "Towards a Theory of Instructional Means." *Educational Psychologist* 12: 14–35.

Orlich, D. C.; Harder, R. J.; Callahan, R. C.; Kauchak, D. P.; Pendergrass, R. A.; and Keogh, A. J. 1990. *Teaching Strategies: A Guide to Better Instruction*. 3rd ed. Lexington, MA: D. C. Heath.

Paris, S. G.; Lipson, M.; and Wixson, K. 1983. "Becoming a Strategic Reader." *Contemporary Educational Psychology* 8: 293–316.

Paul, R. W. 1984. "Critical Thinking: Fundamental to Education for a Free Society." *Educational Leadership* 42 (1): 4–14.

Perkins, D. N. 1984. "Creativity by Design." *Educational Leadership* 42 (1) (Sept.): 18–24.

————. 1985. "Thinking Frames." Presentation at the Thinking Skills Training Institute, Alexandria, VA: Association for Supervision and Curriculum Development.

————. 1991. "What Creative Thinking Is." In A. L. Costa, ed. *Developing Minds: A Resource Book for Teaching Thinking.* rev. ed. Vol. 1: 85–88. Alexandria, VA: Association of Supervision and Curriculum Development.

Perkins, D. N., and Salomon, G. 1988. "Teaching for Transfer." *Educational Leadership* 46 (1) (Sept.): 22–32.

Piaget, J. 1973. *To Understand Is to Invent.* New York: Grossman.

Pogrow, S. 1988. "Teaching Thinking to At-risk Students." *Educational Leadership* 45 (7): 79–85.

————. 1990. "A Socratic Approach to Using Computers with At-risk Students." *Educational Leadership* 47 (5): 61–66.

Polya, G. 1957. *How to Solve It.* 2nd ed. New York: Doubleday.

Pressley, M.; Goodchild, F.; Fleet, J.; and Zajchowski, R. 1987. *What is Good Strategy Use and Why Is It Hard to Teach? An Optimistic Appraisal of the Challenges Associated with Strategy Instruction.* Paper presented at the meeting of the American Educational Research Association, Washington, DC.

Pressley, M.; Johnson, C. J.; Symons, S.; McGoldrick, J. A.; and Kurita, J. A. 1989. "Strategies That Improve Children's Memory and Comprehension of Text." *The Elementary School Journal* 90: 3–32.

Pressley, M.; Levin, J. R.; and Ghatala, E. S. 1984. "Memory Strategy Monitoring in Adults and Children. *Journal of Verbal Learning and Verbal Behavior* 23: 270–88.

Raths, L. E.; Wassermann, S.; Jonas, A.; and Rothstein, A. 1986. *Teaching for Thinking: Theory, Strategies, and Activities for the Classroom.* New York: Teachers College Press.

Research for Better Schools. 1990. *Resources for Teaching Thinking.* Philadelphia: Research for Better Schools.

Resnick, D. P., and Resnick, L. B. 1977. "The Nature of Literacy: An Historical Exploration." *Harvard Educational Review* 47 (3).

Resnick, L. B. 1987. *Education and Learning to Think.* Washington, DC: National Academy Press.

Santrock, J. W. 1992. *Life-span Development.* 4th ed. Dubuque, IA: W. C. Brown.

Segal, J. W.; Chipman, S. E.; and Glaser, R., eds. 1985. *Thinking and Learning Skills.* Vols. 1 & 2. Hillsdale, NJ: Lawrence Erlbaum Associates.

Simon, H. A. 1974. "How Big is a Chunk?" *Science* 183: 482–88.

Smith, G. P., and Dee, M. S. 1988. "The Delaware Study of Higher Order Thinking for All Children" (Doc. No. 01/01/88/03/01). Dover, DE: State of Delaware.

South Carolina State Board of Education. 1989. "Definition and Dimensions of Higher Order Thinking" approved October 11, 1989. Columbia, SC: South Carolina State Department of Education.

Spearman, C. 1927. *The Abilities of Man*. New York: Macmillan.

Sternberg, R. J. 1985a. "Teaching Critical Thinking, Part I: Are We Making Critical Mistakes?" *Phi Delta Kappan* 67 (3): 194–98.

———. 1985b. "Teaching Critical Thinking, Part II: Possible Solutions." *Phi Delta Kappan* 67 (4): 277–80.

———. 1986. *Intelligence Applied: Understanding and Increasing Your Intellectual Skills*. San Diego: Harcourt Brace Jovanovich.

Sternberg, R. J., and Bhana, K. 1986. "Synthesis of Research on the Effectiveness of Intellectual Skills Programs: Snake-oil Remedies or Miracle Cures?" *Educational Leadership* 42 (2): 60–67.

Swartz, R. J., and Parks, S. 1993. *Infusing Critical and Creative Thinking in Content Areas: Elementary*. Pacific Grove, CA: Critical Thinking Press & Software. (Prepress copy)

———. 1993. *Infusing Critical and Creative Thinking in Content Areas: Secondary*. Pacific Grove, CA: Critical Thinking Press & Software. (Prepress copy)

Swartz, R. J., and Perkins, D. N. 1990. *Teaching Thinking: Issues and Approaches*. Pacific Grove, CA: Midwest Publications (now Critical Thinking Press & Software).

Taba, H. 1966. *Teaching Strategies and Cognitive Functioning in Elementary School Children*. Coop. Research Project #2404. Washington, DC: United States Office of Education.

———. 1967. *Teachers Handbook to Elementary Social Studies*. Reading, MA: Addison-Wesley.

Terry, S. J. 1990. "A Comparison of Three Strategies to Induce Analogical Reasoning." Unpublished doctoral dissertation, University of South Carolina, Columbia.

Thorndike, E. L. 1906. *Principles of Teaching*. New York: A. G. Seiler.

———. 1913. *The Psychology of Learning, Educational Psychology II*. New York: Columbia University Press.

Thurstone, L. L. 1938. *Primary Mental Abilities*. Chicago: University of Chicago Press.

Tiedt, I. M.; Carlson, J. E.; Howard, B. D.; and Watanabe, K. S. 1989. *Teaching Thinking in K–12 Classrooms*. Boston: Allyn & Bacon.

Torrance, E. P. 1966. *Torrance Tests of Creative Thinking*. Princeton, NJ: Personnel Press.

Torrance, E. P., and Palm, H. 1959. *The Measurement of Inventive Level and Constructiveness as Aspects of Creative Thinking*. Minneapolis: Bureau of Educational Research, University of Minnesota.

Vygotsky, L. S. 1978. *Mind in Society: The Development of Higher Psychological Processes*. Cambridge, MA: Harvard University Press.

Weber, A. 1990. "Linking ITIP and the Writing Process." *Educational Leadership* 47 (5): 35–39.

Weikart, D. P.; Rogers, L.; Adcock, C.; and McClelland, D. 1971. *The Cognitively Oriented Curriculum*. Urbana, IL: University of Illinois.

Weiner, B. 1974. *Achievement Motivation and Attribution Theory*. Morristown, NJ: General Learning Press.

Whimbey, A., and Lockhead, J. 1982. *Problem Solving and Comprehension*. Philadelphia: Franklin Institute Press.

Whimbey, A., and Whimbey, L. S. 1975. *Intelligence Can Be Taught*. New York: E. F. Dutton.

Wiggins, G., and Swartz, R. 1992. *Performance and Portfolio Assessment: Testing for Understanding and Craftsmanship*. Handout at course on assessment, The Third Greater Boston Summer Institute, Infusing Critical and Creative Thinking into Content Instruction, July 13–31, 1992.

Winocur, S. L. 1985. *Project IMPACT Manual*. Huntington, CA: Center for the Teaching of Thinking.

Wycoff, J. 1991. *Mindmapping: Your Personal Guide to Exploring Creativity and Problem Solving*. New York: Berkeley Books.

Yavorsky, D. K. 1984. *Discrepancy Evaluation: A Practitioner's Guide*. Charlottesville, VA: University of Virginia.

Index